D1204022

Benedict de Spinoza

TWAS 351

Benedict de Spinoza

Benedict de Spinoza

By HENRY E. ALLISON

University of California, San Diego

TWAYNE PUBLISHERS

A DIVISION OF G. K. HALL & CO., BOSTON

Library of Congress Cataloging in Publication Data

Allison, Henry E
Netherlands)
   Bibliography: pp. 229–32.
   Includes index.
   1.l Spinoza, Benedictus de, 1632–1677.
B3997.A44 199^1.492 [B]   75–2059
ISBN 0-8057-2853-8

To the memory of my father

Contents

About the Author

Henry E. Allison is Professor of Philosophy at the University of California, San Diego, and Associate Editor of the *Journal of the History of Philosophy*. He received a B.A. from Yale University (1959), an M.A. from Columbia University (1961), and a Ph.D. from the Graduate Faculty of the New School for Social Research (1964). He has taught previously at the State University of New York, the Pennsylvania State University, and the University of Florida. Dr. Allison is the author of *Lessing and the Enlightenment, The Kant-Eberhard Controversy*, and of numerous journal articles on various topics and figures in the history of modern philosophy and the philosophy of religion.

Preface

The purpose of this book is to provide an introduction to the thought of Benedict de Spinoza, a Dutch Jew of the seventeenth century, who is universally regarded as one of the greatest figures in the history of Western philosophy. Although intended primarily for the general reader and student, it is hoped that it may be of some interest to the specialist and philosopher. Both limitations of length and the need to treat Spinoza's thought as a whole prevent either an intensive criticism or a detailed discussion of any particular aspect of his thought. I have, to be sure, offered criticisms at various points, and, as is inevitable, I have emphasized certain features of his philosophy at the expense of others. Nevertheless, my goal throughout has been to present a balanced picture, one which will give to the reader a sense of the breadth as well as the depth of this unique philosophy. In so doing, I have tried not only to provide an accurate account of Spinoza's main doctrines, and the historical context in which he developed them, but also to explain, as clearly and sympathetically as possible, the main arguments which he offered in support of these doctrines.

I have learned a great deal from the previous literature on Spinoza. Works drawn on in support of specific points of interpretation are, of course, cited in the notes. Other works, which I have often found to be no less important, but which I did not feel necessary to cite on specific points, are listed in the Bibliography. The main virtue which I claim for my own modest contribution—and here the reader must judge for himself the accuracy of this claim—is that, more than similar works, it helps the reader to follow the actual course of Spinoza's argument. It is both important and interesting to see what aspects of a past philosopher are of immediate relevance to contemporary philosophic concerns. Before this can be profitably done, however, it is first necessary to understand what the philosopher in question in fact said, and how his doctrines relate to the intellectual concerns of his own age. While not neglecting the question of relevance, I have given my prime attention to the latter question. This has been done in the firm conviction that the purpose of an introductory work is to provide a guide to, not a substitute for, the actual study of the philosopher in question.

The organization of this book is fairly traditional. The first chapter offers a brief account of Spinoza's background, the main events of his life, and the circumstances underlying the composition and publication, or lack thereof, of his various writings. The second chapter sketches the basic features of seventeenth-century thought that are directly relevant to an understanding of Spinoza's philosophy and also attempts to provide an initial nontechnical characterization of the main thrust or "spirit" of this philosophy. Chapters Three through Five, which form the heart of the book, deal with the central themes of the *Ethics*, that is, with Spinoza's metaphysical, epistemological, psychological and moral theories. The sixth chapter discusses Spinoza's political philosophy, while the seventh outlines his views on traditional religion and his method for interpreting the Bible. The Epilogue offers a very brief account of the influence of Spinoza's philosophy on subsequent thought.

Since this book is designed primarily as a general introduction, all citations are from, and all references are to, standard and readily accessible English versions of Spinoza's works. These are all listed in the Bibliography. On certain occasions, however, when I felt that it was important for an understanding of the argument, I have cited the original Latin expressions. References to the *Ethics* are by proposition; to the *Political Treatise* by chapter and section; and to the correspondence by recipient and date. Thus, the reader who wishes to check the cited passages with the Latin text will have no difficulty in so doing.

Finally, I should like to express my gratitude to my students in two Spinoza seminars at the University of Florida, with whose help I endeavored to rethink the thought of the master; to my colleague Thomas Mark, who read a draft of this work and made a number of helpful suggestions; and to Wayne Stromberg, who proofread the entire manuscript and compiled the index. Especial thanks, however, are due to two people. One is my wife, Norma, who continues to be an inspiration to me, and who once again deciphered my illegible handwriting and typed a complete draft of the manuscript.

The second is Patricia McCorry, who in preparing the entire manuscript in its final form, used her keen eye for detail and considerable editorial skill to save me from a number of embarrassing errors. Those errors that remain are, of course, my own.

My thanks also to the Clarendon Press, Oxford, for permission to quote from *Benedict de Spinoza: The Political Works*, edited and translated by A. G. Wernham, 1958, and to George Allen & Unwin, Ltd., London, for their permission to quote from *The Correspondence of Spinoza*, edited and translated by A. Wolf, 1966.

The portrait of Spinoza that appears on the frontispiece is modeled on the well-known engraving that appears in some copies of Spinoza's *Opera Posthuma*. It is a drawing, in brown ink, signed "J. Faber 1691." In the eighteenth century, the drawing was inserted into a copy of Spinoza's *Nagelate Schriften* that was found in Amsterdam in 1972. That copy is now in the private collection of Salomon S. Meyer, in Amsterdam, and the portrait is reproduced with his permission.

Chronology

1632 November 24: Spinoza is born in Amsterdam.

1638 November: Spinoza's mother dies.

1639 Spinoza begins his studies at the Jewish boys' school in Amsterdam.

1652? He begins his secular studies with Francis Van Den Ende.

1654 March: Spinoza's father dies.

1656 July 27: He receives the final excommunication from the synagogue.

1660 He moves from Amsterdam to Rijnsburg.

1660 He composes *Short Treatise on God, Man, and His Well Being*.

1661 He begins the treatise *On the Improvement of the Understanding*.

1663 He publishes *The Principles of Descartes' Philosophy* together with *Cogitata Metaphysica*. In June he moves to Voorburg.

1670 He publishes anonymously the *Theological-Political Treatise* and moves to The Hague.

1672 August 20: A mob murders the republican leaders John and Cornelius De Witt.

1673 February: Spinoza receives and refuses an offer of a professorship of philosophy at the University of Heidelberg from Karl Ludwig, the Elector Palatine. May: He journeys to Utrecht to see the Prince Condé.

1676 He is visited in The Hague by Leibniz.

1677 February 21: Spinoza dies. November: Spinoza's *Opera Posthuma* is published by J. Rieuwertsz.

CHAPTER 1

The Life of Spinoza

I The Jewish Community in Amsterdam and Spinoza's Life Within It

BARUCH DE SPINOZA was born in the city of Amsterdam on November 24, 1632.[1] His parents were members of the community of Jewish immigrants which had been living in the Netherlands since 1593. Spinoza remained within this community until his excommunication from the synagogue in 1656. This excommunication was undoubtedly one of the central events in Spinoza's life. Not only did it make official and permanent his break with the Jewish religion, which he had long since renounced anyway, but more importantly, it resulted in a complete rupture with his family and the abandonment of any thought of a commercial career, thereby making possible a life devoted exclusively to the pursuit of philosophy. In order to understand this event, however, we must consider not only Spinoza's own character and beliefs, but also some of the salient characteristics and history of the unique Jewish community in which he grew up.

This community was composed largely of descendants of the Marranos, also called "New Christians" or "crypto-Jews." These were the names applied to the Spanish Jews who were forcibly converted to Christianity by the Inquisition in the late fifteenth century. After this "conversion," which was usually, but not always, merely nominal, many of these Jews had risen to positions of great prominence in the intellectual, economic, political and even ecclesiastical life of Spain. Precisely because of their success, however, they were again persecuted by the Inquisition and expelled from the country. The first stop in this new diaspora was nearby Portugal, where even from the beginning life was far from pleasant. Moreover, when the Inquisition officially arrived in that country in the late sixteenth century, they were once again subject to wholesale persecution and were forced to flee.

The logical place to seek refuge was the Republic of the Netherlands, which had recently declared its independence from Spain
and was engaged in war with that country. Not only did the young
Dutch Republic share with the Marranos a common hatred of Spain
and the Inquisition, but it also was the most enlightened country in
Europe at the time and allowed some measure of religious toleration. Furthermore, this was the time of the formation of the East
India and West India companies and the emergence of the Republic
as a great commercial power. For this reason both the capital and
the commercial abilities of the Marranos were welcome, and they
were allowed to settle in Amsterdam, which, with their help, soon
became the commercial center of Europe. It should be noted, however, that even in the Republic religious toleration was far from
complete. The political strength of the Calvinist clergy was far too
great to allow that. Thus, although the first Marranos settlers arrived in Amsterdam in 1593, it was not until 1619 that they received
official permission to hold public worship, and not until 1657 that
they were granted citizenship.[2] This common experience, together
with the role which it played in the economic life of the Republic,
helped to determine some of the special characteristics of the Jewish
community in Amsterdam. As a direct result of this experience,
many of the leaders of this community were highly cultivated men,
but because of their roots, this culture was more Iberian and general
European than Jewish. They had been educated in Spanish universities and trained in scholastic ways of thinking. Their native languages were Spanish and Portuguese, and they were more at home
in Latin than in Hebrew. Furthermore, their commercial adven-
tures had brought them into contact with a wide variety of peoples
and tended to further inculcate a cosmopolitan rather than a ghetto
outlook. Nevertheless, their commitment to Judaism was quite real.[3] As Spinoza himself was later to note, their common experience
of suffering and persecution served only to reawaken and strengthen
their adherence to the Jewish faith, and to intensify their resolve to
affirm and preserve their Jewish identity as a people chosen by God.

In addition to this religious factor, economic interests also served
as a powerful unifying force in the community and a source of shared
values. It has been claimed that the Amsterdam Jewish community
was not only a religious group, but also "a virtually autonomous
socio-economic entity which negotiated with other nations, cities
and Jewish communities."[4] Even if this may be regarded as some-

what of an overstatement, the facts remain that the community was a tightly knit economic group; that as a result of the capital and expertise of some of its members the community as a whole was fairly prosperous; and that commercial success was a focal point of community concern.

As one might expect, this was reflected in a basically conservative political stance. Externally, the Jewish community was a strong supporter of the House of Orange, the source of the Stadtholders who had served as its protectors. Power within the community was concentrated in the hands of the wealthy commercial leaders. The synagogue was the real seat of this power and its ruling council functioned as a virtual dictatorship, exercising almost absolute control over all aspects of community life. Dissent was prohibited, and the publication of allegedly libelous writings or the expression of disrespect for the presiding authority was punished with excommunication.[5] Such control was rendered necessary, not only by the desire of the commercial oligarchy to remain in power, but also by the precarious position of the community within the Republic. Having recently escaped from the clutches of the Inquisition, and being keenly aware of the far from liberal attitude of the Reformed clergy, they were understandably anxious to keep their own house in order. This sense of danger was exacerbated by the activities of notorious heretics such as Uriel Acosta, who was excommunicated in 1640. In many ways a precursor of Spinoza, Acosta not only aroused the wrath of the leaders of the Jewish community by ridiculing their religious practices and materialistic values, but also openly denied the immortality of the soul, an act which was sure to arouse the attention of the Reformed clergy.

Both Baruch de Spinoza's grandfather, Abraham Espinoza, and his father, Michael Espinoza, were among the leaders of the community. His father in particular was a fairly prosperous, although not wealthy, merchant and held several honorary positions. Thus Spinoza was by birth part of the commercial establishment, and was undoubtedly instilled with its values as a child. Apart from the fact that the Espinoza family suffered a number of domestic sorrows, with Michael outliving all three of his wives and all but two of his six children (Baruch and Rebecca, an older half-sister), not much is really known about the philosopher's early homelife. We do, however, have considerable information concerning his early education. This was entirely religious in nature, and it took place at the Jewish

boys' school in Amsterdam, of which Spinoza's father was a war-
den, and which all the boys in the community attended as a matter
of course. This school consisted of seven grades with a precisely
prescribed curriculum. In the early grades the students began to
learn prayers in Hebrew and were introduced to the study and
translation of the Hebrew Bible. In the higher grades they studied
Hebrew grammar and selections from the Talmud and from the
later codes. At the final stage they were introduced to some of the
great medieval Jewish philosophers such as Maimonides.[6] It was
thus within this purely religious context (secular subjects being
taught at home) that Spinoza received his first introduction to
philosophical thought. Much of what he learned there he was soon
to repudiate, but as we shall see, some of it exerted a considerable
influence on his intellectual development and became integrated
into his final philosophical position.

Not even the briefest account of Spinoza's education would be
complete without some mention of his teachers. Foremost among
these were the rabbis Saul Morteira and Manasseh ben Israel, two
classical representatives of Marranos culture. Morteira was at the
time of Spinoza's education the senior rabbi in Amsterdam. Born in
Venice around 1596, he studied medicine under Montalto, the Mar-
rano court physician of Marie de Medici. Upon Montalto's sudden
death in 1616 he came to Amsterdam in search of a Jewish cemetery
for his teacher. While there he accepted a call to the rabbinate of
the older of the two synagogues which existed at that time. A third
synagogue was started two years later, and when all three were
amalgamated in 1638 Morteira was appointed senior rabbi, a post in
which he served until his death in 1660. Although his orientation
was basically medieval and orthodox he had some training in
philosophy, and as a result of his experience in the Medici court,
Morteira obviously knew something of the world. It is reported that
when Spinoza was but fifteen years old the rabbi marveled at the
boy's intelligence and predicted a great future for him. It must
therefore have been with a heavy heart that he presided over the
court of rabbis that excommunicated Spinoza in 1656.

Manasseh ben Israel, a major figure in seventeenth-century
Judaism, was a far more positive influence on Spinoza. Born in
Lisbon in 1604, he was brought as an infant to Amsterdam, where
he lived almost all of his life. He became rabbi of the second
Amsterdam synagogue in 1622; he started a Hebrew printing house

in 1627; and in 1640, when about to emigrate to Brazil, he received an appointment to the senior department of the Amsterdam Jewish school. It was in that capacity that he taught the young Spinoza. In 1655 Manasseh went to England on a special mission to Oliver Cromwell for the purpose of securing the readmission of the Jews into England. He remained there for two years, and thus was absent from Amsterdam at the time of Spinoza's excommunication. He died soon after his return in 1657.

Exceedingly well educated in secular subjects, Manasseh ben Israel was the author of numerous, but not particularly original, philosophical and theological writings. These are replete with references not only to traditional Jewish writers, but also to figures such as Euripides, Virgil, Plato, Aristotle, Duns Scotus and Albertus Magnus. He also had many Gentile friends; corresponded with people of the stature of Queen Christina of Sweden and Hugo Grotius; and sat for a portrait by Rembrandt. His great service to Spinoza was to introduce him to this rich secular culture. It was in all probability Manasseh ben Israel who first induced him to undertake the study of Latin, non-Jewish philosophy, modern languages, mathematics and physics.

The actual result of this study, however, was far different from the one intended. For while the abiding concern of Manasseh ben Israel had been to reconcile his rather mystical and traditional Jewish faith with secular thought, an acquaintance with this thought led Spinoza to a complete abandonment of Jewish beliefs and practices. Spinoza's secular studies were begun under the tutelage of Francis Van Den Ende. An ex-Jesuit, bookseller, diplomat and classicist, Van Den Ende opened a school in Amsterdam in 1652 to instruct the sons of the merchants of the city in Latin and the sciences. As his background suggests, he was quite an unorthodox figure, and, in fact, he acquired considerable notoriety as a freethinker, atheist and political radical. As a result of this notoriety he was eventually forced to close his school. In 1671, while living in France, he was involved in a revolutionary project for founding a republic in which all men would be equal. The project backfired, and its leaders, including Van Den Ende, were imprisoned and later executed.

Under Van Den Ende, Spinoza not only studied Latin and the sciences, but was introduced to the philosophy of Descartes, as well as the underground world of free thought and radical politics. More than that, they became intimate friends, and after the death of

Spinoza's father in 1654, Van Den Ende took him into his own house, asking in return only that Spinoza occasionally help with the instruction of his pupils. Spinoza is reported to have said years later that he had wished to marry Van Den Ende's daughter, Clara. He apparently lost out, however, to a wealthier suitor; and so the only reported romantic episode in Spinoza's career ended in disappointment.[7]

Although he continued to appear occasionally at the synagogue, by living at the home of Van Den Ende, Spinoza had, in effect, already removed himself from the Jewish community. This removal reflected his growing alienation from Jewish beliefs and practices, as well as from the materialistic, commercial values of the community. For Spinoza, the philosopher, this alienation was a spiritual and intellectual affair, grounded in his recognition of the inadequacy of the rational foundations of Biblical religion and the Rabbinic tradition, and the emptiness of a life devoted to the pursuit of wealth. This process was certainly accelerated by Spinoza's contact with Van Den Ende and his circle and by his study of philosophers such as Descartes and possibly Giordano Bruno, but its roots undoubtedly lie in his childhood experience and his first encounter with Jewish thought.

The actual "official" break with Judaism was forced upon Spinoza by the actions of the leaders of the Jewish community. Both the motives of the rabbis and the actual course of events are the subject of some dispute. Strict doctrinal orthodoxy has never been a central concern in Judaism and it certainly would not have been in the Amsterdam community. Similarly, as men of the world, the rabbis would not have been upset by the mere fact of Spinoza's association with Gentiles. But due to all that they had suffered for the right to practice their faith, they would have been deeply offended by any aspersions cast on the uniqueness and significance of the Jewish people and their way of life. In addition, they would have been concerned by any reports that Spinoza was adversely influencing the youth of the community, or that his heretical views, which were fairly close to those of Acosta, might become public knowledge. Finally, as a recent interpreter has suggested, the rabbis' concern could have been directed not at Spinoza's theological beliefs, but at his alleged revolutionary activities and associations.[8]

In any event, an investigation was launched. This led first to the charge that Spinoza had been contemptuous of the Mosaic law, and sometime in June, 1656, he was called before the council of rabbis to answer this charge. Spinoza promptly denied it, only to find new charges brought forth concerning his views on the authority of the Bible and the doctrine that the Jews were the chosen people. This time Spinoza could not deny the charges, and instead he submitted a written defense of his beliefs. Unfortunately, this document has been lost, but it is generally believed that many of its arguments appear in the *Theological-Political Treatise*, which Spinoza published some fourteen years later. Needless to say, this defense did not satisfy the rabbis and he was excommunicated for a period of thirty days. This temporary action was probably done in the hope that he might still repent. He did not, and on July 27, 1656, the final and permanent ban was pronounced against him publicly in the synagogue. In response to this news Spinoza is reported to have remarked:

All the better; they do not force me to do anything that I would not have done of my own accord if I did not dread scandal; but, since they want it that way, I gladly enter on the path that is opened to me, with the consolation that my departure will be more innocent than was the exodus of the early Hebrews from Egypt. Although my subsistence is no better secured than was theirs, I take away nothing from anybody, and whatever injustice may be done to me, I can boast that people have nothing to reproach me with.[9]

This path led to his permanent isolation from the Jewish community. One of his first acts was to replace his Hebrew name, Baruch, with its Latin equivalent, Benedict, by which name he has come to be known in the history of philosophy. He also left Amsterdam for a time to stay with friends at Ouwerkerk, a small village just south of the city. He soon returned, however, and seems to have spent most of the next four years in Amsterdam. As the above passage suggests, Spinoza at this time was very much concerned with the question of earning a living. With his father deceased, and the estate going to his sister Rebecca, he was totally without financial resources. Moreover, with a commercial career neither possible nor desirable, he was forced to learn a trade. The trade which he chose for himself was the highly skilled one of making and polishing lenses for spectacles, microscopes and telescopes. He was engaged in this activity for the rest of his life and it was his reputation in this field which first attracted the attention of leading figures such as Christian Huygens, the mathematician and physicist, and Leibniz, the philosopher. Unfortunately, the unhealthy nature of the work, which made the inhalation of glass dust unavoidable, greatly weakened his already frail constitution and probably contributed significantly to his early death by consumption.

During this period Spinoza acquired for the first time a circle of admirers. These men were largely followers of the Cartesian philosophy and members of the Mennonite and Collegiant sects. In opposition to the rigid orthodoxy of the Reformed Church, these sects offered a simple, ethically oriented, nondogmatic form of Christianity, which emphasized the role of reason and the necessity for toleration in religious affairs. Although Spinoza could not really share in their Christian commitment, he must certainly have found much in common with them. It is believed that Spinoza joined in study clubs with members of these groups and that they therein discussed not only the Cartesian philosophy which served as a common point of departure, but Spinoza's own emerging philosophy as well. In any event, it was to these men that he eventually communicated his own revolutionary philosophical doctrines which he did not dare to make public.

Within this group are some who figure prominently in Spinoza's subsequent career and what we have of his philosophical correspondence. These include Peter Balling, a merchant who translated Spinoza's *The Principles of Descartes' Philosophy* into Dutch in 1664; Jarig Jelles, another merchant, who abandoned his business career and wrote a book showing that Cartesianism was compatible with Christianity; Lodewijk Meyer, a physician and apparent leader of the group, who wrote the preface for the above-mentioned work; Simon Joosten De Vries, still another Amsterdam merchant, who became a disciple of Spinoza and who, just before his premature death, tried to make the philosopher his heir; and Jan Rieuwertsz, a bookseller in Amsterdam, who published the writings of Spinoza, as well as of many other unorthodox authors.

II *The Rijnsburg Years, 1660–1663*

Sometime early in 1660, Spinoza left Amsterdam for the village of Rijnsburg, which is located about six miles northwest of Leyden. The move was probably made at the suggestion of his Collegiant friends, as the village contained the main headquarters of the sect.

Its purpose was no doubt to give Spinoza the time and repose to pursue his own philosophical reflections, something which he was not always able to do in the bustling city with its many distractions. This change of environment proved to be highly successful; for it was during this period that Spinoza not only produced his first philosophical writing, but actually worked out the main lines of his mature system.

Spinoza's earliest known philosophical work, undoubtedly based largely on lines of thought already worked out in Amsterdam, but completed while at Rijnsburg, is the *Short Treatise on God, Man and His Well Being*. Although originally written in Latin, like all of Spinoza's other writings, this work has only come down to us in a Dutch translation, and it was not published or generally known until its discovery in the nineteenth century. This rather strange fate for the work of such a major figure as Spinoza is no doubt due to the caution of the philosopher, the loyalty of his friends, and the mistaken assumption of the editors of his posthumous works that it was merely an early and discarded draft of the *Ethics*. Spinoza composed this work for the circle of friends with whom he had been discussing philosophical issues, not for general publication, and his caution is clearly reflected in the note on which it ends.

So, to make an end of all this, it only remains for me still to say to my friends to whom I write this: Be not astonished at these novelties; for it is very well known to you that a thing does not therefore cease to be true because it is not accepted by many. And also, as the character of the age in which we live is not unknown to you, I would beg of you most earnestly to be very careful about the communication of these things to others. I do not want to say that you should absolutely keep them to yourselves, but only that if ever you begin to communicate them to anybody, then let no other aim prompt you except only the happiness of your neighbor, being at the same time clearly assured by him that the reward will not disappoint your labor. Lastly, if, on reading this through, you should meet with some difficulty about what I state as certain, I beseech you that you should not therefore hasten at once to refute it, before you have pondered it long enough and thoughtfully enough, and if you do this I feel sure that you will attain to the enjoyment of the fruits of this tree which you promise yourselves.[10]

This note of caution was well justified; for among the "novelties" contained in this work are the identification of God with nature, and thus the repudiation of the Judeo-Christian doctrine of the creation of the world; the affirmation of the necessity of God's activity, and thus the denial of any purpose in nature or of any divine providence; and the denial of the freedom of the will. In all of these points, which remained central to his mature system, Spinoza had already clearly broken with the more conservative Cartesian position which attempted to combine an understanding of nature based on the new mathematical physics with a basically theistic world view. Spinoza's friends, it will be recalled, were all Cartesians, and this fact certainly underlies his admonitions to them not to reject his doctrines without careful consideration.

But while Spinoza had arrived at many of the fundamental doctrines of his philosophy, he had not yet determined the manner in which they could best be presented and demonstrated. This led him directly to a consideration of the problem of method, which was a central issue in seventeenth-century thought. Modern thinkers—that is, those who took as their point of departure the new, mathematical science of nature—were united in their repudiation of the essentially syllogistic method of scholastic philosophy and science. They differed profoundly among themselves, however, concerning just what was to be put in its place. The issues involved are subtle and go to the very heart of the intellectual life of the period. We therefore cannot hope to describe them adequately here.[11] Suffice it to note that the broad line of division was between a basically inductive-empirical approach, as advocated by Francis Bacon and his followers, and a more deductive-mathematical approach, which was most forcefully advocated by the Cartesian school. The actual text of the *Short Treatise* shows us a philosopher torn between these two poles and casting about for an appropriate form in which to present his philosophy and for the best manner in which to demonstrate its doctrines. For example, a priori and a posteriori proofs of the existence of God are juxtaposed, and straightforward narrative is combined with dialogue forms. It is only in an appendix, obviously written somewhat later than the main text, that we find a crude anticipation of the geometrical method of Spinoza's masterpiece, the *Ethics*.

The decision to side with the Cartesians in the advocacy of a deductive-geometric method is reflected in the important, but unfortunately unfinished, essay *On the Improvement of the Understanding (Tractatus de Intellectus Emendatione)*. This work, which probably dates from 1661, was initially intended as a systematic treatise, wherein the discussion of method was to serve as an introduction to Spinoza's metaphysics. This discussion, in turn, is prefaced by a quasi-autobiographical prologue which has often been compared with the opening of Descartes's *Discourse on Method.* In it Spinoza relates the concerns which led him to philosophy in a way that not only resembles many classical religious, and even mystical, writings, but also seems to reflect the spiritual crisis which he must have undergone after his excommunication. The basic theme is the quest for a true and lasting good. The "ordinary objects of desire," i.e., wealth, honor, and sensual enjoyment, are dismissed as transient and empty and the true good is said to lie in "a knowledge of the union existing between the mind and the whole of nature."[12] The location of the true good in knowledge leads to a consideration of the best method for attaining this knowledge. The essay breaks off in the middle of the discussion of method and thus never gets to the metaphysical issues. The completed portion does, however, delineate a conception of knowledge as a deductive system which naturally suggests the geometrical method as the most suitable means for ordering and demonstrating such knowledge.

Meanwhile, in 1662 Spinoza was visited by one Johannes Casearius, a student of theology at the University of Leyden. He came to Spinoza for instruction in the newest philosophy, and while Spinoza liked the young boy and was willing to help him, he was quite understandably hesitant about initiating him into his own thought. He decided instead to teach him the essentials of scholastic metaphysics as it was then being taught at most of the universities and introduce him to the basic principles of the Cartesian philosophy. Toward this latter end, and in line with his recent methodological reflections, he put into geometrical form the second and a portion of the third part of Descartes's *Principles of Philosophy.* While on a visit to Amsterdam, Spinoza apparently showed this work to his friends. They promptly persuaded him to do the same thing with the first part of the *Principles* and to publish the entire work. Spinoza agreed not only to do this, but also to add some supplementary metaphysical thought as an appendix, on the condition that Meyer edit the work, polishing the Latin wherever necessary and adding a preface explaining that the author was not in complete agreement with the Cartesian philosophy. Meyer readily agreed, and it was published in 1663 by Rieuwertsz as *The Princi-*

ples of Descartes' Philosophy, with the appendix entitled *Cogitata Metaphysica*. This was the casual origin of the only work of Spinoza's to appear in his lifetime with his name attached.

By this time Spinoza was already hard at work on the *Ethics*, and he continued to work on it intermittently from 1662 until sometime in 1675.[13] Moreover, as the correspondence with Simon De Vries clearly shows, his Amsterdam friends were in possession of a substantial portion, if not the whole, of the first part by February, 1663, and were engaged in the process of discussing it in their philosophical club.[14] This discussion led to some questions which De Vries, in his role as spokesman for the group, raised concerning the nature of definitions and their role in Spinoza's demonstrations. These questions are answered by Spinoza in two letters of March, 1663, which not only show the stage of his thought at the time, but are important documents for the interpretation of his philosophy.[15]

Shortly after this time, Spinoza decided to leave Rijnsburg, probably for much the same reason that brought him there in the first place, viz., the desire for peace and quiet. This move was made necessary by the constant stream of visitors that came to see him from Leyden. One such, the young Casearius, has already been noted, but another, and far more significant one, must also be mentioned. This man is Henry Oldenburg, and his interest in Spinoza is not only a good indication of the force of Spinoza's personality, but also a barometer of the reputation which he had already achieved at that early date.

Oldenburg, a native German who was some twelve years older than Spinoza, is one of the more interesting figures in the European intellectual circles of the time. Far from being a creative philosopher or scientist in his own right, he was nevertheless in constant contact with those who were. He specialized in the dissemination of information concerning the research activities of others, and he thus functioned as a vital link between scientists working in various parts of Europe. While on a diplomatic mission to London in 1660, he helped to found the Royal Society and served as its first secretary. During a visit to Leyden in 1661, Oldenburg was evidently told about the young philosopher and lens-maker, and eager as usual to make the acquaintance of anybody who was in any way remarkable, he decided to visit Spinoza. This visit had a profound effect upon Oldenburg, and it led to an important correspondence between the two men, which deals with both scientific and philosophical subjects. In the scientific realm, Oldenburg tells Spinoza about the latest developments at the Royal Society, asking for news in return, and serves as intermediary between Spinoza and the famous chemist Robert Boyle, founder of the "Corpuscular Philosophy." This led to a series of letters in which Oldenburg reports the results of Boyle's experiments on nitre (potassium nitrate) and other matters, while Spinoza responds with his own criticisms and reflections. This shows Spinoza's knowledge of, and concern with, current scientific research, but the exchange proved to be of little significance, as Boyle stuck to his empirical-inductive method and Spinoza advocated a more deductive model of scientific explanation. The philosophical side of the correspondence proved to be even less fruitful. Here the basic problem was simply that, despite constant requests for explanation, which Spinoza gladly provided, Oldenburg was unable to grasp the implications of Spinoza's thought. Moreover, when the real nature of Spinoza's unorthodox religious views became known to him after the publication of the *Theological-Political Treatise*, Oldenburg's interest cooled considerably and he ceased encouraging him to publish the *Ethics*.

III   *The Years at Voorburg, 1663–1670*

Spinoza's next place of residence was Voorburg, a small village about two miles from The Hague. Its size provided him the desired peace and quiet, and its proximity to The Hague, then the seat of the States-General and the capital of the United Provinces, placed him near powerful protectors who could make it possible for him to pursue and publish his philosophy without fear of harassment. Such protectors were to be found in the De Witt brothers, and especially the younger and more powerful one, John De Witt, with whom Spinoza shared both a deep concern for the republican form of government and a strong interest in mathematics and physical science.

John De Witt was not only the leader of the republican cause against the royalist-federalist supporters of the House of Orange, but also, as the Grand Pensionary of Holland, since 1653 the effective ruler of the United Provinces. Moreover, at the time in which Spinoza first settled at Voorburg, De Witt was at the height of his powers. Having successfully extricated his country from a disastrous war with England that had begun before his ascendancy, he was not yet involved in the second English war, which started in 1665. In addition, by promising to withhold support from the Stuarts in England, he had gained, to some extent at least, the support of the House of Orange. Beyond that, he had managed to put the financial affairs of the country in order and to secure religious toleration and the freedom of the press. Despite this, however, he had never been able to achieve great popularity. The masses had always been and remained supporters of the House of Orange and the monarchist cause; and De Witt's defense of religious toleration and of the supremacy of the civil power earned the bitter enmity of the Reformed clergy, who desired to establish a state church.

Although he was an ardent supporter of De Witt and the republican cause, Spinoza's central concern was philosophy rather than politics. He had, after all, moved to Voorburg so as to be better able to continue his work on the *Ethics*; and from a letter to a friend, John Bouwmeester, dated June, 1665, we learn that the work had advanced as far as what in the final version became the fourth part.[16] In September of the same year, however, we find Oldenburg chiding Spinoza: "I see that you are not so much *philosophizing* as, if one may say so, *theologizing*, since your thoughts are turning to angels, prophecy and miracles."[17] This suggests that in the interim Spinoza had informed Oldenburg that he had set aside the *Ethics* and was already hard at work at what was to become the *Theological-Political Treatise*. Spinoza confirms this in his response in which he admits that he is currently writing a treatise on the interpretation of Scripture and lists the following reasons:

1. The Prejudices of the Theologians; for I know that these are among the chief obstacles which prevent men from directing their mind to philosophy; and therefore I do all I can to expose them, and to remove them from the minds of the more prudent. 2. The opinion which the common people have of me, who do not cease to accuse me falsely of atheism; I am also obliged to avert this accusation as far as it is possible to do so. 3. The freedom of philosophizing, and of saying what we think; this I desire to vindicate in every way, for here it is always suppressed through the excessive authority and impudence of the preachers.[18]

Clearly, behind the reasons given to Oldenburg lies a sense of urgency created by the political situation. In 1665 the Republic was in a state of crisis. The immediate cause of this crisis was the renewal of the war with England and Sweden, as a result of which the Dutch forces were so hard pressed that they had to employ French troops, an action which only served to increase the popular discontent. In addition, the situation was greatly exacerbated by the actions of the Reformed clergy. Still bent upon Calvinizing everyone and resenting the liberalism of De Witt's party with its strong advocacy of religious liberty, the clergy used the military situation as an occasion for mobilizing public opinion behind the young Prince of Orange and against De Witt. They did this by citing the progress of the war as evidence of divine judgment on the country because of the godlessness of its rulers. Furthermore, the transfer of power to the House of Orange was claimed to be necessary not only for the military but also for the spiritual well-being of the country.[19]

Similar outcries had earlier been raised against that great champion of liberalism and republicanism John Van Oldenbarnevelt, who at the instigation of the clergy had been executed for treason in 1619. Thus, De Witt and his supporters were well aware of the potential danger of the situation, as well as of the urgent need for people willing to speak out on the issue and to argue for the principles of republican government and religious liberty. Spinoza likewise saw this need; and it is perhaps the strongest proof of the fact that he was not an "ivory tower" thinker, divorced from the cares of the world, that he set aside his lifework in order to meet it. As a philosopher, however, his concern was not simply to produce another pamphlet in favor of freedom of thought, but rather to get to the very heart of the matter and expose the foundations of the "Prejudices of the Theologians" which stand in the way of such freedom. The basis of the clerical position was the Bible, especially the belief that the Bible was a divinely inspired, infallible book which, as such, functions as the supreme authority on all matters with which it deals. It was through an appeal to the Bible, thus construed, that the clergy justified their repressive stance; and it was thus only by exposing the illegitimacy of this appeal that their position could be completely undermined and freedom of thought defended.

With this in mind, Spinoza returned to a study of Scripture and to the arguments against its alleged infallibility which he had raised some years earlier in the defense of his beliefs before the rabbinic tribunal. The result is what is generally regarded as the first modern work on the Bible, the initial attempt at "higher criticism." Confining himself mainly to the Hebrew Bible or Old Testament, with which he was far more familiar, he treats it in a thoroughly naturalistic and historical fashion, demonstrating that the various books date from different times and reflect widely different conditions and points of view. This is combined with a thoroughgoing critique of prophecy and miracles which shows that the authors of the Biblical books were not men of extraordinary intellectual gifts. We are thus led to the conclusion that, aside from the inculcation of true virtue, which is the only divine aspect of the Bible, there is in it no consistent message or set of doctrines. But since the Bible does not contain any uniform teaching or any special speculative insights, it can hardly serve as an authority in these matters. Finally, having undermined the authority of the Bible, Spinoza proceeds in the final chapters to offer his positive arguments for freedom of thought and expression, and against any interference by a church in the affairs of state.

The seriousness with which Spinoza approached this task is reflected in the time it took him to complete it: some five years, most of which was devoted to research into the text of the Bible, Jewish history and the Hebrew language. Unfortunately, when the book finally appeared in 1670, the political situation had deteriorated to such an extent that there was little hope of achieving its main purpose of providing an effective support for the policies of the De Witts, and absolutely no hope of achieving its subsidiary purpose of defending Spinoza against charges of atheism. Spinoza himself, keenly aware of the dangers involved, and giving up any hopes of justifying himself in the eyes of the public, decided to publish the *Theological-Political Treatise* anonymously and under a false imprint (the place of publication being listed as Hamburg rather than Amsterdam). This stratagem, however, proved to be completely ineffective; his authorship was soon common knowledge and both he and the book became the object of frequent and violent attack. Typical of these attacks is a description of the work as a wicked instrument "forged in hell by a renegade Jew and the devil, and issued with the knowledge of Mr. De Witt."[20] These attacks were further intensified as a result of the rapid spread of the work. By the end of 1670, there had already appeared four reprints of the first edition in Germany and the United Provinces, with many others under false titles. This naturally led to efforts to suppress the book, all of which were frustrated by De Witt. Thus, the project, which began as an effort to defend De Witt and his cause, ended up requiring defense in its own right. Spinoza was clearly disillusioned by the whole affair and came to the realization that he could never publish the *Ethics* during his lifetime.

IV *The Years at The Hague, 1670–1677*

In 1670 Spinoza moved once again, this time to The Hague, where he remained until his death in 1677. Once again, he was probably motivated by desire for peace and once again this desire was frustrated; for these years proved to be the most eventful of his life, especially in terms of his involvement in the affairs of the country.

Upon settling in The Hague, Spinoza returned to work on his *Ethics*. The long period of neglect had brought with it the need and desire for substantial revisions, and he worked on these revisions until 1675, when the book attained its final form. In the meantime, Spinoza was either actually working on or contemplating a number of projects. These included a Dutch translation of the Hebrew Bible, a scientific treatise on the Hebrew language, a treatise on political science, a work on natural science to supplement the very sketchy discussion in the *Ethics*, and a new exposition of the principles of algebra. Of these projects, the only visible fruits found at his death were the unfinished texts of the *Hebrew Grammar* and the *Political Treatise*, and two essays: *On the Rainbow* and *On the Calculation of Chances*. The first two works were published together with the similarly unfinished *On the Improvement of the Understanding*, the complete text of the *Ethics*, and a selection from Spinoza's correspondence in the *Opera Posthuma*, which was edited by a number of his friends and appeared in the very year of his death. As an indication of the way in which Spinoza was generally viewed at the time, it is noteworthy that it was felt necessary to remove all names and other means of identification from the correspondence, and to omit the names of the editors and publisher, as well as the place of publication. Not even the full name of the author was mentioned, and only Spinoza's initials (B.D.S.) appeared on the title page.

Many of these projects were not completed simply because of Spinoza's ill health and early death. But political developments during the last years of Spinoza's life must certainly have been a contributing factor, especially in regard to the *Political Treatise*, which

we shall consider in some detail later. The first and most shattering
of these developments was the brutal murder of the De Witt
brothers by a frenzied mob. This act was the culmination of a long
series of events and of continued rabble-rousing by the clergy, but
its immediate cause was the joint declaration of war against the
Republic by England and France in 1672. The resulting military
crisis led to a popular outcry for the Prince of Orange to take over
the country and save it from its enemies as his father had done
previously. Moreover, this was combined with a demand for ven-
geance against De Witt, who was treated as a scapegoat in the whole
affair. This demand was satisfied on August 20, 1672, when a mob
broke into the prison at The Hague where John, who had resigned
his post as Grand Pensionary of Holland on August 4, was visiting
his brother Cornelius, who had been arrested on a charge of con-
spiring against the Prince. Finding the brothers together, the mob
murdered both of them, practically tearing them to pieces in the
process and then hanging their mangled remains from a post.

When he heard of this deed, Spinoza, for once in his life at least,
lost all of his philosophic calm. He is said to have burst into tears
and then written out a placard on which he expressed his utter
abhorrence of "the very lowest of barbarians" who had committed
this heinous murder. His intent was to place this placard near the
scene of the crime, but fortunately his landlord, Van Der Spyck,
realized the true nature of the situation and locked Spinoza in the
house.[21] Otherwise, it is quite probable that Spinoza would have
suffered a fate similar to that of the De Witts.

The next major episode in Spinoza's life took place the following
year and was likewise occasioned by the war with France. The
French army at the time, under the leadership of Prince Condé,
was occupying Utrecht. Condé was a man of liberal views with an
interest in science and philosophy. One of his officers, a Colonel
Stoupe, who was a former Calvinist minister serving a Catholic king
in the invasion of a Calvinist country, and who later wrote a pamphlet attacking Spinoza, informed the Prince that the philosopher
lived nearby and suggested that he might invite him to visit. Condé
agreed and sent, through Stoupe, an invitation to Spinoza to visit
him at Utrecht.

Spinoza seems to have regarded this invitation as a possible opening for peace negotiations, and being anxious to do what he could for

the cause of peace, he decided, after getting permission from the Dutch authorities, to accept. Thus, armed with the necessary safe-conducts, Spinoza traveled across enemy lines to Utrecht in May, 1673. In the meantime, however, his host had been unexpectedly called away. Spinoza was invited to remain and await his return, which he did, and during this period he was well treated. While waiting, he was offered a pension on the condition that he dedicate a book to Louis XIV. Spinoza respectfully declined, and when, after several weeks of pleasant conversation, the word came that Condé could not return, he decided to leave.

Upon learning of Spinoza's visit to the enemy, the people of The Hague immediately jumped to the conclusion that he was a spy or traitor. They threatened to break into his house and murder him, just as they had previously murdered the De Witts. Spinoza, however, came out of his house and, confronting the mob directly, proclaimed his innocence and concern for the Republic. This frank and fearless conduct in the moment of danger must have allayed the suspicions of the mob, as they dispersed and left him alone.[22]

That same year Spinoza received another and greater honor which he found considerably more difficult to reject than the offer of a pension from Louis XIV. In February, 1673, the Elector Palatine, Karl Ludwig, brother of the Princess Elizabeth who had befriended and corresponded with Descartes, offered him the professorship of philosophy at the University of Heidelberg. Karl Ludwig had spent many years in Holland and was a strong advocate of the republican philosophy of religious and economic freedom. The existence of a distinguished faculty, which included Samuel Puffendorf, the great authority on international law, and a Jewish rector, bears ample witness to the fact that these principles were in force at the University of Heidelberg, which Karl Ludwig had founded in 1652.[23] Moreover, the offer included a promise of absolute freedom of thought and expression, so long as he did not disturb the public religion. Despite his years of solitude and lack of experience of academic life, Spinoza was greatly tempted by this offer and the attendant opportunity to abandon his trade and devote more of his time to philosophy. Thus, he considered it for some six weeks before finally deciding to decline it. His reasons for this decision, as expressed in a polite letter of refusal to Professor Johann Ludwig Fabritius, a Heidelberg philosopher who had tendered the offer to

Spinoza on the part of Karl Ludwig, were a hesitancy to embark on a teaching career at that stage of his life and a characteristic refusal to compromise, at any price, the independence for which he had paid so dearly. Spinoza's affirmation of this latter point is worth citing in full:

I think that I do not know within what limits that freedom of philosophizing ought to be confined in order to avoid the appearance of wishing to disturb the publicly established religion. For schisms arise not so much from an ardent love of religion as from men's various dispositions, or the love of contradiction, through which they are wont to distort and to condemn all things, even those that have been correctly stated. I have already experienced these things while leading a private and solitary life, much more then are they to be feared after I shall have risen to this degree of dignity.[24]

Although he decided to remain in the mode of life to which he had grown accustomed, Spinoza did increase his circle of acquaintances. Indeed, the last years of Spinoza's life are amongst the most significant in this regard; for it was during this period that he first met and began a correspondence with the promising young scientist Ehrenfried Walter von Tschirnhaus and through him became acquainted with the great philosopher Gottfried Wilhelm von Leibniz, who at the time was in the process of developing his own philosophical system.

Tschirnhaus was a German count who studied at the University of Leyden from 1668 to 1675, but he served for a part of this time as a volunteer with the Dutch army in the war with France. In 1674 he made the acquaintance of Spinoza's physician, George Hermann Schuller, who told him about Spinoza. Having already studied the works of Descartes, Tschirnhaus became immediately interested in Spinoza, began a correspondence, and visited him that same year. This correspondence is of considerable philosophical importance, as Tschirnhaus succeeded in pointing to many of the basic difficulties in Spinoza's system and elicited in return some significant responses from Spinoza. Accordingly, we shall have frequent occasion to refer to it in our treatment of Spinoza's thought. The following year Tschirnhaus visited London, where he met Oldenburg and Boyle, and the communication with Oldenburg apparently led directly to the resumption of his long-interrupted correspondence with Spinoza. After leaving London, Tschirnhaus went to Paris, where he met the young Leibniz and told him of Spinoza's work, specifically about

some of the doctrines in the *Ethics* which he had read in a manuscript copy. For his own part, Tschirnhaus later proved to be a man
of some accomplishments in the sciences. He is credited with having discovered the tangential movement of circles and with the
invention of porcelain. His main philosophical work, *Medicina Mentis*, 1683, was essentially a development of some of the views expressed by Spinoza in *On the Improvement of the Understanding*.

In the meantime, upon hearing Tschirnhaus's reports, Leibniz became immensely interested in Spinoza's work. He had already read
the *The Principles of Descartes' Philosophy* and in 1671 had sent
Spinoza a copy of his "Notice on the Progress of Optics." In return
Spinoza had sent him a copy of the *Theological-Political Treatise*.
Leibniz had also already read this work and had, in fact, described it
as "an unbearably free-thinking book." Apparently, however, he
had not known that Spinoza was its author. Now, after hearing about
the *Ethics*, he was desirous of reading it for himself and requested
Tschirnhaus's assistance in procuring a copy for him. Tschirnhaus
wished to oblige but could not show Leibniz his own copy without
Spinoza's permission. When, however, he wrote to Dr. Schuller in
order to obtain this permission from Spinoza, it was denied. Spinoza, who as a result of his experiences had become increasingly cau-
tious, simply did not trust Leibniz and suspected (quite accurately)
that Leibniz, a German, was in Paris on a mission for the reunion of
Protestants and Catholics, an effort which, if successful, would inevitably lead to the suppression of all liberal tendencies. Nevertheless, Leibniz would not give up. He came to The Hague in the fall of
1676 and managed to gain Spinoza's confidence. While there he not
only acquired a firsthand knowledge of the *Ethics* but also engaged
in frequent conversations with the dying philosopher. Because of
the importance of Leibniz's own philosophy, and its kinship in many
ways to the thought of Spinoza, the interchange between these two
men must be ranked as one of the major intellectual events of the
seventeenth century.

Spinoza himself was at this time declining rapidly. Nevertheless,
he continued to be active and to go about his business until the end.
This end came suddenly and peacefully at three o'clock on the
twenty-first of February in the presence of Schuller. Numerous
reports of deathbed confessions, of frantic recantations, and of requests for divine forgiveness began circulating immediately after
the death was announced, and some seem to have gained consider-

able credence. It is clear, however, from all the evidence that Spinoza died as he had lived, that is, in accordance with his own description of a free man as one who "thinks of death least of all things" and whose "wisdom is a meditation not of death but of life."

CHAPTER 2

Spinoza's Philosophy in Its Historical Context

SPINOZA'S *Ethica Ordine Geometrico Demonstrata (Ethics Dem-onstrated in a Geometrical Manner)* is an extremely difficult and forbidding book. Both its obscure, scholastic terminology and its stark, geometrical form provide formidable barriers for even the philosophically trained reader, and undoubtedly help to explain the great diversity of ways in which the work has been interpreted. Thus, rather than plunging immediately into the argument of the work, with its strange format of definitions, axioms and propositions, and its bewildering talk of substance, attributes and modes, it would seem to be far preferable to consider briefly the historical context in which Spinoza wrote, and, in light of this, to introduce the central themes of his philosophy. This will be the task of the present chapter, and it is hoped that it will help to guide the reader through the more systematic and technical investigation which is to follow.

I *The Roots of Spinoza's Philosophy in the New Science and Its Conception of Nature, and the Relevance of Descartes*

We have already seen that as a youth, Spinoza studied and was profoundly influenced by medieval Jewish philosophy, and it is also generally assumed that in the course of his development he came under the influence of Renaissance philosophers of nature such as Bernardino Telesio and Giordano Bruno. A full-scale intellectual biography of Spinoza would, therefore, have to deal with these and a wide variety of other influences, e.g., the Kabalah, to which a Jewish intellectual living in seventeenth-century Holland would inevitably be exposed.[1] Nevertheless, it remains the case that, from the point of view of understanding the distinctive features of his metaphysical vision, the single most important factor is the development of the mathematical science of nature, which was occurring at a rapid rate during Spinoza's lifetime. Spinoza was not, like Descartes, a creative scientist, but as his relationships with men like Huygens and Oldenburg clearly reveal, he was a keen student of contemporary developments in a number of sciences and of the fundamental problems of scientific methodology. This new science certainly inspired Spinoza's naturalistic approach to ethical questions, but beyond this it provided him with the basis, although not all of the details, of his conception of nature. It is in the knowledge of the union between the mind and nature, so conceived, that Spinoza placed the highest good for man in his early treatise *On the Improvement of the Understanding*, and it is this same infinite and law-abiding nature that he identified with God in the *Ethics*.

The modern scientific conception of nature, like most philosophical conceptions, can best be understood by contrasting it with that which it replaced.[2] This was the medieval view, in both its Jewish and Christian expressions, which was itself based on a precarious synthesis of Aristotelian physics and cosmology with Biblical doctrines of God, man and creation. According to this view, the world of nature was in the original sense a cosmos, that is, a finite ordered whole, in which everything had its determinate place and particular function. The earth stood at the center of this cosmos, and the allegedly incorruptible heavenly bodies, including the sun, revolved about it. The world was created by God, largely for the benefit of man, who was "made in His own image." The doctrine of the creation of the world ran counter to the Aristotelian view of its eternality, and this gave rise to some of the most difficult problems for thinkers, like Maimonides and Thomas Aquinas, who endeavored to synthesize Aristotle and Scripture. Nevertheless, apart from the affirmation of the divine creation of the world, they basically followed Aristotle in conceiving of it as composed of distinct types of substances, falling into fixed genera or "natural kinds," each obeying its own set of laws.

The laws in accordance with which each substance acted were dependent upon its particular function, and this function, according to the medievals, was assigned to it as part of God's providential scheme, which was essentially directed toward the salvation of man. Such a world was perfectly intelligible in principle, although not in fact, for man naturally was not privy to all of the details of God's great plan. Nevertheless, the understanding that was available to man, which, thanks to Aristotle, was thought to be fairly extensive, was primarily in terms of the function or purpose of the substance under examination. This function or purpose was characterized by Aristotle as the "final cause" in his famous analysis of the four causes, and such causes played a very significant role in scientific explanation. In more modern terms, the prime manner of explaining an event was teleological, i.e., in terms of the end achieved. Consequently, the basic scientific question was: "Why did X do something?" and the first place one looked for an answer was to the peculiar nature or function of X. This would provide the final cause of the action in question. It was only if the action did not accord with X's function, i.e., was "accidental" rather than "natural," that one looked for an external cause. Thus, in accordance with this style of explanation, one might well think that one has understood why the rain falls when it is seen that this provides water for the crops, which are, in turn, necessary to support human life. This is, of course, a gross oversimplification of the way in which medieval thinkers viewed the problem of explanation. Not all scientific explanation was teleological and not all teleological explanation was, or need be, as crude as the above-cited example. It remains the case, however, that this characterizes the basic way in which the medieval mind, even the philosophic mind, viewed the world, and that the world, so viewed, was certainly a place in which man felt at home.

The conception of nature which finally emerged in the seventeenth century, after a long process of development, and which we associate primarily with such names as Kepler, Galileo, Descartes and Newton, differs in almost every respect from its predecessor. Whereas the older universe is finite, teleologically and hierarchically ordered, with each kind of substance obeying its unique set of laws, the modern one is infinite, mechanically ordered, and governed by a single set of universal laws which apply to all phenomena celestial and terrestial alike. The key to this new conception is the role given to mathematics in scientific explanation. In the famous and oft-quoted words of Galileo:

Philosophy is written in that great book which ever lies before our eyes—I mean the universe—but we cannot understand it if we do not first learn the language and grasp the symbols, in which it is written. This book is written in the mathematical language, and the symbols are triangles, circles, and other geometrical figures, without whose help it is impossible to comprehend a single word of it; without which one wanders in vain through a dark labyrinth.[3]

The universe of Galileo and the new science is thus fundamentally geometrical in character. Geometrical reasoning had already led Copernicus to abandon the geocentric hypothesis, and Kepler to conclude that the orbits of the planets about the sun are elliptical rather than circular (the supposedly perfect motion). Similarly, the telescope had revealed spots on the sun and thus corruption in the allegedly incorruptible heavenly bodies. The privileged status of these heavenly bodies, as well as the central position of the earth, was therefore abandoned, and the closed cosmos of medieval thought gave way to the infinite, geometrically ordered universe of modern science. The denizens of this universe are not unique substances with their natural places, functions and purposes, but rather phenomena completely describable in mathematical, i.e., quantitative terms. All salient relations between these phenomena are expressible in such terms, and it is precisely this factor which makes possible the discovery and formulation of a set of universal laws.

It is important for our purposes to realize that in the minds of Galileo and the other great founders of modern physical science, the mathematical structure of reality was not merely a convenient assumption or hypothesis which proved useful for scientific description and prediction. This, after all, was what the dispute between Galileo and the Church was all about. Rather this mathematical structure was viewed as the truth about the nature of things. The "real world" was quite simply the geometrical-quantitative world of the mathematical physicist. It consisted solely of bodies moving in space and interacting with each other according to precise, mathematically expressible laws. Not only was teleological explanation thus rejected as "unscientific," but final causes were themselves banished from nature and placed either in the inscrutable will of God or the imagination of man.

As a direct result of this changed perspective, the whole world of ordinary human experience, values and concerns, with its colors, sounds and odors, and its striking, inexplicable happenings, was at best granted a kind of secondary status and at worst relegated to the realm of illusion. This "scientific" outlook is perfectly exemplified in the widely held distinction between primary and secondary qualities. The primary qualities of a body, in this view, were such features as shape, size, mass and motion, all of which can be measured and dealt with quantitatively. It was of these qualities that the body was really composed. Secondary qualities, on the other hand, which include the above-mentioned colors, sounds and odors, were regarded as subjective or in the mind. Galileo himself characterized these secondary qualities as "mere names" having no place in nature; and for him, as for many others, man's perceptual experience of these qualities was understood to be the result of an interaction between the real physical object, composed solely of primary qualities, and the sentient organism.[4]

This changed conception of nature obviously brought with it a whole host of philosophical problems. What, for instance, is the relationship between this conception and the Biblical view of God, man and nature? Does the truth of science imply the falsity of divine revelation? Also, what is the place of man in nature so conceived? Is he completely subject to its mathematical laws, and, if so, what becomes of the freedom of his will, in virtue of which he earns either salvation or damnation? Finally, there is the problem of knowledge, which here arises in a distinctively modern form: how can the human mind, whose only access to reality is through sense experience, ever acquire knowledge of this non-sensible, abstract world of mathematical physics? The very truth which the physicists claim about the world seems to entail a hopeless skepticism, as it renders the "real" world inaccessible to the human mind. Galileo himself was a physicist, not a philosopher, and he therefore did not attempt to deal in a systematic fashion with these crucial issues. This task was left to Spinoza's great predecessor, René Descartes, who for that very reason is generally regarded as the father of modern philosophy.

Descartes came to philosophy as both a scientist and a Christian, or at least a professed Christian. As a scientist, he was motivated by the dream of a "universal mathematics," an all-embracing science of order and proportion through which all fields of knowledge could be integrated into a single whole and mastered by a single method, that of mathematics. The greatest fruit of this endeavor toward a unified science was analytic geometry, wherein Descartes showed that one and the same set of relations or proportions could be expressed either algebraically or geometrically. The attempt to apply this method to nature resulted in a purely geometrical physics which proved to be not nearly so successful. As a professed Christian, Descartes conceived of man as possessing a free will and an immortal soul. He also tended to resolve any conflicts between faith and science or philosophy by assigning them to different realms and

claiming that the sacred truths of the former are beyond the capacity
of human reason or the "natural light."

As a philosopher, Descartes developed the split between mind
and nature, which was implicit in Galileo, into a full-fledged
metaphysical dualism. The key to this dualism is the concept of
substance, a concept which likewise plays a crucial role in Spinoza's
philosophy. Substance is defined in the *Principles of Philosophy* as
"that which so exists that it needs no other thing in order to exist."[5]
Strictly speaking, only God fits the definition; for only God is totally
independent, and all created things depend on God for their creation and conservation. Nevertheless, since the realm of nature or
matter and the realm of thought are independent of one another, in
the sense that each can be conceived without the other, they are
classified as created substances. The former is called corporeal,
material or extended substance *(res extensa)* and the latter mind or
thinking substance *(res cogitans)*. Each kind of substance has one
principal property or attribute which constitutes its essence. The
essence of the former is extension in length, breadth and depth.
Thus, all of the properties of this substance (matter) can be expressed geometrically, whence Descartes arrived at his idea of a
geometrical physics. The essence of the latter (mind) is simply
thought, as all other specifically mental functions, e.g., imagining,
willing, feeling, are merely diverse forms of thinking. The perfect
symmetry of this scheme is, however, vitiated somewhat by the fact
that whereas there is only one extended substance of which all
physical bodies are merely modifications, each individual mind is
conscious of itself, and of its independence from all things save God
(which is the basis for the belief in its immortality), and thus constitutes a distinct thinking substance.

Having split the worlds of mind and matter (which includes the
human body) in so uncompromising a fashion, Descartes was obviously faced with the problem of explaining their relationship. This
problem, however, is itself complex, and it arises in at least two
distinct forms. The first, the epistemological form, requires an explanation as to how thinking substance, which has immediate access
only to its own thoughts, can ever attain to a certain knowledge of
matter or extended substance. This is equivalent to the question of
how the science of physics is possible. The second, the metaphysical
form, concerns the interaction between two distinct substances.
How can events in nature affect the mind, and how can thoughts

and free volitions have any effect in the corporeal world, e.g., how can my decision to raise my arm lead to the physical act? This issue has come to be known as the "mind-body problem."

Descartes's solution to the epistemological problem, as presented in his *Meditations on First Philosophy*, is certainly the best-known aspect of his philosophy and has been, and continues to be, the topic of countless discussions. Its most characteristic and controversial feature is the attempt to overcome skepticism from within by doubting everything until one arrives at something that simply cannot be doubted. This indubitable truth would then be able to stand firm against any skeptical attack and serve as the "Archimedean point" upon which Descartes can confidently proceed to erect the edifice of scientific knowledge. The first beliefs to fall to this procedure of methodical doubt are those based on sensory evidence, including the belief in the existence of one's own body and the external physical world. It is, after all, at least conceivable that all life is a consistent dream, and, in any event, the senses themselves do not furnish any sure criterion for distinguishing between waking and dreaming. But far-reaching as it already is, this doubt does not stop here. By means of the ingenious hypothesis of a deceiving God, Descartes even finds it possible to cast doubts (albeit feeble ones) on the basic truths of mathematics. However, just when it appears that the victory of skepticism is going to be complete, Descartes arrives at his indubitable truth. This concerns one's own existence while thinking. Even if one is being systematically deceived, one must still exist in order to be deceived. Thus: "I am, I exist is necessarily true each time that I pronounce it, or that I mentally conceive it."[6]

This, however, does not take us very far, and in order to progress to other truths, which have temporarily been abandoned by the process of methodical doubt, we must see just what it is about this truth that exempts it from doubt. Descartes's more or less technical answer is that we "clearly and distinctly perceive" it to be true. Now to clearly and distinctly perceive a proposition to be true really amounts in the end, for Descartes, to either grasping it immediately through intuition as self-evident or seeing that it can be deduced from self-evident truths (intuition and deduction being the two sources of rational knowledge). Thus, the crucial problem of Cartesian epistemology is whether everything which we perceive in this manner can be safely regarded as true. Descartes is able to answer this affirmatively by demonstrating that God exists and that he is no deceiver, which suffices to remove all grounds for doubting such propositions. God, in other words, functions for Descartes as the guarantor of our clear and distinct perceptions. This does not, of course, guarantee the truth of all our propositions or beliefs, but it does of those which deal with our geometrical conceptions of extension. We can therefore be sure that extended substance (the external world) exists and has the characteristics assigned to it by the science of physics.

Descartes's attempted solution to the mind-body problem is much less systematic. It basically amounts to the admission that the problem is insoluble, at least in terms of the appeal to clear and distinct perceptions, which is the standard of scientific evidence. This appeal led Descartes to the separation of mind and body in the first place, and it hardly enables him to explain the union between the two radically disparate substances. Instead, Descartes simply appeals to experience, a procedure which he likewise followed in his defense of the freedom of the will: "Everyone feels that he is a single person with both body and thought so related by nature that the thought can move the body and feel the things which happen to it."[7] The relationship must therefore be accepted as a brute fact, even though it cannot be adequately explained. Yet Descartes did not abandon all efforts to explain how mind and body interact, and he even tried to provide a physiological account of their interaction. This account is based on the hypothesis, later ridiculed by Spinoza, that the pineal gland in the brain is the "seat of the soul," and that it serves as the point of union between the immaterial thoughts, passions and volitions of the mind and the "animal spirits," which are the small particles of matter by which messages are allegedly relayed from the brain to the rest of the body and vice versa.[8] Through this rather fanciful explanation Descartes evidently hoped to unite his completely mechanistic physiology (the conception of the human body as a machine) with his conception of an immaterial, independent and immortal soul or thinking substance.

Such was the first great attempt to construct a philosophy based on the mathematical conception of nature, and to resolve the problems concerning man and his place in nature which inevitably arose as a result of this conception. It can, indeed, to use Spinoza's significant phrase, be seen as an effort "to understand the union existing between the mind and the whole of nature," with "nature" being construed as the infinite, extended realm of mathematical physics. As such, however, it clearly failed, and the dream of a unified science, which would include a science of man in one universally applicable system of explanation, and which was already at least suggested by Descartes's idea of a universal mathematics, remained unfulfilled. Partly because of his basically Christian starting point and partly because of some of his metaphysical assumptions, e.g., the concept of substance, Cartesian man is never really integrated into nature. With his free will and immaterial and immortal soul he remains an alien being, whose very knowledge of nature can only be assured by a question-begging appeal to divine veracity, and whose actual interaction with it is an inexplicable fact and a manifest exception to its universal lawfulness.

II *Some Central Themes in Spinoza's Philosophy*

In his editorial preface to the *The Principles of Descartes' Philosophy,* Meyer, speaking for Spinoza, notes several areas in which his philosophy differs from that of Descartes. These include the conception of the will and its alleged freedom and the notion that the human mind constitutes a distinct thinking substance. Special attention is given, however, to the Cartesian notion *"that this or that surpasses human knowledge."* As Meyer points out in reference to Spinoza: "He believed that all these things, and even many things more subtle and more sublime, could not only be clearly and distinctly conceived by us, but even readily explained if only the human mind were led in the way which Descartes opened up and made possible for investigating truth and for acquiring knowledge."[9] Thus, in opposition to the Cartesian appeal to the limits of knowledge, an appeal which was undoubtedly motivated by theological considerations, Spinoza affirms an absolute rationalism. Given the proper method, reality as a whole is intelligible to the human mind, and Spinoza claims in his *Ethics* to have done nothing less than to demonstrate this truth.[10]

Above and beyond this, however, the greatest single difference between the philosophies of Descartes and Spinoza, and the root of most of the others, lies in the fact that the main thrust of Spinoza's philosophy is ethical. He is before everything else a moralist, concerned, like the great Greek thinkers, to determine the true good for man. This is not at all to suggest that Descartes was unconcerned about ethical issues, but simply to point out that they never had the centrality in his thought which they had for Spinoza. Thus, although

questions about the nature and limits of human knowledge, the
nature and existence of God, and the relationship between the
human mind and the body are given considerable attention in the
Ethics, and they will occupy us to a large extent in our analysis of
Spinoza's philosophy, it must never be forgotten that Spinoza's
treatment of these issues is based upon, and often colored by, his
ethical concern.

Speaking in general terms, Spinoza's moral philosophy can be
placed within the intellectualistic tradition, which goes back to the
classical Greek moralists, Socrates, Plato and Aristotle. Common to
all of these thinkers is the identification of virtue, or in the case of
Aristotle, the highest virtue, with knowledge. Otherwise expressed,
the highest virtues are intellectual, while the so-called "moral virtues" or virtues of character, such as self-control, courage, and benevolence, are seen either as effects of intellectual virtue or as
preparatory stages necessary for its realization. Spinoza accepts this
doctrine in an unqualified form, and he contends that it is only
through knowledge that one can overcome the bondage to the passions which constitutes the essence of human misery. He is therefore also willing to affirm the hard doctrine that only the wise man
can be truly happy and truly free.

In at least verbal agreement with Maimonides and other representatives of medieval Jewish, Christian and Islamic religious
traditions, Spinoza regards God as the prime object of knowledge.
The attainment of a genuine knowledge of God is therefore viewed
as the ultimate goal of human life and the key to the achievement of
blessedness. Moreover, not only does Spinoza see human existence
as culminating in a knowledge of God, but also he claims, again in
agreement with the religious tradition, that this knowledge necessarily leads to love. Thus, the entire argument of the *Ethics* culminates in the "intellectual love of God" *(amor intellectualis Dei)*
through which the human mind is allegedly able to transcend its
finitude and unite with the eternal. This conception constitutes
Spinoza's purely philosophical alternative to the Beatific Vision, and
it provides much of the religious and perhaps even mystical tone
which some have found in his philosophy.

The ground of this conception, however, must be placed in
Spinoza's thoroughgoing rationalism rather than his religious sensitivity. As we have already noted, this rationalism involves the
belief in the total intelligibility of the real. Given Spinoza's

mathematically oriented conception of knowledge, this in turn means that all reality can be explained within a single deductive system. This is not, of course, to claim that particular facts can be deduced by the human mind, but rather that, given these facts, which are provided by experience, they can all be understood in terms of this universal system of explanation. The concept of God serves as the first principle of this system, from which all else follows with logical necessity. Thus, it is only with reference to the concept of God that we can have adequate knowledge of anything in nature, including our emotions and their causes. Any knowledge that does not have its source in rationally grounded principles, and ultimately in God, is attributed by Spinoza to the imagination, which is in turn viewed as the source of man's bondage to the passions and hence of human misery. We can therefore see that two of the major tasks incumbent upon Spinoza are to show how genuine knowledge differs from the products of the imagination, and how a knowledge of God is possible for man. These are the central themes of his epistemology.

Although much of Spinoza's language is reminiscent of the religious tradition, his overall point of view is really quite different from, if not completely antithetical to, that tradition. The God who functions as the first principle of knowledge, and who is the object of a purely intellectual love, has very little in common with the God of Abraham, Isaac and Jacob. Spinoza describes this God in the *Ethics* as "a being absolutely infinite, that is, a substance consisting in infinite attributes, of which each expresses eternal and infinite essentiality" (Part I, Def. VI). This definition is deliberately intended to correct the traditional notion of God as a most perfect or supremely perfect Being, which in Spinoza's opinion leads to an inadequate idea of God and therefore to dangerous anthropomorphisms.[111] These difficulties can be overcome by conceiving of God as substance; and, as we shall see in the next chapter, the logical development of this conception leads to the rejection of the Cartesian dualism and to the establishment of a monistic metaphysics, wherein thought and extension, which for Descartes were created substances, are viewed instead as attributes of God, the unique, infinite substance.

For the present, however, we can only note that when Spinoza speaks in the *Ethics* about the knowledge of God, he means precisely the same as he had meant in *On the Improvement of the*

Understanding by the "knowledge of the union existing between the mind and the whole of nature." Spinoza's God is thus not a being beyond nature but rather nature itself. Yet it is just at this point that misunderstanding is apt to arise; for by the identification of God with nature, Spinoza is not referring to nature as the sum total of particular things which we find about us, but to nature as an infinite system of laws and forces in which these things have their determined and necessary place, and through which they must be understood. The divinity of nature, so conceived, consists in its infinity and necessity. As truly infinite, in Spinoza's technical language "absolutely infinite," there is nothing beyond nature on which it depends, nor any external purpose which it can be thought to embody. As a necessary system of laws and forces, nothing in it is contingent, nothing could possibly be other than it is. Moreover, man's knowledge of such a God is obviously equivalent to the knowledge of the infinite and necessary order, in which man, like everything else, has his determinate place; and the intellectual love that springs from this knowledge is the joyful acceptance and affirmation of the very same necessary order.

This complex activity of knowledge, acceptance and affirmation constitutes, for Spinoza, man's highest destiny and chief good. It is not a means to happiness, but happiness itself, in its most authentic and lasting form. Similarly, virtue, so conceived, is its own reward, and not, as the religious tradition so often affirms, merely a means for acquiring future rewards or avoiding future punishments. Finally, Spinoza tells us that this very same activity is the source of man's freedom. But freedom here is not to be conceived, as Descartes and others have conceived it, as some mysterious power which in some inexplicable way exempts man from the laws and power of nature. Rather, it consists entirely in the apprehension of the necessity of these very laws. Spinoza's point is essentially the same as the claim which was later brought home so forcefully by Freud. We gain control of our emotions, and thus become free in the most meaningful sense in which we can use this expression, solely by acquiring knowledge of these emotions and of their causes.[12]

This view, which we have only attempted to sketch in its broadest outlines, can be seen as the most fully developed defense of the ideal of scientific objectivity as a life task to be found in the history of Western thought. The maxim "Know thyself," which for Socrates expressed the sum and substance of human wisdom, but which led only to the ironic conclusion that the only thing that one can know about oneself is that one knows nothing, became for Spinoza the demand to become aware of one's place in the infinite and necessary scheme of things. This demand is grounded in the conviction that things are, indeed, necessary and determined; that through the proper use of his intellect, man is capable of comprehending this necessity; that the course of infinite nature is completely indifferent to human purposes; and, consequently, that moral and religious categories such as good and evil or sin and grace have no basis in reality but are merely products of human thought and desire. It is also, however, based on Spinoza's firm conviction that the recognition of these facts is the source of peace and satisfaction; not the "peace that passeth understanding" of religious ecstasy, but the true and lasting peace that does not so much derive from, as actually consist in, understanding.

Spinoza himself provided the clearest statement of his basic standpoint in the critique of final causes which he appended to the first part of the *Ethics*. Final causes there stand for almost everything that Spinoza opposes. Not only does he reject any appeal to them as an inadequate, unscientific mode of explanation, an attitude which he shares with all of the proponents of the new science, but he treats this conception as an important expression of the theistic, pluralistic world view which stands in the way of achieving the desired understanding of man and his place in nature.

According to Spinoza's analysis: "All such opinions spring from the notion commonly entertained, that all things in nature act as men themselves act, namely, with an end in view."[13] When combined, as it has been since the Middle Ages, with the Judeo-Christian conception of God, it leads to the familiar doctrine that God created all things for the benefit of man. But such a belief is the result of viewing things through the imagination rather than through the intellect, which alone grasps things through their true causes. Given human nature, however, such a procedure is inevitable; for everyone ought to be willing to admit "that all men are born ignorant of the causes of things, that all have the desire to seek for what is useful to them, and that they are conscious of such desire." From this it follows that all men think themselves free and act with an end in view (what they take to be useful). Moreover, being ignorant of true causes, they tend to judge other natures by their own, and when they find many things in nature that prove useful to them, e.g., "eyes for seeing, teeth for chewing, herbs and animals for yielding food, the sun for giving light, the sea for breeding fish, etc., they come to look on the whole of nature as a means for obtaining such conveniences." Now being aware that they did not themselves create all of these great conveniences, men were naturally led by their imagination to the belief that "some ruler or rulers of the universe endowed with human freedom . . . arranged and adapted everything for human use." Thus arises the belief in the gods, and with it, as we can clearly see, although Spinoza does not here make it explicit, the superstitious idea that human virtue consists in doing what is pleasing to these gods, so that they will continue to confer their benefits upon us. Yet one soon realizes that these benefits are not distributed equitably, that "good and evil fortunes fall to the lot of pious and impious alike." This gives rise to what has come to be known as the "problem of evil," viz., the problem of reconciling the apparent evil in the world with the goodness of God. This problem, in turn, is generally resolved by an appeal to ignorance in the form of the pious claim that "God's judgments far transcend human understanding." As Spinoza well knew from personal experience, this appeal can lead to the grossest superstition and the most irrational acts, for it serves as the great justification for religious oppression in all its forms. Furthermore, he reflects, "such a doctrine might well have sufficed to conceal the truth from the human race for all eternity, if mathematics had not furnished another standard of verity in considering solely the essence and properties of figures without regard to their final causes."[14]

With this total repudiation of final causes, Spinoza is, in effect, advocating the universalization of the method of mathematics, that is, the method whereby things are understood in terms of their logical, lawful relationships to each other, not in terms of their imaginative, contingent relationship to our needs and desires. In the preface to Part III of the *Ethics* he points out that "there should be one and the same method of understanding the nature of all things whatsoever, namely, through nature's universal laws and rules." The central point here is that man, with his mental and emotional life, the realm of *res cogitans*, which Descartes had separated from nature, is no exception to this principle. Spinoza emphasizes this by proclaiming that he will "consider human actions and desires in exactly the same manner, as though I were concerned with lines, planes, and solids."[15] Not only is such a mode of explanation alone scientific, but even more importantly for Spinoza, it is the way in which we have to regard our own actions and desires, as well as those of our fellowman, if we are ever to achieve virtue, happiness and freedom.

III   *The Geometrical Method*

We cannot complete our brief overview of Spinoza's philosophy without taking at least some note of the geometrical form in which he cast it. The geometrical order or method of demonstration is modeled after that of Euclid's *Elements*. It normally begins with the presentation of a set of definitions, axioms and postulates; and it proceeds, on the basis of these, to demonstrate a number of theorems or propositions. This is equivalent to what Descartes had called the synthetic method of demonstration, which he opposed to the analytic method of discovery. Descartes himself had made use of this method, at the request of some of his critics, for the presentation of some of the basic principles of his philosophy.[16] Moreover, such an endeavor was not unique to Descartes, but rather very much in the spirit of the seventeenth century, with its emphasis on mathematics as the standard of intelligibility and of scientific explanation.[17] But while Spinoza was neither the first nor the last to attempt this, he was the first to do so on such a large scale, and it must have cost him a great effort. Each of the five parts of the *Ethics* begins with a set of definitions and axioms, and the argument is, as with Euclid, presented in a series of propositions, each with its own demonstration. These propositions, in turn, are interspersed with frequent scholia in which Spinoza abandons the formal manner of presentation and adds significant illustrative material and occasional criticisms of opposing views. Finally, a number of the parts have prefaces and appendices which introduce and supplement the argument in important ways.

Like much else in Spinoza, the significance of the geometrical method of demonstration has been the object of considerable dispute. The basic issue is quite simply whether this form or method of demonstration is really required by the content, or whether the connection between the two is more external, with the choice of a geometrical form being motivated purely by extrinsic factors such as its pedagogical value. Moreover, as is unfortunately so often the case with Spinoza scholarship, the master himself has left us with no real information as to his own views on the matter, so that the question must be resolved by more indirect means.

It is true that one can point to a number of distinguished scholars and philosophers on each side of the issue.[18] If, however, we are to take Spinoza seriously as a philosopher, we must likewise take his method seriously. Perhaps the best way to begin is through a consideration of the way in which Spinoza viewed his definitions and the role which he gave to them in his argument. This information is not provided by the *Ethics*, which does not attempt to justify or even explain its own mode of procedure, but it is to be found in Spinoza's correspondence and in *On the Improvement of the Understanding*.

The modern reader, and especially the philosophically trained reader, has a good deal of trouble with Spinoza's definitions, of which the already cited definition of God can serve as an example. Such a reader is often left with the impression that Spinoza simply and arbitrarily defines his key terms in such a way as to arrive at his desired conclusions. The argument of the *Ethics* is thus viewed as an impressive and intricate chain of reasoning which nowhere touches reality. Now, regardless of how we may ultimately come to view this judgment, we must at least realize that Spinoza himself was keenly aware of the problem. In a letter to his young friend Simon De Vries, he distinguishes between two kinds of definitions in a way which parallels the traditional distinction between nominal and real definitions. The former kind stipulates what one means by a word, or what one thinks in a given concept. Such a definition can be conceivable or inconceivable, clear or obscure, helpful or unhelpful, but since it is arbitrarily concocted by the human mind, it cannot, strictly speaking, be called either true or false. The latter kind of definition (real definition), which in Spinoza's terms "explains a thing as it exists outside of the understanding," defines a thing rather than a name. It therefore can be either true or false, and it is in fact a proposition, differing from an axiom only in its specificity.[19]

At first glance the definitions which we find in the *Ethics* seem to be of the former variety. They are introduced by expressions such as "by . . . I mean that" or "a thing is called . . ." which suggest that we are merely being told how the term in question is being used, and it is just this feature of Spinoza's definitions which gives rise to the above-mentioned objections. The actual course of the argument, however, makes it clear that Spinoza intends his definitions to be considerably more than that; for merely nominal definitions cannot provide us with any information about reality. Like the definitions of geometrical figures found in Euclid, Spinoza's definitions are designed to describe not only the names used, but also the objects named. They therefore are presented as true propositions describing the essence of things. Thus, just as the mathematician can deduce the properties of a figure from his real definition, so Spinoza, the metaphysician, proposes to deduce the basic properties of reality or nature from his fundamental real definitions.[20]

But then the obvious question arises: How does Spinoza know that he has arrived at a true definition which, in his own terms, provides us with an adequate or clear and distinct idea of the object in question? Here, perhaps more than in any other area, we can discern the influence of the geometrical way of thinking in Spinoza, and especially the approach of the analytic geometry as developed by Descartes. What Spinoza does, in effect, is to ask how the mathematician knows that he has arrived at a real definition of a figure. This is found to occur when he is able to construct it. His definition is thus a rule for the construction of a figure, what is often called a "genetic definition," and from such a definition alone, all of the properties of the figure can be deduced. To cite Spinoza's own example, the nominal definition of a circle as "a figure, such that all straight lines drawn from the center to the circumference are equal" is rejected in favor of the genetic definition as "the figure described by any line whereof one end is fixed and the other free."[21] This definition tells us how such a figure can be constructed, and from the rule for construction we can deduce all of its properties.

Spinoza's central point is that the same principles apply to our knowledge of nature or reality as to our knowledge of abstract entities such as mathematical objects. Thus, we have a real definition, adequate, true or clear and distinct idea of a thing (all of these terms, as we shall see later being more or less interchangeable) insofar as we know its "proximate cause" and can see how its properties necessarily follow from this cause. "For, in reality," Spinoza writes, "the knowledge of an effect is nothing else than the acquisition of a more perfect knowledge of its cause."[22] Moreover, in such instances there is no room for doubt of the kind envisioned by Descartes. When the mind has a true idea it immediately knows it to be true; as it grasps the logical necessity with which the proper-

ties of the object follow from the idea.[23] The metaphysician as well
as the mathematician can therefore arrive at genetic definitions of
things, and it is through these definitions that he acquires rationally
grounded knowledge.[24]

If, however, the knowledge of a thing is equivalent to the knowledge of its cause, which Spinoza identifies with its logical ground, or
the principle in terms of which it is understood, then either we find
ourselves involved in an infinite regress, which would in turn lead
to a hopeless skepticism, or the whole cognitive enterprise must be
grounded in a single first principle. Furthermore, this first principle
in terms of which everything is to be explained obviously cannot
itself be explained in terms of anything else. It must therefore have
the reason or ground of its existence in itself, or in the language of
the schools, which Spinoza likewise adopts, be *"causa sui"* (self-
caused). The first principle is, of course, the concept of God, and we
can thus see how Spinoza's method leads necessarily to his concept
of God.[25] As Spinoza himself clearly tells us:

> As regards the order of our perceptions, and the manner in which they
> should be arranged and united, it is necessary that, as soon as is possible
> and rational, we should inquire whether there be any being (and, if so, what
> being), that is the cause of all things, so that its essence, represented in
> thought, may be the cause of all our ideas, and then our mind will to the
> utmost possible extent reflect nature. For it will possess, subjectively, na-
> ture's essence, order, and union.[26]

How then do we know that our thoughts are arranged in the
proper logical order, that they "possess, subjectively, nature's essence, order and union"? Spinoza's answer is that we know this in
precisely the same way in which the mathematician knows that he
has arrived at the correct idea of a circle. In both instances the
properties follow with strict logical necessity from the cause and the
mind is able to see that nothing is undetermined, nothing left unexplained. The argument of the *Ethics* is intended to lead us to
understand reality as a whole in just this way. We must come to see
"that from God's supreme power, or infinite nature, an infinite
number of things—that is, all things have necessarily flowed forth in
an infinite number of ways, or always follow from the same necessity; in the same way as from the nature of a triangle it follows from
eternity and for eternity, that its three interior angles are equal to
two right angles" (*Ethics* I, Prop. XVII, Scholium). The necessity

with which the truth about the interior angles of a triangle follows from the nature of the triangle is strictly logical, and it is based on the real definition of the triangle. But if, as Spinoza claims, things follow from God with *precisely the same necessity* and in *precisely the same manner*, then it would seem to be highly appropriate, to say the least, for the method of demonstration to be the same in the one case as in the other.

We can therefore conclude that the geometrical form of Spinoza's philosophy is, indeed, intimately related to, if not actually inseparable from, its content; and we shall have to keep this constantly in mind throughout our investigation of the argument of the *Ethics*. This is not to suggest that the geometrical form of presentation is "demanded" or "required" by the philosophy in the strong sense that its basic conclusions cannot even be accurately expressed apart from it. No philosopher, with the possible exceptions of Plato, Hegel and Kierkegaard, has ever achieved such an interpenetration of form and content. Furthermore, as already noted, the geometrical method is a method of demonstration, not of discovery, so that it would be nonsensical to try to argue that Spinoza actually arrived at his philosophy by beginning with certain definitions and axioms and proceeding from these to deduce his conclusions. As he affirms explicitly, method presupposes a certain body of knowledge and serves only to put it into the best possible logical order.[27] Nevertheless, given the assumptions about the nature of knowledge which we have just touched upon and shall examine in more detail later, the geometrical method is the most adequate vehicle for presenting this philosophy. Not only does it allow Spinoza to deduce, or at least attempt to deduce, all of his conclusions from a single first principle, viz., the concept of God, and to illustrate the absolute necessity governing all things, but for these very reasons, it presents his view of the universe in the form in which, according to his theory of knowledge, it can be adequately grasped by the intellect. Such a form is therefore, from Spinoza's point of view, necessary for the realization of his moral ideal.

CHAPTER 3

God

THE first part of the *Ethics*, *"De Deo"* (Concerning God), is devoted to an analysis of the nature of God and to the delineation of the main outlines of the relationship between God and the world. It contains Spinoza's analysis of the basic structure of reality (his metaphysics) and his criticisms of the Judeo-Christian conception of God. This discussion falls roughly into three parts, which determine the three divisions of this chapter. The first (Props. I-XV) offers an exposition of the nature or essence of God, i.e., an account of what God is, together with a set of demonstrations that God, so conceived, necessarily exists. Here Spinoza introduces his fundamental category of substance, in light of which he develops his conception of God as "a substance consisting of infinite attributes, of which each expresses eternal and infinite essentiality." The second section (Props. XVI-XXIX) considers the divine power or causality, which is equivalent to the infinite power of nature. This naturally leads to an analysis of the relationship between God and the world, and within the context of this analysis, Spinoza presents a first characterization of particular things in nature as finite modes. The last section (Props. XXX-XXXVI) makes explicit many of the results which have already been established and uses them as the basis of a polemic against the whole Judeo-Christian religious tradition. This polemic culminates in the appendix dealing with final causes which we have already considered.

I *God as Substance*

By developing his doctrine of God in light of the concept of substance, Spinoza made a rather original use of one of the most important concepts in the history of Western philosophy. The concept arose with the Greeks in connection with their attempt to resolve a fundamental problem about the universe, viz., the problem of change. The explanation of change seems to require the recognition of something permanent or abiding which underlies change and in relation to which it can be understood. The concept of substance fulfilled this function. It was introduced to refer to the permanent element or elements in the universe, the abiding substratum of change, while the changing features of experience were viewed as its states or qualities. Thus, Aristotle, who provided the first systematic treatment of the concept of substance, writes: "The most distinctive mark of substance appears to be that, while remaining numerically one and the same, it is capable of admitting contrary qualities."[1] Aristotle also claimed, however, that substances are not only the substrata of change but also the subjects of predication.[2] Intelligible talk about the world seems to require expressions both for qualities and for things or subjects which have these qualities. Moreover, since we can conceive of a thing or a subject without at least some of its qualities, which are therefore called accidental, but cannot conceive of a quality except in relation to a thing or subject, it follows that the latter are more fundamental. The various subjects of predication, that is, the particular things in nature, e.g., men, horses, trees, were thus viewed by Aristotle as substances in the primary sense, the basic elements in the universe in terms of which everything else is to be understood.

By the time of Descartes the concept of substance had changed considerably, and in a way which accords with the development of the mathematical science of nature. Descartes, it will be recalled, had defined substance primarily in terms of independent existence, as "a thing which so exists that it needs no other thing in order to exist." Each substance, so conceived, has one fundamental attribute or property, which constitutes its nature or essence, and through which it is known. As we have seen, the essence or essential property of corporeal substance is extension, and it is on the basis of this conception that Descartes argued for the possibility of a completely geometrical science of nature. Like Aristotle, Descartes used the concept of substance to refer to what is fundamental in nature, that in terms of which everything else is to be explained (this is accomplished by defining it in terms of independent existence), but in accordance with his radically different view of scientific explanation, he conceived of what is "substantial" in a quite different manner. Nevertheless, there is a residue of Aristotelianism in Descartes's theory, for in addition to his well-known account, which we have just considered, he also defined substance as "Everything in which there resides immediately, as in a subject, or by means of which there exists anything that we perceive, i.e., any property, quality, or attribute, of which we have a real idea."[3] He thus conceived of substance as a subject of predication, as a *thing* which has *properties*, and is, in fact, only known in terms of these properties. Moreover, it is in light of this conception that he used the expression "attribute" to designate the principal or essential property through which each substance is known,[4] and "mode" to refer to the nonessential properties, which cannot be conceived without substance, but without which substance or its principle attribute can be conceived.[5]

Given the role attributed to substance (as the ultimate principle of explanation) by thinkers as diverse as Aristotle and Descartes, and given Spinoza's attempt to explain everything by reference to God, it was perfectly natural for Spinoza to endeavor to understand God in terms of the concept of substance. But in light of his unique view of nature and of the manner in which things depend on God, we should expect that Spinoza would construe substance in a rather different fashion. This difference is implicit in the definitions which Spinoza presents at the beginning of the first part of the *Ethics*. Substance is here defined as "that which is in itself, and is conceived through itself: in other words, that of which a conception can be formed independently of any other conception" (Def. III). Substance, so defined, is distinguished first from *attributes*, by which Spinoza means "that which the intellect perceives as constituting the essence of substance" (Def. IV), and then from *modes*, by which he means "the modifications [*affectiones*] of substance, or that which exists in, and is conceived through something other than itself" (Def. V).

Central to this conception is the total abandonment of the view of substance as the subject of predication or bearer of properties. Neither attributes nor modes are viewed by Spinoza, as they were for Descartes, as properties of substance, and thus they are not related to substance as qualities to a thing or predicate to a subject.[6] There has been considerable debate concerning the precise status of attributes and this debate revolves around the meaning of the phrase "that which the intellect perceives as [*tanquam*] constituting." Some scholars, emphasizing the simplicity of substance and the identity of the attributes, have interpreted this in a basically subjective fashion and have contended that the diversity of attributes is merely a result of the way in which the intellect perceives substance and does not therefore really pertain to substance as it is in itself. Others contend, on the contrary, that the diversity of attributes reflects a real or "objective" diversity in the nature of substance.[7] Once again we cannot go into the details of this seemingly endless debate, but it does appear that the bulk of the evidence supports the objective interpretation. Spinoza's God is, after all, "a substance *consisting of* [italics mine] infinite attributes," and, as we have already seen, his whole philosophy culminates in a knowledge of God, who functions as the very principle of intelligibility. Now, as the definition makes clear, it is through the attributes that the intellect understands God, or substance, and it would seem to follow from this that if this knowledge is to be adequate, and Spinoza claims that it is, then these attributes must really pertain to the nature of God. To deny this would lead one to the rather paradoxical and un-Spinozistic conclusion that the principle of intelligibility is itself unintelligible.

But if attributes are neither properties of substance nor subjective interpretations foisted upon it by the perceiving intellect, what are they? How are we to understand the strange doctrine that substance consists of infinite attributes, of which the human intellect grasps only two, viz., thought and extension? We shall turn later to the problem of the infinite attributes, but for the present our concern must be directed to the general notion of attribute. The view which we here offer is that attributes can best be regarded as aspects of substance or perspectives in terms of which it can be conceived. In an effort to make this somewhat clearer, let us briefly consider an analogy between the way in which the intellect perceives substance and the way in which we ordinarily perceive objects in sense perception. Every object, it can be claimed, is necessarily perceived from a certain perspective or point of view. We never simply perceive the table, but always from the front, behind, above, etc. The "real table" would only be fully revealed through the sum of all possible perspectives. Nevertheless, each distinct perspective does not merely acquaint us with a property, or even a separable part of the table, but rather with the table as a table, i.e., as a distinct, unified entity, albeit perceived from a particular limited point of view. Much the same can be said about Spinoza's attributes. Each of them *is* substance, although substance as grasped from a particular point of view. This helps us to understand why Spinoza should make many of the same claims about attributes that he does about substance, e.g., that they are conceived in themselves and through themselves, and why in the *Short Treatise* and in his early correspondence he tended to indentify them.[8] Nature, after all, *is* extension in the sense that the physicist can give a complete and coherent account of reality in physical terms, without bringing in any nonphysical presuppositions, e.g., final causes. But nature, so conceived, is an object of knowledge, and it is therefore equally possible to view reality as a system of thought. Like any analogy, the present one cannot be pressed too far, and it seems to break down in at least two important respects. First of all, each attribute of substance, unlike each visual perspective of a thing, is self-contained and does not refer to other attributes. Secondly, no attribute, again unlike the various perspectives, is in any way privileged. Each provides us with an equally adequate knowledge of substance. Even allowing for these differences, however, the point remains that although the finite intellect necessarily interprets nature from a particular perspective, it nevertheless is able to comprehend the true nature or essence of substance, and not merely some of its properties. Leibniz was later to express a similar thought with his contention that each monad (finite substance) represents or perceives the universe from a particular point of view, and both Spinoza and Leibniz drew from this thought the rather significant consequence that human knowledge is similar in kind, although not in scope, to God's knowledge.

Futhermore, modes which are conceived through and dependent upon substance are likewise not to be construed as properties or qualities which inhere in and are predicated of substance. This is certainly true of "infinite modes," which, as we shall see, are basically general principles or categories, but it also holds of "finite modes," which are particular things. These things stand to substance in the relation of effect to cause, not of predicate to subject or property to things; and it is precisely this causal dependence of all particular things on God that Spinoza is concerned with establishing in the first part of the *Ethics*.[9]

In light of these basic definitions or conceptions, Spinoza proceeds in the opening propositions to prove that there can only be one substance, that existence pertains to its very nature, and that it possesses infinite attributes. The demonstration of the unity of substance, which is the central thesis of Spinoza's monism and the heart of his critique of Descartes, is itself divided into three parts which more or less refer to three possible pluralistic positions that are being refuted. Spinoza first argues (Props. I-V) that there cannot be more than one substance having the same nature or attribute. As is typical of Spinoza, his argument takes the form of the demonstration of the absurdity of the contrary hypothesis, of which Descartes's doctrine of a plurality of thinking substances is a perfect example. Since an attribute is not a property but an expression of the nature of substance, two substances with the same attribute would have the same nature; they would, in short, be one and the same identical substance. This argument is based on what Leibniz later called the principle of the "identity of indiscernibles," and it is interesting to note that a principle which was used by Spinoza to help establish the unity of substance, was taken by Leibniz as one of the bases of his pluralism.

The second alternative to be considered is that there exist a number of different interacting substances with distinct natures. This view is of particular importance to Spinoza; for it is reflected both in Descartes's distinction between extended and thinking substances (which have nothing in common but which interact with one another) and in the Judeo-Christian doctrine of creation with its conception of man as a created substance. The refutation is simple, as much of the groundwork has been laid in the early propositions. Since *"two substances, whose attributes are different, have nothing in common"* (Prop. II), and since *"things which have nothing in common cannot be one the cause of the other"* (Prop. III), which is itself based on the axiom "Things which have nothing in common cannot be understood, the one by means of the other" (Axiom V), it follows that *"one substance cannot be produced by another substance"* (Prop. VI), and, as he goes on to add in the demonstration, "one cannot be the cause of another."

One possibility still remains, and that is the view, which was actually adopted by Leibniz, viz., that there are a plurality of distinct substances which do not stand in causal relation to one another or interact in any way. Spinoza proceeds to repudiate this view, and thus, in effect, to refute Leibniz in advance. This argument, however, is somewhat more complex, and before Spinoza can complete it, he must first establish two additional central features of his doctrine of substance: (1) that existence belongs to its nature, and (2) that it possesses an infinity of attributes.

The claim that existence belongs to the essence of substance is actually equivalent to the assertion that substance necessarily exists. But although Spinoza was much concerned to establish this latter thesis, the overall goal of his argument, viz., the identification of God with substance, seems to have led him to delay making this connection until somewhat later. As Spinoza develops his proof in the present instance, the unique relationship between the essence of substance and its existence is a direct consequence of the just-established fact that it cannot be produced or caused by anything external to itself. Since substance cannot be so produced, he argues that "it must, therefore, be its own cause—that is, its essence necessarily involves existence, or existence belongs to its nature" (Prop. VII). This argument obviously rests on what has been called, at least since Leibniz, the principle of sufficient reason, i.e., the principle that everything must have a ground, reason or cause (these terms being generally used synonymously) which determines its existence. Spinoza, like most rationalists before Kant, seems to have simply assumed this. In fact, he even argued that a cause or reason must be assigned not only for the existence, but also for the nonexistence of anything (Prop. XI, second proof). Nothing, in other words, can simply exist or not exist; in either case there must be a rational ground or cause through which its existence or nonexistence can be understood. In light of this principle, he reasons that since substance cannot have the cause or reason for its existence in anything external to itself, for then it would not be substance, it must have it in itself. Substance is therefore self-caused or self-sufficient being, and as such existence belongs to its very nature. As he goes on to add, however (in a scholium which for some reason is attached to the next proposition), this proof is really unnecessary. If only people kept in mind the true nature of substance (that which is in itself and conceived through itself), the proposition would be viewed as "a universal axiom and accounted a truism" (Prop. VIII, Scholium II). Spinoza's point here is that this manner of existence follows logically from the very definition of substance—as, indeed, it must if this definition is to function in the required manner in his arguments.

This, in turn, provides the basis for the demonstration of the infinity of substance, but since Spinoza uses the notion of infinity in two distinct senses, the argument falls into two parts. The two senses of infinity between which Spinoza is careful to distinguish (Defs. II and VI) are "infinite after its own kind" and "absolutely infinite." A thing is infinite in the first sense when it cannot be limited by another thing of the same nature. This applies to the attributes, thought and extension, which are each coextensive with reality as a whole. A particular thought or body, on the other hand, is limited or determined by another thought or body, and is therefore "finite after its kind" *(suo genere finitas.)* The infinity of substance *in this sense* can be directly inferred from its mode of existence; for if it were limited, determined or produced, it could only be by another substance of the same nature, which has already been shown to be impossible (Prop. VIII).

Spinoza's concern, however, is not to show that substance is infinite in this sense (which applies to his attributes and to Descartes's created substances), but that it is "absolutely infinite." A being is infinite in this strong sense if it possesses complete reality and no negation. This simply means that there is nothing outside of it or apart from it in any way, even in the manner in which thought and extension, as distinct expressions of one reality, are apart or distinct from one another. Another way of making the same point is to say that such a being possesses infinite attributes, and this is precisely what Spinoza proceeds to affirm. The basis for this claim is the principle that *"the more reality or being a thing has the greater the number of its attributes"* (Prop. IX). As Spinoza indicates, this follows from the very definition of attributes, and his point can be grasped if we keep in mind that attributes are to be construed as aspects of substance, or perspectives in terms of which it is perceived, rather than as properties. In this view, the claim that something possesses more reality or attributes than something else is equivalent to the assertion that there are more aspects to it, or more perspectives from which it can be viewed. For example, one might say that a man has more reality than a stone because he has a more complex nature, which includes a mental life as well as a material body. He therefore has aspects of his being which the stone lacks, or at least possesses in an extremely primitive form, and as a result man, unlike the stone, can be the subject matter of the science of psychology as well as that of physics. Now a being that possessed all reality would, by definition, lack nothing. It would therefore contain within itself all possible aspects, with each of these aspects

providing a perspective in terms of which this being can be understood, at least by an infinite intellect. But this is precisely the case
with substance, and hence Spinoza can conclude that substance
possesses infinite attributes.

Despite its medieval tone, which has led some scholars to reject it
as an anachronism, inconsistent with the main thrust of Spinoza's
metaphysics,[10] the doctrine of infinite attributes is really an integral
part of Spinoza's philosophy. First of all, it gives a philosophical
expression to the notion of the infinity of nature, which is characteristic of modern science. By saying that thought and extension are
merely two of the infinite attributes, he is really claiming no more
than his contemporary Malebranche, who warned that one should
not jump to the conclusion that thought and extension exhaust the
infinite reality of nature.[11] Secondly, although Spinoza does not
definitively state his conclusion until somewhat later (Prop. XIV),
this doctrine plays a key role in his argument for the unity of substance, as it provides the means whereby he can repudiate the third
and last version of pluralism. Since substance possesses infinite attributes or all reality, there is literally nothing which could conceiv-
ably exist apart from substance, so that the possibility of a plurality
of substances with different natures, which do not stand in causal
relations with one another, is no longer available. Moreover, the
abandonment of this possibility really involves, although Spinoza
does not put it in quite this way, the abandonment of all attempts to
conceive of substance as an entity of a particular kind, and the
adoption of the view that it must be conceived as the whole of
reality—not, to be sure, as the whole of reality in the sense of the
sum or aggregate of things, but as the principle of their intelligibility.

The true significance of this result can be gleaned from the little
that we have already seen of the history of the concept of substance.
As noted, substance was generally viewed *both* as the ultimate
ground of explanation, which amounts to saying that it functions as
the principle of intelligibility, and as a particular entity, i.e., a
bearer of properties. The problem with such a conception is that it
made it virtually impossible to conceive of nature as consisting of a
single universal order, to which all particular things belong. In this
respect it directly violated a basic assumption of modern natural
science. Spinoza overcomes this difficulty precisely by abandoning
the conception of substance as a particular entity and by identifying

it with the universal order of nature itself. In the last analysis, then, the claim that there is one substance with infinite attributes can be interpreted to mean that there is one universal order in relation to which all things must be understood. This is the order of nature.

Substance, so conceived, possesses one of the basic functions (ultimate explanation) and some, although certainly not all, of the characteristics which have also commonly been attributed to the Deity. It is therefore no surprise that Spinoza identifies God with substance and affirms that *"God, or substance, consisting of infinite attributes, of which each expresses eternal and infinite essentiality, necessarily exists"* (Prop. XI). In support of this proposition, Spinoza provides three proofs for the existence of God, which are modeled after arguments found in Descartes and other philosophers, but which, given the unorthodox nature of Spinoza's God, are put to a rather different purpose.

We have room here only to discuss the first of these proofs, but even a brief consideration of it, seen in relation to parallel arguments in his predecessors, suffices to reveal the main thrust of Spinoza's thought. The first proof is Spinoza's unique version of the ontological argument, which was first developed by St. Anselm and later reformulated by Descartes. The characteristic feature of this famous argument is its attempt to derive existence from the mere concept of God. Thus, Descartes argued that God must necessarily exist on the grounds that "existence can no more be separated from the essence of God than can its having three angles equal to two right angles be separated from the essence of a triangle, or the idea of a mountain from the idea of a valley."[12] This contention is based on the definition of God as an all-perfect being, and the assumption, which has often been challenged, that existence is a perfection. Since existence is a perfection, and since God (by definition) possesses all perfections, we cannot, without contradicting ourselves, deny existence of God; and this is equivalent to saying that God necessarily exists. Spinoza's version of this argument makes reference neither to the notion of perfection, which he later equates with reality, nor to the definition of God. Instead, it simply draws the logical consequence from the already established principle that "existence belongs to the nature of substance" and applies it to God, who is identified with substance in the very formulation of the proposition: "God or substance . . . necessarily exists." This argument consists of two stages which really do little more than provide two equivalent expressions for the above principle. We are first told that this principle implies that we cannot conceive of God or substance as not existing, and this, as with Descartes, is then said to mean that God exists necessarily.

Nevertheless, it is not immediately clear either what, if anything, Spinoza has shown to exist necessarily, or what the assertion that something exists necessarily really means. No matter what we may think of his argument, it is at least clear that Descartes uses it to establish the existence of a being (God) about whom one was previously in doubt. Spinoza, on the other hand, has shown that substance, consisting of infinite attributes, and therefore encompassing all reality, possesses the peculiar characteristic of existing necessarily. Yet not only is Spinoza's substance not the sort of being about whose existence one can have doubts, but, as we have just seen, it is not *a being* at all. Thus, despite their many formal similarities, we find (and precisely the same can be said of the other proofs) that Spinoza's argument leads to a radically different result than Descartes's. It does not prove that any being (God) exists, but that reality, as conceived under the category of substance, exists necessarily. Moreover, since necessary existence means independent existence or being self-caused, and since this is applied to substance or reality as a whole rather than to a transcendent Deity, Spinoza's argument has the effect of denying the very creator God whose existence Descartes endeavored to establish. His argument is thus, in a very real sense, a demonstration of the nonexistence of God!

The real intent of Spinoza's argument, however, is not negative, but is designed to establish something important about the nature of reality. Exactly what this is can best be understood in light of his rationalistic method, which is itself intimately related to his ethical concern. As already noted, a basic assumption of this method is that thought must find a resting place in a single first principle, which not only serves to explain everything else, but which is itself perfectly intelligible in its own right. Moreover, since a first principle cannot, by definition, be explained in terms of anything prior, it must somehow be self-explicating or self-justifying. Anything less would fail to satisfy the demands of thought. It would provide us with a principle of explanation which itself stands in need of explanation, and this would obviously lead to an infinite regress and a hopeless skepticism. But explanation, for Spinoza, is in terms of causes: "The knowledge of an effect depends on and involves the knowlege of a cause" (Axiom IV). To understand something, or to have an adequate idea of it, involves seeing how its existence and nature follow necessarily from its cause. When dealing with a first principle, however, which is intelligible in itself, or in Spinoza's terms "conceived through itself," we cannot look for a prior or external cause. Its existence must therefore follow from its own nature, or it must be self-caused; both of which are equivalent to having necessary existence. The conclusion that God or substance necessarily exists thus seems to be demanded by Spinoza's method, as it alone serves to ensure the ultimate rationality of the whole order of nature.

But such a mode of argumentation can be subjected to severe criticism. For instance, one can claim with some justification that it is simply a mistake to look for the kind of explanation which Spinoza attempts to provide. It may be perfectly proper to assume that everything in nature has a cause in terms of which it may be understood and from which it necessarily follows, but one cannot say the same thing of reality as a whole. To attempt to do so is to treat the whole of reality as if it were another particular thing (which is just the view that Spinoza wished to avoid), and this, in the technical language of contemporary philosophy, is to commit a "category mistake." Moreover, one would further argue that this basic mistake generates, in turn, the misguided need to make use of contradictory expressions such as "self-caused" and "necessary existence."

Yet even if the force of this line of objection is acknowledged, and it raises profound issues which we cannot hope to begin to deal with adequately here, it must at least be recognized that Spinoza's argument answers a deep metaphysical need, and that his philosophy as a whole contains one of the most forceful expressions of this need to be found in the history of Western thought. (Perhaps the only other philosophers who can compare with him in this regard are Plato, Kant and Hegel.) This is the need for reason to arrive at an ultimate which is truly self-contained, in reference to which one cannot meaningfully ask the question "Why?" Most philosophers in the Judeo-Christian tradition have found such an ultimate in God the creator. Spinoza repudiated this ultimate as a figment of the imagination, but neither his rationalistic method nor his moral concern for a true and lasting good allowed him to stop there. It was not enough for him to show that nature, conceived under the category of substance, cannot possibly depend on a transcendent God. He likewise could not accept the view, expressed by some twentieth-century existentialists, that reality is simply there, a brute, inexplicable, and ultimately absurd fact. This would effectively introduce sheer contingency at the very heart of things, and it would not only render the order of nature unintelligible, but also undermine any possibility for man to achieve a lasting good.

But if reality is not, so to speak, simply there, if the order of nature, from which all things necessarily follow, is itself a necessary and rational order, then this can only mean that it is the only conceivable order. When reason recognizes this, all questions cease; for to see that no alternative is even conceivable, that the matter could not possibly have been otherwise, is to understand in the fullest possible sense. We should not, therefore, be surprised to find Spinoza affirming, after two propositions dealing with the indivisibility of substance, that "*besides God no substance can be granted or conceived*" (Prop. XIV). The importance of this contention, which follows from the definition of God and his necessary existence, does not lie in the assertion that there is no other substance besides God, or that there is only one substance in the universe (this has already been effectively established through the demonstration that substance possesses infinite attributes), but in the addendum that another substance *cannot be conceived.* If we keep in mind what we have already learned about substance in Spinoza, we can see that he is here providing us with the strongest possible affirmation of the rationality and necessity of the order of nature. The only remaining question concerns the all-inclusiveness of this order, that is, whether there may be things or events which stand outside it and are not subject to its laws. Spinoza provides a decisive answer to this question in the last proposition of this section when he asserts: "*Whatsoever is, is in God, and without God nothing can be, or be conceived*" (Prop. XV).

II   *Divine Causality and the Modal System*

With Proposition XV we arrive at the decisive expression of Spinoza's monism. Nothing exists or can be conceived apart from this one, infinite, self-contained system, which can be characterized either as God or substance. Nevertheless, the very formulation of this thesis involves a dualism of a sort. In giving up the distinction between God *and* nature, we are forced to distinguish between two aspects of God *or* nature, that is, between God and nature as source or principle of intelligibility, which exists through itself and is conceived through itself, and the same God or nature as the system of laws and particular things which are conceived through and depend upon this principle or source. Moreover, it is through the formulation of this distinction that Spinoza first identifies God with nature, just as he had previously identified substance with God.[13] The first of these aspects is termed *natura naturans* (active or generating nature) and the second *natura naturata* (passive or generated nature). The former refers to God as conceived through himself, i.e., as substance with infinite attributes, and the latter as the modal system which is conceived through these attributes (Prop. XXIX, Scholium).[14] Furthermore, this distinction within God or nature entails a similar distinction with regard to divine causality. In treating of this subject, Spinoza first considers this causality as it is in itself, that is, in its inherent nature or as *natura naturans* (Props. XVI-XX), and then as it is expressed in the modal system or *natura naturata* (Props. XXI-XXIX).[15]

Spinoza establishes the essential features of his theory of divine causality at the very beginning of his analysis. *"From the necessity of the divine nature,"* he asserts, *"must follow an infinite number of things in infinite ways [infinita infinitis modis]—that is, all things which can fall within the sphere of infinite intellect"* (Prop. XVI). He thereby determines (1) the *nature* of the divine causality or power, affirming that it operates through the "necessity of the divine nature," and (2) the *extent of its power*, maintaining not only that it produces an "infinite number of things in infinite ways," by which he means an infinite number of modes, each reflected in each of the infinite attributes, but also that this includes "everything which can fall within the sphere of the infinite intellect," i.e., everything conceivable.

By locating the causality or power of God in the very "necessity of the divine nature," Spinoza is not only rejecting any appeal to the "will of God" as a causal force or to final causes in any form, but also conceiving of the causal relation between God and the world in terms of the model of the logical relation between ground and consequent. God functions in Spinoza as the logical ground of things. They follow from His nature in precisely the same way that the conclusion of a valid deductive argument follows from its premises. Such a conception of causality is not only consistent with, but actually required by, Spinoza's deductive model of explanation. If

genuine knowledge involves the realization of the necessary consequences of our adequate ideas, and if these ideas are themselves
ultimately grounded in the idea of God, then it follows that these
same ideas are derivable from the idea of God as conclusions from a
premise. Furthermore, if this whole logical chain of reasoning is to
be something more than a consistent dream, if it is to yield truth, as
Spinoza certainly believes that it does, then it must reflect the
structure of reality. "A true idea," he affirms, "must correspond
with its ideate or object" (Axiom VI). The logical order of our
adequate ideas is thus, for Spinoza, the expression in the attribute of
thought of the necessary causal order of reality. As we shall see in
more detail in our consideration of Spinoza's theory of knowledge,
we have genuine knowledge precisely to the extent to which the
order of our ideas reflects this necessary order.

In light of the above considerations, it is both significant and
understandable that Spinoza bases his demonstration of the infinite
extent of the divine causality on his theory of definition. From the
proper definition of a thing, Spinoza reasons, it should be possible
to infer several properties of that thing. Moreover, "in proportion as
the essence of the thing defined involves more reality," more properties can be inferred from it. This contention was sharply criticized
by Tschirnhaus, who claimed, on the basis of geometrical examples,
that from the definition of a thing taken alone only one property can
be deduced.[16] Spinoza responded by granting that this may perhaps
be true in regard to the "most simple things" or to "things of reason"
(including geometrical figures), but that it does not apply to "real
things." As an example, he cites the possibility of deriving several
properties, e.g., necessary existence, immutability, infinity,
uniqueness, from the very definition of God as a "Being to whose
essence belongs existence."[17] Spinoza seems here to be operating
with the same conception of reality and degrees of reality which we
have already encountered in our discussion of attributes. Thus, pur-
suing our previous analogy, we can say that more properties can be
inferred from the definition or adequate idea of man than of a stone,
because a man has more reality, i.e., more aspects to his being. But
since, as has already been established, God has absolutely infinite
attributes, each of which "expresses infinite essence after its kind,"
Spinoza concludes that an infinite number of things must necessarily follow from the divine nature.

This is, of course, exactly the same thought which we have previously encountered in the assertion that from "God's supreme power," which is equated with his "infinite nature," an infinite number of things necessarily follow "in the same way as from the nature of a triangle it follows from eternity and for eternity, that its three interior angles are equal to two right angles." This statement is itself presented as an explication of the proposition presently under consideration, and it seems perfectly clear from both passages that Spinoza is explicitly and deliberately identifying what most philosophers, at least since Kant, have taken pains to distinguish, viz., causal and logical necessity, or cause and logical ground.[18] Thus God, who is described as the "efficient cause" of all things (Prop. XVI, Corollary I) and as the "absolutely first cause" (Prop. XVI, Corollary III), must be conceived as the logical ground from which all things follow, and in terms of which they can alone be adequately understood.

At this point we must be especially careful, if we are to avoid misunderstanding. Spinoza does, to be sure, hold that things follow from God with logical necessity, and that the number of things which follow in this manner is infinite. Nevertheless, he does not claim, or need to claim, that it is possible to deduce any particular thing from the infinite essence of God. Particular things, as we shall see in our analysis of finite modes, do, indeed, follow necessarily from God. They do not, however, follow from the infinite essence of God, but from God qua modified in a particular way, i.e., from another finite mode. Furthermore, since the infinite essence of God is really equivalent to the universal order of nature as expressed in the various attributes, the claim that an infinity of things follows logically from God means essentially that this infinity of things necessarily falls within this order, and consequently that all things can be understood in terms of one set of universal laws.[19]

Finally, we must keep in mind that Spinoza asserts not only that an infinite number of things necessarily follow in infinite ways from the very nature of God, but also that these encompass everything "which can fall within the sphere of the infinite intellect." This addition is not without its importance. The infinite intellect, which, as we shall see, is regarded as an eternal and infinite mode of thought, corresponds to the complete comprehension of everything conceivable. The conceivable defines the limits of the possible, so that anything not falling within the scope of such an intellect is inconceivable and impossible. This, in turn, entails the conclusion that everything possible follows necessarily from the nature of God, and thus that everything that could possibly exist does in fact exist—or, correlatively, whatever does not exist is impossible. Expressed in theological terms, this means that God created everything that was possible.

The subsequent propositions of this section specify more precisely the nature of divine causality. The first point to be made is that *"God acts solely by the laws of his own nature, and is not constrained by anyone"* (Prop. XVII). As the demonstration indicates, the assertion that God acts "by the laws of his own nature" means precisely the same as the just-established claim that things follow from the necessity of the divine nature. The further qualification that God acts *solely* in this manner and "is not constrained by anyone" follows logically from the proposition that there is nothing outside of God, and so nothing which could possibly constrain Him. On the basis of this proposition he concludes that nothing can possibly move God to act "besides the perfection of his own nature" (Corollary I), and that "God is the sole free cause" (Corollary II). The expression "free" here must be understood in the special sense which Spinoza gives to it. According to this sense "free" does not mean undetermined, but self-determined. The basic opposition is therefore not between freedom and necessity, for everything in the universe is necessary, but between being self-determined, or acting according to the laws of one's own nature, and being determined to act by an external cause. In the development of his moral philosophy, Spinoza applies this conception of freedom as self-determination in a limited extent to man, but as the present discussion makes clear, in its full sense it is really only applicable to God, who is by nature absolutely self-determined.

Continuing his analysis of divine causality, Spinoza makes use of some scholastic distinctions, which were apparently current in contemporary textbooks, and affirms that *"God is the indwelling and not the transient cause of all things"* (Prop. XVIII). By a transient cause was meant one which is separable from its effects, while an immanent cause was one which is inseparable. Accordingly, by characterizing the divine causality in this manner, Spinoza is merely underlining his already established doctrine that God is not a being apart from the world, but the immanent ground of its intelligibility. God is not, however, immanent in the sense that He is "in the world," but rather that the world is in Him in the manner in which a consequent is "in" its logical ground.[20]

A traditional theological doctrine which Spinoza does retain, albeit in a manner consistent with his view, is that of the eternality of God. *"God, and all the attributes of God,"* he writes *"are eternal"* (Prop. XIX). The crux of the demonstration is the definition of eternity, by which is meant "existence itself, in so far as it is conceived necessarily to follow solely from the definition of that which is eternal" (Def. VIII). As he goes on to add in his explanation of this key definition, eternity here means essentially necessary existence, so that the existence of something eternal is itself an "eternal truth," i.e., a logically necessary truth.[21] Moreover, eternity, thus construed, is absolutely opposed to time or duration, even though this duration may "be conceived without a beginning or end." The eternity of God is thus to be conceived as a logical consequence of—or, better, as identical with—His necessary existence, and not viewed imaginatively as endless duration or as existing "forever and ever." Furthermore, since the attributes express the "essence of the divine substance," they likewise are eternal in precisely the same sense.

On the basis of the above proposition, Spinoza concludes his analysis of *natura naturans* with the assertion that *"the existence of God and his essence are one and the same"* (Prop. XX). This is another traditional theological doctrine. It functions as a way of making the point that God does not just happen to exist. Not only does existence follow from His nature, but His very nature, i.e., essence, is to exist.[22] For Spinoza this is really nothing more than another expression for the eternality of God, but he draws two consequences from it. The first is that the existence of God is an eternal truth, i.e., a logically necessary truth (Prop. XX, Corollary I), and the second is that "God, and all the attributes of God, are unchangeable" (Prop. XX, Corollary II). Any change in God's mode of existence would, in light of the above proposition, be likewise a change in the divine nature. But if God could change in this manner, it would mean that God could cease to be God, which is absurd. Traditionally this doctrine has been used to prove that God does not change his mind, that the divine decrees are inviolable, but with Spinoza, for whom God is the order of nature and the "decrees of God" are equivalent to the laws of nature, the unchangeableness of God really means nothing more than the unchangeableness and necessity of these laws.[23]

This doctrine of the eternality and immutability of God both completes the discussion of *natura naturans* and serves as a transition to *natura naturata*, the modal system, which exists "in" and is conceived through God. Spinoza's treatment of this theme seems to have been explicitly modeled after the theory of emanation, which was developed by Neoplatonic philosophers and their medieval followers in the Jewish, Christian and Islamic tradition.[24] Expressed in its simplest terms, this theory held that the universe "flowed" or followed from God in a series of necessary stages, beginning with immaterial beings such as the "intelligences" and finally ending with the material world. This notion of the progression or emanation of things, and especially of the material world, from God, was intended to provide an alternative to the orthodox theory of creation, wherein the material world was created by God out of nothing (*ex nihilo*), and to the dualism of the kind advocated by the Gnostics, which allows for a preexisting matter out of which the world was fashioned. The problem with the first view is that it does not explain how something finite and allegedly "imperfect" (matter) can be produced by an infinite and perfect deity; while the difficulty with the second is that it grants to matter an existence independent of God (thereby denying divine omnipotence). By making matter ultimately dependent on God, yet conceiving of this dependence in such a way that it is mediated by several stages, and is thus indirect, the emanationists hoped to overcome the difficulties of both alternative theories. As is immediately apparent, however, the mere positing of stages between God and matter does not really help to explain how the latter can depend on and be derived from the former.

Spinoza, as we have seen at length, likewise rejected the doctrine of creation, as well as any view which would grant to matter or the material world an existence independent of God. Moreover, he can be said to have viewed the relation between *natura naturans* and *natura naturata* in terms of emanation, albeit with the quasi-mythical notion of "flowing" replaced by the strictly logical relation of ground and consequent. This view is expressed in his highly complex and often obscure theory of modes. Unlike the emanationists, however, Spinoza does not use his doctrine as a device to somehow bring together an infinite God and a world of finite things. He does not do so because he never viewed them as apart, and by making extension an attribute of God, he effectively dismissed the whole problem of deriving a material world from an immaterial deity.[25] Instead, Spinoza's theory of modes offers, first, an explanation of the relation between the basic principles and categories of scientific explanation and the order of nature (as expressed in the attributes of thought and extension) and, second, an account of how finite things express and are related to this order.

Modes, it will be recalled, were defined by Spinoza as "modifications of substance, or that which exists in or depends on something else." A mode is therefore by definition a dependent being, and that on which it depends is God or substance. But not all modes relate to God in the same way or have the same status. Spinoza's first concern is to establish the eternality and infinity of those modes which follow directly from God. To this end he writes: *"All things which follow from the absolute nature of any attribute of God must always exist and be infinite, or, in other words, are eternal and infinite through the said attribute"* (Prop. XXI). The basic point is simply that whatever follows directly from God or substance partakes to some extent of the nature of that from which it follows. Such modes must therefore, like substance, or rather the relevant attribute, be eternal and infinite. Yet they obviously cannot be eternal and infinite in the precise sense that substance and its attributes are; for this would mean that they exist necessarily and are therefore themselves substances. Spinoza indicates this difference by asserting that they are "eternal and infinite through the said attribute," that is, in virtue of their cause. The very formulation of the proposition makes it clear that eternality in this context really means endless duration or unceasing existence; while the assertion that modes are infinite through the said attribute, rather than being absolutely infinite, means simply that they are unlimited by another modification under the same attribute. Spinoza goes on to maintain that this not only holds for modes which follow immediately from any attribute of God, but also for modes which follow directly from these, that is, which are "modified by a modification, which exists necessarily and as infinite, through the said attribute" (Prop. XXII). We thus find a distinction between "immediate" and "mediate" eternal and infinite modes, with the former derived directly from an attribute, and the latter directly from the former (Prop. XXIII).

Unfortunately, within the confines of the *Ethics* Spinoza gives us precious little information about these modes. The only one even mentioned by name is the "idea of God" (Prop. XXI), which is equivalent to what is elsewhere described as the "absolutely infinite intellect," and which is an immediate eternal and infinite mode of the attribute of thought. Thus, in order to learn even the names of some of these modes and to gain some understanding of their nature and function, it is necessary to go beyond the text of the *Ethics* to some of Spinoza's other writings and his correspondence.

In this regard, it is first of all helpful to consider a passage in *On the Improvement of the Understanding* wherein Spinoza discusses "fixed and eternal things," which are generally viewed as identical with the eternal and infinite modes of the *Ethics*. [26] This notion is introduced within the context of a consideration of the proper ordering of our ideas, and of the necessity of referring all of our ideas to the idea of a being (God) who is the cause of all things. The basic principle which is proclaimed is the necessity of deducing all of our ideas from "true causes" or "real things" which are opposed to the abstract universals, i.e., the genera and species, of the Aristotelians. Against any empiricism, however, Spinoza points out that by "true causes" and "real things" he does not mean the objects of ordinary experience, i.e., "the series of particular mutable things," but rather "the series of fixed and eternal things." An empiricistic approach, which would attempt to ground knowledge in the first series of things, is rejected as both impossible and unnecessary. The impossibility stems from the fact that this series is infinite both in extent and complexity, so that any given thing could be brought into existence or destroyed by an infinite number of possible causes. Thus, the human intellect can never arrive at adequate knowledge of any particular thing by tracing its chain of causes. This effort is unnecessary because the essence or true nature of these things is not to be found in this manner. Instead, Spinoza goes on to claim:

This inmost essence must be sought solely from fixed and eternal things, and from the laws inscribed (so to speak) in those things as in their true codes, according to which all particular things take place and are arranged; nay, those mutable particular things depend so intimately and essentially (so to phrase it) upon the fixed things, that they cannot either be or be conceived without them. [27]

This passage makes it quite clear that we can only come to a knowledge of particular things through, and in terms of, the series of "fixed and eternal things," which are equivalent to the eternal and infinite modes of the *Ethics*. We find in them the essences of particular things, as opposed to the mere fact of their existence, which depends on external causes and is only learned through experience. Spinoza's highly metaphorical characterization of these "fixed and eternal things" as the codices in which the particular laws of nature are inscribed calls attention to their essential function as ultimate principles or categories of scientific explanation. They are not themselves particular laws, which obviously can only be learned from experience, but the a priori or necessary presuppositions of all such laws. It is, of course, somewhat strange that Spinoza should characterize these principles as things, and later in the *Ethics* as modes, but this is done in order to emphasize their uniqueness and their distinction from the class concepts of the Aristotelians. These latter, as we shall see in our discussion of Spinoza's epistemology, were regarded by him as mere products of the imagination, having no real basis in the nature of things. The "fixed and eternal things," however, are more real than the particular things, as they are the source of the very essences of these things. They are, in fact, precisely what Hegel later called "concrete universals," that is, universals which as unique wholes contain the particulars within themselves. Spinoza himself says as much when he writes: "Whence these fixed and eternal things, though they are themselves particular, will nevertheless, owing to their presence and power everywhere, be to us as universals, or genera of definitions of particular mutable things, and as the proximate causes of all things."[28]

This extremely schematic account becomes a bit more intelligible if we consider some of the examples of eternal and infinite modes which Spinoza offers. Together with the already mentioned idea of God or absolutely infinite intellect, we find motion introduced in the *Short Treatise* as a "Son of God" and an eternal and immutable creation.[29] Furthermore, in response to a query by his friend Schuller, Spinoza again cites the absolutely infinite intellect as an eternal and infinite mode of the attribute of thought which is paralleled by motion and rest (*motus et quies*) in the attribute of extension, and he adds the "face of the whole universe (*facies totius Universi*) which, although it varies in infinite modes, yet remains always the same"[30] as a mediate eternal and infinite mode in the attribute of extension.

Leaving for later the whole discussion of the absolutely infinite intellect, we can see that the "motion and rest" of the letter to Schuller provides us with more of an insight into Spinoza's thinking than the bare "motion" of the *Short Treatise*. Spinoza's point, which he develops in connection with his analysis of body in the *Ethics*, is that each particular physical body must be conceived of as a particular proportion of motion and rest. This proportion, together with the effort (*conatus*) to preserve it, constitutes the very essence of body. He is thus claiming that "motion and rest" functions as a basic category of scientific explanation, and in so doing Spinoza is certainly operating in terms of the model of Galilean physics where the fundamental laws of nature are laws of motion (which are therefore "inscribed" in "motion and rest" as a codex). Furthermore, by giving "motion and rest" the status of an eternal and infinite mode, which, as such, is derived directly from the attributes of extension, Spinoza endeavored to overcome a basic difficulty in Cartesian physics. Descartes, it will be recalled, identified material substance with extension. He had also recognized, however, that matter, so conceived, could not have a principle of motion (force) and hence of individuation within itself. He thus found it necessary to introduce the action of God in order to explain the origin of motion and the division of matter into distinct bodies.[31] Such a view was, as we have seen repeatedly, completely unacceptable to Spinoza, and his doctrine that "motion and rest" is derived directly from the attribute of extension not only involves a corrective to Cartesian physics, but also provides the basis for a dynamic conception of matter.[32]

The "face of the whole universe" can be understood in a similar manner. As a mediate eternal and infinite mode of extension, it must follow immediately from "motion and rest." Like all eternal and infinite modes, "motion and rest" is held to be immutable. But since the proportion of "motion and rest" in particular portions of corporeal nature is constantly changing, this immutability can only mean that the proportion in corporeal nature as a whole is constant. Spinoza is thus able to "deduce" the principle of the conservation of motion, which was a basic principle in Cartesian physics.[33] Now the "face of the whole universe" is identical with corporeal nature as a whole, insofar as it maintains a constant proportion of "motion and rest." Furthermore, in the portion of the *Ethics* to which Spinoza refers Schuller in connection with this notion, it is argued that, precisely because it maintains such a constant proportion, corporeal nature as a whole can be regarded as a distinct individual "whose parts, that is, all bodies, vary in infinite ways, without any change in the individual as a whole" (*Ethics* II, Prop. XIII, Lemma VII). Since they are identical, the same can be said of the "face of the whole universe," and it is thus, like the other "fixed and eternal things," a universal individual or concrete universal, which includes its particulars within itself, and in terms of which these particulars can alone be understood.

But neither the general category "motion and rest" and the knowledge that it constitutes the essence of body, nor the fact that its proportion in corporeal nature as a whole remains constant is enough to determine or deduce the behavior of particular bodies. Indeed, it is impossible to deduce particular processes, things or events in nature solely from a set of universal principles and laws, i.e., from the "series of fixed and eternal things." As we have suggested, however, this should not be viewed as a weakness in Spinoza's scheme, pointing to the "limits of deduction," but rather a basic fact about scientific method which Spinoza accepts, and for which he endeavors to account.

The doctrine of finite modes is the direct result of this endeavor. Spinoza's specific problem is to show that although such modes or particular things cannot be deduced directly from any of the attributes of God or the eternal and infinite modifications thereof, they nevertheless follow from and can only be conceived through these attributes and modifications. In developing this doctrine, Spinoza first affirms that *"the essence of things produced by God does not involve existence"* (Prop. XXIV), which simply means that such things are not created substances, and that *"God is the efficient cause not only of the existence of things, but also of their essence"* (Prop. XXV), which means that they cannot even be conceived as possible apart from the infinite power of God or nature. God is thus said to be the cause of all things "in the same sense as he is called the cause of himself" (Prop. XXV, Scholium), that is, both their actual existence and their very possibility (essence) follow necessarily from the nature of God. From this he infers that "individual things are nothing but modifications of the attributes of God, or modes by which the attributes of God are expressed in a fixed and definite manner" (Prop. XXV, Corollary). Continuing this line of reasoning, he points out that anything which has been conditioned to act must have been conditioned by God, and that anything which has not been so conditioned cannot condition itself (Prop. XXVI). Moreover, once conditioned, such a being cannot render itself unconditioned. A being capable of either conditioning or unconditioning itself would be a god and not a mode. But the preceding analysis has also shown that everything which follows directly from God or from some eternal and infinite modification of God is itself eternal and infinite. Finite things therefore cannot follow directly from God, and this leads Spinoza to conclude:

Every individual thing, or everything which is finite and has a conditioned existence, cannot exist or be conditioned to act, unless it be conditioned for existence and action by a cause other than itself, which also is finite, and has a conditioned existence; and likewise this cause cannot in its turn exist, or be conditioned to act, unless it be conditioned for existence and action by another cause, which also is finite, and has a conditioned existence, and so on to infinity. (Prop. XXVIII)

The problem seems to be to reconcile this last claim with the prior and crucial claim that all things in nature, finite and infinite alike, follow from and are conditioned by God. This problem disappears, however, when we note that these finite things are themselves modifications of God. As Spinoza puts it in his demonstration of the above proposition, these finite things "must follow from, or be conditioned for, existence and action by God or one of his attributes, in so far as the latter are modified by some modification which is finite, and has a conditioned existence." This condition or cause must likewise be conditioned in a similar manner, and so we arrive at an infinite series of finite modes, each conditioning other modes while being conditioned in turn. There is thus no direct transition from the infinite to the finite, or from general categories, principles and laws to particular things. Nevertheless, since each particular thing is, as a "modification of a modification," itself an instance or expression of a general law or principle, and only as such serves as the condition of another thing, it can be claimed that all things in nature follow from, and are conditioned by, these general laws and principles, and thus ultimately by God.

The upshot of this whole discussion is that within the theological framework in which Spinoza presents his theory of divine causality, one can detect at least the outlines of a thoroughly modern conception of scientific explanation.[34] The basis of this conception is the view that every event or thing in nature must be understood in terms of two intersecting lines of explanation. There must first of all be a set of general principles or universal laws (infinite modes) which the event or thing in question instantiates, and secondly, there must be a set of antecedent conditions (finite modes), which likewise instantiate these principles or laws. Given both of these, everything in nature is determined, and since the latter are themselves instantiations or expressions of the former, and thus of the power of God, Spinoza can conclude his argument in this section with the sweeping claim that "*nothing in the universe is contingent, but all things are conditioned to exist and operate in a particular manner by the necessity of the divine nature*" (Prop. XXIX).

III *Some Theological Implications*

The traditional conception of God as a person endowed with intellect and free will and the associated doctrine of the creation of the world have been left far behind by the relentless progress of Spinoza's argument. Nevertheless, apart from a brief aside (Prop. XVII, Scholium) where Spinoza affirms that "neither intellect nor will appertain to God's nature," the repudiation of the traditional doctrine of God as well as some of the other doctrines which we have already touched upon remains, more or less implicit and beneath the surface. The main function of the final section of the first part of the *Ethics* (Props. XXX-XXXVI and the already discussed appendix dealing with final causes) is to make all of this perfectly explicit, and to underline the radical distinction between the God of the *Ethica ordine geometrico demonstrata* and the God of the religious tradition.

The first target is the notion of the divine intellect, which has traditionally been viewed as archetypal, that is, as the source of the plan in accordance with which the world was actually created by an act of divine will. This is contrasted with the ectypal human or finite intellect, which derives its ideas from preexisting objects. Now Spinoza, as we have already seen, does not completely reject the whole notion of a divine or infinite intellect, but he does deny it any creative or archetypal function, and he carefully interprets it in such a way as to avoid any anthropomorphic implications.

The former of these tasks is accomplished through the proposition that "*intellect, in function (actu) finite, or in function infinite, must comprehend the attributes of God and the modifications of God, and nothing else*" (Prop. XXX). This innocent-sounding assertion is based on the truism that "a true idea must agree with its ideate or object" (Axiom VI), and the already established contention that there are literally no other objects for any mind to consider except the attributes of God and their modifications. The significance of this lies in the fact that it effectively undermines any effort to establish a qualitative difference, or a difference in kind, between a human or finite and a divine or infinite intellect. Any intellect, whether finite or infinite, must relate to its object in precisely the same way. This further implies, on the one hand, the already discussed view that man, insofar as he possesses adequate knowledge, apprehends his object in precisely the same manner as an infinite intellect, and on the other hand, that by an infinite intellect can be meant nothing more than one which answers or corresponds to the sum total of adequate knowledge.[35] In other words, far from being an archetypal or creative intellect, the infinite intellect in Spinoza is not really an actual intellect at all, but the mere idea of the sum total of possible knowledge or the knowledge of the whole order of nature as it is expressed in and through each of the infinite attributes. Nevertheless, because it refers to the complete knowledge of a unique whole (nature), Spinoza attributes to it a certain specificity and concreteness, and hence views it, like the other "fixed and eternal things," as a kind of universal individual, having a reality above and beyond that of the particular individuals of which it is composed.

This already presupposes that the infinite understanding is a mode, belonging to *natura naturata* rather than to *natura naturans*, and Spinoza proceeds to make this explicit: *"The intellect in function, whether finite or infinite, as will, desire, love, &c., should be referred to passive nature and not to active nature"* (Prop. XXXI). The point of this, of course, is that one cannot meaningfully apply the notion of intellect to God and affirm, in the manner of the religious tradition, that "God has an intellect." Yet, given the fact that Spinoza does regard thought as a genuine attribute of God, the exclusion of intellect from the divine nature might seem to be a bit strange. The actual argument, however, turns on the very distinction between thought as an attribute or "absolute thought" and intellect. As Spinoza affirms in the scholium, by intellect is meant "the very act of understanding" and not some mysterious capacity or potentiality, e.g., the "potential intellect" of Aristotle. But this act, as well as other modes of thought such as volitions and desires, depends on, and can only be conceived through, thought itself. Spinoza thus seems to view the act of intellection or understanding as the affirmation of a particular, determinate portion of the total realm of thought, which therefore presupposes this realm as a pre-given totality, precisely in the manner in which a particular body for Descartes presupposes the whole of extension. The limitation to a particular affirmation applies only to a finite intellect; but since Spinoza has just shown that the infinite intellect does not differ in kind from the finite variety, but rather affirms, in precisely the same manner, the whole realm of adequate ideas, it too can be said to presuppose the attribute of thought, and thus to be a mere mode.

As the formulation of the above proposition makes clear, this result holds not only for intellect, but for other modes of thought, including the will. It has already been established, therefore, that will does not pertain to the nature of God. Nevertheless, Spinoza proceeds to argue that *"will cannot be called a free cause, but only a necessary cause"* (Prop. XXXII). The point here is to show that even if one wishes to attribute will to God or to talk about an infinite will, one could not conclude that God acts from freedom of the will. God, to be sure, has been defined as a "free cause," and this was shown to be equivalent to being self-determined; but what we now see is that God is not such a cause in virtue of a free will. This really follows from the very definition of will as "only a particular mode of thinking," from which Spinoza concludes: "However it be conceived, whether as finite or infinite," it requires a cause by which it should be conditioned to exist and act. "Thus (Def. vii) it cannot be called a free cause, but only a necessary or constrained cause."

But if things follow necessarily from the nature of God, rather than from an act of free will, then it certainly holds that *"things could not have been brought into being by God in any manner or in any order different from that which has in fact obtained"* (Prop. XXXIII). This is another affirmation of the absolute necessity of things, or, equivalently, of the inconceivability of another order of nature or course of events. Like the other propositions in this section, it therefore adds little to the actual course of the argument. Nevertheless, it is not without its importance; for it formulates this central Spinozistic thesis in such a way as to bring into clear focus the precise nature of the opposition of his views to those of the religious tradition, while at the same time allowing Spinoza to argue with that tradition on its own terms. Perhaps no belief is more integral to the Western religious tradition, which includes Judaism, Christianity and Islam, than that God created the world through an act of free choice and that, if He had so desired, He could have created either a different world or no world at all. Only such a God, it is commonly believed, can be considered in any meaningful sense a person to whom one can appropriately apply moral qualities such as goodness and mercy, and only such a God can be a suitable object of worship. After all, if God had no choice in the matter, how can we possibly call creation good, or God a perfect being? Indeed, what is the difference between a God who functions without free choice and blind fate? Spinoza had already touched upon this problem in passing (Prop. XVII, Scholium), but he now confronts it head on and attempts to show that even on the basis of the theologians' own assumptions, they must accept his conclusions.

First of all, assuming for the sake of argument that God acts out of freedom of the will, a God who could change his desires or decree other than he has done would necessarily have a different intellect and will. But since, as the proponents of this theory assume, God's intellect and will pertain to His nature, this implies that God's very nature would be different. Yet these same theologians also assume that God's actual nature is supremely perfect, so they are forced to conclude that if God had in fact decreed other than He has done, He would have been less perfect, and therefore not God. Against this it might be objected that there is no intrinsic perfection or imperfection in things, and that what is perfect or imperfect depends solely on the will of God, so that "if God had so willed, he might have brought it about that what is now perfection should be extreme imperfection, and *vice versa*." This is, in fact, the view of Calvin and Descartes, and Spinoza is easily able to show that it succumbs to precisely the same dialectic. Since God necessarily understands what He wills, Spinoza reasons, this view amounts to the claim that God might understand things differently from the way in which He does understand them, which leads to the same absurdity as before. God's will, after all, cannot be different from God's perfection, and therefore, on the theologians' own assumption, neither can things be different. But while Spinoza totally repudiates the theory which "subjects things to the will of an indifferent deity, and asserts that they all depend on his fiat," he nevertheless suggests that it is less far from the truth than the theory which holds that "God acts in all things with a view of promoting what is good." This doctrine, which was later developed by Leibniz, is dismissed with the utmost contempt. By conceiving of God as acting for the sake of some preestablished goal (the good), it submits God to a kind of external control, and therefore, like the other view, really undermines His divinity.

But it may be granted that God could not have created any world other than the perfect one which He has in fact created without somehow becoming less than God, which is admittedly absurd. Nevertheless, it still does not follow from this that God had to create any world at all. Perhaps, then, in the sheer contingency and unfathomable mystery of the decision to create, we can locate the cherished element of divine choice. To such a claim Spinoza has a ready answer: *"God's power is identical with his essence"* (Prop. XXXIV). This conclusion is derived from the principle that things follow from the very nature or essence of God, and its clear implication is that the suggestion that God might not have exercised His power, i.e., not created at all, is once again equivalent to the absurd claim that God has the power not to be God. On the basis of this, Spinoza can therefore conclude against the theologians that *"whatsoever we conceive to be in the power of God, necessarily exists"* (Prop. XXXV), which amounts to an explicit denial of the suggestion that the world might not have come into existence. The final proposition of the first part of the *Ethics, "There is no cause from whose nature some effect does not follow"* (Prop. XXXVI), does not seem to fall within this line of argument. It does, however, reflect Spinoza's view that every particular thing participates in or expresses the infinite power of God or nature in a conditioned manner,[36] and it perhaps also serves as a transition to the discussion of final causes, which are in fact regarded by Spinoza as "causes" from which no effects follow.

Despite his diametrically opposed point of view, Spinoza had no qualms about meeting the theologians on their own grounds and showing either that their views can be reduced to absurdity or that they entail his own. By so doing, he completed his project of replacing the traditional conception of God as a superhuman person with the scientifically inspired conception of nature as an infinite, necessary, self-contained, and above all thoroughly intelligible system. It is important to realize, however, that Spinoza did not merely wish to keep the word God while emptying it of all significance. Rather, his intent was to show that, properly understood, this concept referred to nature, and to nature alone. This nature does not possess an intellect or will, and it thus does not act for the benefit of man. Yet although not *intelligent*, it is *intelligible*, which the God of the theologians was not, and, as Spinoza proceeds to argue, man finds his true good in the knowledge of its necessary order. Moreover, since there is literally no power apart from it which can in any way limit it, this nature is in the fullest sense of the word omnipotent. Thus, no matter what one may think about Spinoza's logic, there can be no doubt about his sincerity and the depth of conviction with which he identified God and nature. For Spinoza, as for other thinkers of a similar persuasion, such as Goethe, who have no use for the traditional conception of God, the above-mentioned features of nature were more than enough to consider it divine.

CHAPTER 4

The Human Mind

IN his brief Preface to the second part of the *Ethics* Spinoza
writes:

I now pass on to explaining the results, which must necessarily follow from
the essence of God, or of the eternal and infinite being; not, indeed, all of
them (for we proved in Part. i., Prop. xvi., that an infinite number must
follow in an infinite number of ways), but only those which are able to lead
us, as it were by the hand, to the knowledge of the human mind and its
highest blessedness.

We have here another clear indication of the essentially practical
nature of Spinoza's thought. The elaborate metaphysical analysis of
the first part of the *Ethics*, with its rigorously developed conception
of substance, its identification of substance, so conceived, with God,
and its criticisms of the traditional notion of God, was not presented
as an end in itself, but, given Spinoza's deductive method, as a
necessary first step in the acquisition of adequate knowledge of the
nature of the human mind. Since this mind, like all other particular
things in nature, is a finite mode and not an individual substance,
knowledge of its true nature can only be derived from a prior
knowledge of its eternal and necessary causes, which in this case
turn out to be the attribute of thought and the infinite intellect. Yet
as the passage cited above suggests, even this project, which is the
chief concern of this portion of the *Ethics*, is not undertaken for its
own sake, but as a necessary prelude to the determination of the
true good for man or human blessedness.

The three specific topics which Spinoza discusses under the general subject "Of the Nature and Origin of the Mind" are (1) the
nature of the mind and its relation to the body (Props. I-XV); (2) the
intellect and the nature and extent of human knowledge (Props.
XVI-XLVII); and (3) the will and its alleged freedom (Props.

87

XLVIII-XLIX). Unlike most contemporary philosophers, and even
to some extent Descartes, Spinoza does not treat these problems in
isolation. His solution to each one is deduced from the same general principles, and his resolution of the mind-body problem serves
as a point of departure for the treatment of the other two. Nevertheless, for the purpose of exposition, it is convenient to divide Spinoza's analysis in this manner, and we shall therefore proceed accordingly.

I *The Mind and its Relation to the Body*

Despite being so cryptic as at times to render interpretation extremely difficult, Spinoza's treatment of the mind-body problem is
one of the most interesting and significant aspects of his philosophy,
and it is of considerable relevance to contemporary discussions of
this issue.[1] Spinoza's theory is primarily designed to account for the
unity of human nature, and to show that the mind as well as the
body is part of universal nature and is subject to a set of universal
and necessary laws. This contrasts sharply with the Cartesian
dualism, with its conception of mind and body as two distinct, yet
interacting, substances. This theory is equally opposed, however, to
any materialistic view, such as that of his contemporary Thomas
Hobbes, which allows for only bodies and motion in the universe,
and therefore not only rejects the whole notion of a thinking substance, but also tends to identify thought with physical processes
(e.g., motions in the brain).[2] Although Spinoza's psychological
theory seems to owe a great deal to Hobbes,[3] he nevertheless
staunchly resisted any attempt to reduce thought to its physical
correlate, or to explain ideas in terms of anything in the realm of
extension.[4]

Spinoza's doctrine of attributes allows him to avoid both of these
unattractive alternatives, and thus to affirm the autonomous, self-
contained nature of thought without making mind into a distinct
substance. As two of the infinite attributes of the one substance,
thought and extension are not separate entities, but irreducible and
distinct expressions of one and the same reality. Moreover, since
the human mind and the human body are finite modifications of
these attributes, the same conclusions can be applied to them.
Thus, while the mind cannot by some mysterious power determine
the body to act, nor the body cause the mind to think, an act of
thought and its physical correlate in the realm of extension are

intimately related as two strictly parallel expressions of the same state of affairs. One could express this in contemporary terms by saying that mind and body are related functionally rather than causally, with "function" being taken in its mathematical sense.[5] Spinoza himself makes this point by asserting that the mind is the idea of the body or, more precisely, that *"the object of the idea constituting the human mind is the body"* (Prop. XIII). This proposition contains the essential expression of Spinoza's conception of mind, but before we are in a position to understand and evaluate it properly, we must first consider the line of argument whereby he arrives at it, and the rather special meaning which he gives to key terms such as "idea."

Let us first briefly consider Spinoza's conception of the nature of ideas; for it is an essential feature not only of his views on the mind-body problem, but also of his treatment of the nature of knowledge and of the will. "By *idea*," he tells us, "I mean the mental conception which is formed by the mind as a thinking thing" (Def. III). As Spinoza's explanation of this definition makes clear through the distinction between conception (*conceptum*) and perception (*perceptionem*), the emphasis falls on the activity of the mind. It does not passively perceive but actively conceives its objects. Indeed, an idea for Spinoza turns out to be the very act of conception or understanding through which a certain content is affirmed. He here differs markedly from Descartes, for whom an idea is essentially an object of consciousness, which belongs in the mind more or less as a property belongs to a thing.[6] This latter view is closely connected with the Cartesian conception of mind as a thinking substance, and it is only natural that in rejecting this doctrine, Spinoza likewise found it necessary to provide a different conception of ideas. A more detailed treatment of this topic must await our consideration of Spinoza's actual argument, but we can already see how this conception of ideas enables Spinoza (as in the proposition cited above) to sometimes identify the mind with its ideas. Since ideas are essentially acts of thinking or understanding, this identification really amounts to the claim that the mind is identical with its acts, that its essence, as a finite mode, like that of God, is its activity, and that its unity and individuality are the unity and individuality of this activity. Such a conception not only enables Spinoza to avoid the pitfalls of Cartesianism, but also is consistent with the basic principles of his metaphysics, and, as we shall see, it has a precise parallel in his conception of body.

As already noted, Spinoza's argument moves deductively from general principles concerning the attributes of thought and extension and their relationship, to specific conclusions concerning the mind and body as finite modifications of these attributes. The first thing to be established is that thought and extension are in fact two of the infinite attributes of God (Props. I and II). From this Spinoza is able to deduce several basic truths. First of all, since thought is an attribute of God and hence an expression of his infinite essence, *"in God there is necessarily the idea not only of his essence, but also of all things which necessarily follow from his essence"* (Prop. III). This serves to affirm the all-inclusiveness of the attribute of thought and that of its immediate mode, the infinite intellect. Such an intellect, as we have already seen, stands for the realization of all possible knowledge. It therefore, by definition, encompasses everything that follows from the nature of God, which means everything conceivable. Moreoever, Spinoza continues, since God is one, the idea of God, i.e., the infinite intellect, is itself one (Prop. IV). This implies that the realm of thought constitutes a unified, closed deductive system, and this becomes explicit in the next proposition: *"The actual being of ideas owns God as its cause, only in so far as he is considered as a thinking thing, not in so far as he is unfolded in any other attribute; that is, the ideas both of the attributes of God and of particular things do not own as their efficient cause their objects (ideata) or the things perceived, but God himself in so far as he is a thinking thing"* (Prop. V). God, "in so far as he is a thinking thing" is really equivalent to thought, viewed as an attribute, so that Spinoza's point is simply that each idea must be caused by another modification of thought, that is, by another idea, and this is what makes the realm of thought a self-contained system. Yet, as he proceeds to remind the reader, this by no means bespeaks any special privilege for thought, but it is applicable to all of the other attributes, each of which is a self-determined, self-contained whole (Prop. VI).

Nevertheless, although self-determined and self-contained, thought, like the other attributes, is not a substance or a world apart, but merely a particular expression of the one substance and its rational order. Thought thus reflects in its own peculiar medium, that of ideas, this universal rational order, and on the basis of this principle Spinoza formulates what is perhaps the single most important proposition in the entire *Ethics:* *"The order and connection of ideas is the same as the order and connection of things"* (Prop. VII).

Given his basic assumptions, this proposition is applicable to the relation between the attribute of thought and each of the infinite attributes. As he admits to Tschirnhaus, there must be a modification of thought corresponding to each modification in each of the infinite attributes,[7] and, as has often been noted, this tends to undermine Spinoza's doctrine of the strict equivalence of the attributes, and to grant a certain preeminence to thought.[8] Within the present context, however, Spinoza means by "things" merely modifications of the attribute of extension, and his concern is to establish not merely the parallelism, but the actual identity of the series of modifications in these two attributes. As he puts the matter in the scholium: "Substance thinking and substance extended are one and the same substance, comprehended now through one attribute, now through the other. So, also, a mode of extension and the idea of that mode are one and the same thing, though expressed in two ways." With this, the Cartesian dualism is decisively overcome, and we are presented with a view of thought and extension as two distinct yet equivalent expressions of one and the same rational order.

The stage is now set for the descent from the attribute of thought to its most interesting finite modification, the human mind. This descent, however, is somewhat circuitous, as Spinoza stops to dwell on some considerations which at first glance do not seem to be directly relevant to the issue. The first point to be considered is the obvious problem of ideas of nonexistent, or what other philosophers might call "potential," things. As infinite, the idea of God, or the infinite intellect, must include the ideas of all possible, i.e., conceivable, things, and not only the ideas of those things which happen to exist at any particular moment. This seems to conflict with the claim that "the order and connection of ideas is the same as the order and connection of things," but the problem is resolved by distinguishing between two senses in which a thing (mode of extension) can be said to exist. It can exist either in the sense that it is deducible from the attribute of extension (possible existence), or that it follows from a given condition and actually exists, which for Spinoza means that it has a certain duration. Given the identity between the two orders, it follows that ideas must likewise exist in this two-fold sense (Prop VIII). Spinoza, in other words, uses the very principle which seems to give rise to the problem in order to resolve it. In the scholium to this proposition he attempts to illustrate his thesis by means of a mathematical analogy. The nature of a circle is such, he points out, that if any number of straight lines intersect within it, the resulting rectangles will be equal to one another. None of these possible rectangles can be said to actually exist unless the circle exists. Nevertheless, given the circle, an infinite number of rectangles possibly exist in the sense that they can be constructed in the circle, and since each of these possible rectangles can be conceived, and thus *is* conceived by the infinite intellect, the same can be said in regard to the ideas of these rectangles. If, however, we suppose that of these infinite rectangles two actually exist, or are actually constructed, then, Spinoza concludes: "The ideas of these two not only exist, in so far as they are contained in the idea of the circle, but also as they involve the existence of those rectangles; wherefore they are distinguished from the remaining ideas of the remaining rectangles."

The importance of this analogy, which Spinoza himself admits to be imperfect, due to the uniqueness of the situation, is based on its implications concerning ideas of actually existing things. Such ideas, the analogy suggests, may be said to endure or continue to exist throughout a period of time (as long as their object endures), and they consist essentially in the affirmation of the existence of their object. We have already seen that ideas are construed by Spinoza as acts of thought through which a particular content is affirmed, so that what we now learn is that these activities can persist through time and that they involve the affirmation of actual existence. Both of these consequences are, as we shall soon see, crucial for the development of Spinoza's theory of mind.

Since an idea of an actually existing thing is a finite modification of the attribute of thought, Spinoza has no difficulty in showing that these ideas do not follow directly from God, or God "*in so far as he is infinite,*" but only from God "*in so far as he is considered as affected by another idea of a thing actually existing, of which he is the cause, in so far as he is affected by a third idea, and so on to infinity*" (Prop. IX). In other words, each of these ideas is caused by another idea, and together they form an infinite causal chain, which corresponds at every point to the causal chain of their objects in the attribute of extension. The main interest of this proposition is found in the corollary which Spinoza attaches to it. This introduces the question of the knowledge of particular existing things, and Spinoza's claim is that such knowledge can only be said to be "in God" insofar as God has the idea of the object in question. But to be in God in this manner really means to be in the corresponding finite mode, i.e., in the idea of the object; so that we now see that these ideas involve the knowledge of their objects.

In order to establish the connection between this conception of ideas and the human mind, Spinoza stops to underline the already amply established fact that man is not an independent substance, but merely a finite mode (Prop. X). Moreover, since it is an undeniable experiential fact that "man thinks" (Axiom II), it follows that at least part of the essence of man is constituted by modifications of thought. Now although Spinoza differs from Descartes in regard to the nature of ideas, he agrees with him in maintaining that ideas are the fundamental modifications of thought, on the grounds that other modifications of thought, or more simply other thoughts, such as desires and volitions, presuppose an idea of an object. Since the human mind does have desires and volitions, which here at least are distinguished from ideas, Spinoza does not simply equate the totality of the mind with its ideas, but he does affirm that "*the first element, which constitutes the actual being of the human mind, is the idea of some particular thing actually existing*" (Prop. XI).

On the basis of this contention, Spinoza adds in a significant corollary that the human mind is "part of the infinite intellect of God." We have already seen enough to realize that this mystical-sounding claim, which is central to Spinoza's epistemological and moral theories, is merely his characteristic way of making the point that the human mind is a member of, and participates in, the absolute or total system of thought. It is a finite, limited member, however, and Spinoza expresses this by noting that statements of the form "The human mind perceives this or that" are equivalent to metaphysical statements of the form "God has this or that idea, not in so far as he is infinite, but in so far as he is displayed through the nature of the human mind." This again is Spinoza's rather elaborate way of saying that perception follows from the particular nature of the perceiving mind and not from the absolute system of thought; and we should also note that "perception" is used here, as elsewhere, in a very broad sense, to include all mental events, of which conscious apprehension is merely one particular manifestation. Perceptions, so construed, can be arranged hierarchically according to the adequacy with which they represent their object, and thus Spinoza introduces an additional important clarification:

"When we say that God has this or that idea, not only in so far as he constitutes the essence of the human mind, but also in so far as he, simultaneously with the human mind, has the further idea of another thing, we assert that the human mind perceives a thing in part or inadequately." An inadequate perception is therefore a partial one, and this occurs when the mind has an idea, or perceives something, without at the same time having the idea of the cause of this perception—a situation which obviously holds in those instances of perception wherein there is something less than conscious apprehension of a particular content.

This broad sense of perception, together with the principle of the identity of the order and connection of ideas with the order and connection of things, forms the basis of Spinoza's contention that *"whatsoever comes to pass in the object of the idea, which constitutes the human mind, must be perceived by the human mind, or there will necessarily be an idea in the human mind of the said occurrence. That is, if the object of the idea constituting the human mind be a body, nothing can take place in that body without being perceived by the mind"* (Prop. XII). Here perception obviously cannot be limited to conscious apprehension, for that would lead to the manifestly false conclusion that the mind is aware of everything that occurs in the body. Spinoza is clearly not maintaining this, but rather he is suggesting that the condition of the idea which constitutes the first element of the human mind, and hence of the mind itself, is a function of the state of the entire body. The mind thus varies according to variations in the physical organism, and nothing occurs in the organism which does not have its mental correlate. It is in this sense, and in this sense alone, that the mind can be said to "perceive" everything that occurs in the body.[9] This conception of perception enabled Spinoza to replace the tenuous, external relation between mind and body, which Descartes established by means of his fanciful appeal to the pineal gland, with a doctrine which allows for the most intimate conceivable correlation between the mental and physical life of an individual human being.

The intimate nature of the correlation between the human mind and the body becomes even more apparent as Spinoza finally affirms that this body, *"in other words a certain mode of extension which actually exists, and nothing else,"* is, indeed, the object of the idea constituting the human mind, that is, the physical object with which the activity of the mind is strictly correlated (Prop. XIII). But, as he goes on to add, this by no means constitutes a peculiarity of the human mind: "For of everything there is necessarily an idea in God, of which God is the cause, in the same way as there is an idea of the human body; thus whatever we have asserted of the idea of the human body must necessarily be asserted of the idea of everything else." More simply expressed, this means that there is an idea or correlate in the attribute of thought for everything that occurs in the physical world. In this very restricted and technical sense, all individual things, "though in different degrees, are animated," which of course does not mean that all things are conscious or possess rational minds. But if this is the case, as the identity of the order and connection of ideas with the order and connection of things seems to clearly imply, how are we to explain the superiority of the human mind to the mind, let us say, of a fly? Spinoza's ingenious answer to this crucial question turns on the distinction between different degrees of animation or levels of mind, with the degree or level being a function of the nature of the body. Thus, he tells us:

In proportion as any given body is more fitted than others for doing many actions or receiving many impressions at once, so also is the mind, of which it is the object, more fitted than others for forming many simultaneous perceptions; and the more the actions of one body depend on itself alone, and the fewer other bodies concur with it in action, the more fitted is the mind of which it is the object for distinct comprehension. (Prop. XIII, Scholium)

By means of his deductive, a priori method, Spinoza was here able to arrive at the thoroughly modern view that mind is a function of organic complexity. The more a body is able to interact with its environment, both to affect it and be affected by it, the greater the power of the mind to perceive this environment. Conscious awareness and rational comprehension stand at the highest end of this scale of power. Moreover, with this conception of mind, not only was Spinoza able to overcome the radical limitation of the Cartesian view, which was simply unable to deal with the problem of the organic basis of mind, but also, by rejecting Descartes's identification of mind with consciousness and rationality, he was able to conceive of mind as manifesting itself throughout nature at various levels.

Nevertheless, Spinoza himself largely ignored the interesting implications of this view in order to concentrate on the primary object of his concern, the human mind. But, as his functional approach makes clear, in order to understand the human mind and its "union with the whole of nature," we must first acquire a more accurate knowledge of the nature of the human body. The deductive method, however, requires that any such knowledge be based on general considerations concerning the nature of all physical bodies. Thus, Spinoza found it necessary to interrupt his analysis of the human mind and to make a brief foray into physics and biology. This occurs in a series of lemmata, axioms and postulates which immediately follow the above proposition. We have already touched on this discussion in connection with our treatment of the eternal and infinite modes, but we must here consider it in a bit more detail if we are to arrive at an adequate understanding of Spinoza's conception of the human body, and therefore of the human mind.

The analysis is divided into three parts. The first deals with the properties of the most simple bodies; the second is concerned with complex, organic bodies; the third consists of a series of postulates dealing specifically with the human body. As one might expect, the basic principle of the whole analysis is that all bodies are combinations of motion and rest. Bodies are thus "distinguished from one another in respect of motion and rest, quickness and slowness, and not in respect of substance" (Lemma I). All bodies therefore agree in certain respects, that is, all bodies are conceived in terms of the same attribute and its principal modification (Lemma II). Moreover, since every body is a finite mode, "a body in motion or at rest must be determined to motion or rest by another body, which other body has been determined to motion or rest by a third body, and that third again by a fourth, and so on to infinity" (Lemma III). From this Spinoza is able to derive one of the basic principles of the science of physics, the law of inertia: "A body in motion keeps in motion until it is determined to a state of rest by some other body; and a body at rest remains so, until it is determined to a state of motion by some other body" (Lemma III, Corollary).

The discussion now shifts to more complex bodies, which are compounded of these simple bodies, and it is in this context that Spinoza deals with the living organism, or, more generally, with the phenomenon of life. The first question to be considered is the problem of identity. More specifically, in light of what principle can one claim that a number of distinct, simple bodies constitute one particular individual? Spinoza's answer, which is based on the preceding analysis, is in terms of contact and of the preservation of the same proportion of motion and rest. Insofar as any given group of bodies "are compelled by other bodies to remain in contact," or if "their mutual movements should preserve amongst themselves a certain fixed relation," Spinoza reasons that we can consider such bodies in union, and claim "that together they compose one body or individual, which is distinguished from other bodies by this fact of union." A complex body can thus retain its identity throughout a change in its component parts, and this conception provides the basis for Spinoza's treatment of organic unity. As Spinoza proceeds to suggest in the following lemmata (IV-VII)—which deal, in terms of motion and rest, with the basic biological functions of metabolism, growth, motion of the limbs, and locomotion—the very essence of such unity, that is, the unity of a living being, consists in its ability to remain identical not only in spite of, but actually by means of a constant change in its component parts (cells) and a constant interaction with its environment. Unfortunately, we cannot here consider this topic in any more detail, but it is certainly worthy of note that within the confines of a very brief space, Spinoza succeeded in developing the outlines of a speculative theory of organism that goes much further and gives promise of dealing in a far more adequate manner with the nature of life, than Descartes's purely mechanistic account of the body.[10]

The entire discussion concludes with a series of postulates which, as already noted, apply these basic principles to the human body. We are told that this body is an individual of a very high degree of complexity, composed of a number of parts (organs) which are themselves complex individuals (Post. I). Some of these parts are fluid, some soft and some hard (Post. II), and each of these parts, and consequently the body itself, is affected in a number of distinct ways by external bodies (Post. III). Not only is the human body so affected, but it also "stands in need for its preservation of a number of other bodies, by which it is continually, so to speak, regenerated" (Post. IV). Moreover, since it contains soft and fluid parts, it is capable of forming and retaining impressions when affected by external bodies (Post. V), while at the same time it can, of course, affect external bodies in a variety of ways. In short, and this is the whole point of Spinoza's analysis, the human body, as an extremely complex organic individual which stands in complex and manifold relation with its environment, is an adequate vehicle for the human mind.

This result is more definitively established in the next two propositions, which conclude the discussion of the mind-body problem and prepare the way for the analysis of human knowledge. Here Spinoza points out that since the human body is capable of affecting and being affected by a large number of external bodies in a variety of ways, the human mind, as the idea of that body or the corresponding modification in the attribute of thought, *"is capable of perceiving a great number of things, and is so in proportion as its body is capable of receiving a great number of impressions"* (Prop. XIV). The perceptual power of the mind is thus a function of the sensitivity of the body. Finally, just as the human body is a complex individual, composed of a great number of bodies, so, Spinoza concludes, *"the idea, which constitutes the actual being of the human mind, is not simple, but compounded of a great number of ideas"* (Prop. XV).

II *The Intellect*

Traditionally, the intellect has been viewed as the faculty of knowledge. The analysis of the intellect is therefore primarily a consideration of the nature and extent of human knowledge, or what is now called epistemology. The ultimate goal of Spinoza's epistemological analysis is nothing less than to demonstrate that *"the human mind has an adequate knowledge of the eternal and infinite essence of God"* (Prop. XLVII). At the same time, however, Spinoza also desires to demonstrate that this knowledge comes from reason, and that insofar as the intellect operates with ideas based on sense perception, it cannot arrive at any adequate knowledge at all. His discussion of knowledge is consequently divided into two parts, with the critique of sense perception preceding the justification of reason, the positive power of the intellect.

One of the keys to this whole analysis is obviously the notion of adequacy, and more specifically the conception of an adequate idea. We have already encountered this expression, and we have likewise referred in passing to knowledge as adequate or inadequate. Now, however, it is time to examine this notion more precisely, and, as usual, the place to begin is with Spinoza's own definition. "By *an adequate idea*," Spinoza tells us at the beginning of the second part of the *Ethics*, "I mean an idea which, in so far as it is considered in itself, without relation to the object, has all the properties or intrinsic marks of a true idea" (Def. IV). In the explanation which follows this definition he further notes: "I say *intrinsic*, in order to exclude that mark which is extrinsic, namely, the agreement between the idea and its object (*ideatum*)." Much the same point is made in response to Tschirnhaus's query concerning the relation between truth and adequacy wherein Spinoza writes:

I recognize no other difference between a true and an adequate idea than that the word true refers only to the agreement of the idea with its ideatum, while the word adequate refers to the nature of the idea in itself; so that there is really no difference between a true and adequate idea except this extrinsic relation.[11]

The point of these statements is that truth and adequacy are strictly correlative. All true ideas are adequate and vice versa, but the most basic notion is that of truth. As we can see, this refers to the agreement of an idea, which philosophers would now tend to call an assertion or a proposition, with its object (*ideatum*). Spinoza calls this characteristic extrinsic because it involves the relation between an idea and something else, namely, its object. His working definition of truth is therefore, verbally at least, very close to one of the traditional conceptions of truth as the correspondence between an idea or proposition and an object or fact.[12] A major difference, which is a direct consequence of Spinoza's doctrine of substance, is that idea and *ideatum* are not regarded as distinct entities, but as one and the same thing expressed in two ways. This can either be in two attributes when the *ideatum* is a modification of extension, or in the attribute of thought itself when the *ideatum* is another idea.[13] In the latter case we have what Spinoza calls the "idea of an idea" (*idea ideae*), which he claims stands in precisely the same relation to the original idea as this idea stands to the corresponding modification in the attribute of extension (Prop. XXI).

Adequacy, for its part, is the inner characteristic of an idea in virtue of which it is judged to be true. This can also be expressed by saying that it is the criterion of truth. The basic feature of an adequate idea is its completeness. As we have already noted in the discussion of Spinoza's methods, an adequate idea is simply one from which all of the properties of its *ideatum* can be deduced. It is therefore equivalent to a real or genetic definition, and following the language of Descartes, Spinoza also sometimes categorizes such ideas as "clear and distinct." For example, we can see that the mathematician's idea of a triangle is adequate because he derives all of the properties of the figure from it, while the conception of a triangle possessed by someone ignorant of geometry is inadequate precisely because he cannot do so. Such a person may have a vague idea of a triangle and be aware of the fact that it is a figure with three sides, but since he does not know what follows from this, he does not really possess the true concept or an adequate idea of a triangle.

This conception of adequacy and its function as a criterion of truth enable Spinoza to avoid the kind of radical skepticism that was generated by Descartes's methodical doubt. *"He who has a true idea,"* Spinoza tell us, *"simultaneously knows that he has a true idea, and cannot doubt of the truth of the thing perceived"* (Prop. XLIII). As he explains in the attached scholium, this is because "to have a true idea is only another expression for knowing a thing perfectly, or as well as possible." Now, as our brief consideration of the notion of adequacy shows, knowing a thing in this manner involves seeing how all of its properties follow necessarily from its nature. In all such instances, nothing remains ambiguous, nothing is left unexplained, undetermined or uncertain. There can then be no rational basis for doubt and no need to appeal to God or, indeed, to anything external to the ideas themselves, in order to guarantee their truth. To cite Spinoza's appropriate and uncharacteristically elegant metaphor: "Even as light displays both itself and darkness, so is truth a standard both of itself and of falsity" (Prop. XLIII, Scholium).

The reference to falsity in this context is likewise extremely significant, for it shows that the very same conception of adequacy which serves as criterion of truth also provides the basis for determining the nature of error or falsity. At first glance, error would seem to be a major problem for Spinoza. Since the order and connection of ideas is the same as the order and connection of things, and since an idea and its object are not two distinct things between which disagreement or lack of correspondence is possible, but merely one and the same thing expressed in two manners, one is tempted to ask how an idea can ever fail to agree with its object, or correlatively, how, on the basis of Spinoza's metaphysical assumptions, such a thing as error or falsity is even conceivable.

Spinoza begins his brief yet significant account of this topic in the *Ethics*[14] by acknowledging that there is a sense in which all ideas are true. They are all true *"in so far as they are referred to God"* (Prop. XXXII). As the proof of this proposition makes clear, this follows from the identification of the order and connection of ideas with the order and connection of things. What, then, does it mean to refer ideas to God? Within the confines of Spinoza's metaphysics, it would seem to mean nothing more than to consider them as apprehended by an infinite intellect, and therefore as agreeing perfectly with their objects. The proposition thus seems to reduce to the not very informative claim that all ideas which are conceived in such a way as to agree with, or adequately express, their objects are true.

Nevertheless, this proposition is not quite as empty as it first appears; for from the fact that an idea in its inherent nature, as a modification of the attribute of thought, must necessarily agree with its object, we can infer that *"there is nothing positive in ideas, which causes them to be called false"* (Prop. XXXIII). Furthermore, since falsity is not a positive characteristic of any idea, which means that there simply are no ideas which do not agree with their objects, error can only be due to the way in which an idea is "in" or grasped by a particular mind. Any given mind can possess or conceive a particular idea either completely or partially, as in our earlier example in which the mathematician possesses the complete and hence adequate idea of a triangle, while the person ignorant of mathematics does not. Thus, while any idea which is conceived adequately, i.e., completely, by the human mind is true and is, in fact, conceived in precisely the same way as an infinite intellect would conceive it (Prop. XXXIV), obviously not very many ideas are conceived by the human mind in this manner. Those that are not, are conceived falsely, so that *"falsity consists in the privation of knowledge, which inadequate, fragmentary, or confused ideas involve"* (Prop. XXXV). Falsity, in other words, is really partial truth, which is mistakenly taken for the complete truth about a state of affairs. This typically occurs when the mind perceives the idea of an effect without considering the idea of its cause. In such cases our ideas are said to be "as consequences without premises" (Prop. XXVIII).

Fortunately, Spinoza illustrates his conception of error with two examples which serve to greatly clarify his meaning. The first is his favorite bête noire, the notion of the freedom of the will. The belief in such freedom, he points out, arises simply because men are ignorant of the true causes of their actions. This ignorance is due to the fact that the inadequate ideas which men have of their actions do not include the ideas of their determining causes. They therefore naturally tend to explain these actions in terms of a mysterious faculty of will "which is a mere phrase without any idea to correspond thereto." The second example is even more revealing, and Spinoza's analysis is worth quoting in full:

So again, when we look at the sun, we imagine that it is distant from us about two hundred feet; this error does not lie solely in this fancy, but in the fact that, while we thus imagine, we do not know the sun's true distance or the cause of the fancy. For although we afterwards learn, that the sun is distant from us more than six hundred of the earth's diameters, we none the less shall fancy it to be near; for we do not imagine the sun as near us, because we are ignorant of its true distance, but because the modification of our body involves the essence of the sun, in so far as our said body is affected thereby. (Prop. XXXV)

The whole point of this is that our imaginative idea of the sun as being only about two hundred feet from us is not intrinsically false. There is, it will be recalled, nothing positive in ideas in virtue of which they can be considered false. In the present instance, the idea of the sun contains an accurate description of how the sun actually *seems* to the eye, or, in Spinoza's language, how it is perceived in virtue of its modification of the body. It still appears in the same way to the person who has an adequate idea, i.e., enough scientific knowledge to know better, and the reason why it appears in this way is itself subject to a scientific explanation (through the science of optics). Error in this instance, which is typical of our perceptual ideas, arises when the mind views its imaginative (perceptual) representation of the sun apart from the ideas of its determining causes and consequently confuses mere appearance with reality. An adequate idea of the sun, on the other hand, such as the one possessed by the scientist, would include the imaginative representation within it in the sense that it provides an explanation for it. In Spinoza's terms, it includes a knowledge of its cause.

Spinoza's treatment of error, especially as discussed in the last example, follows in the text, but provides the basis for, his whole analysis of the nature of sense perception and of its significance for human knowledge. His general term for such perception, and for the thought based upon it, is perception "according to the common order of nature." This refers to the order in which the mind receives its ideas in experience, which naturally corresponds to the order in which the body is affected by the objects of these ideas. Spinoza contends that the mind is passive when it perceives in this manner, and this constitutes one of the bases for his theory of the passions. For the present, however, the important point is that ideas perceived in this manner reflect the condition of the organism in its interplay with the environment, rather than the true nature of the objects of these ideas. As the last example makes clear, it provides ideas of how things *seem*, not of how they *really are*. Thus, insofar as the mind's thought relies on such ideas, it inevitably falls into error. The order of perception, or the "common order of nature," is contrasted with the "order of the intellect." This refers to the order of logical dependence, "whereby the mind perceives things through their primary causes." This order, unlike the former, is "in all men the same" as it does not depend on external causes, but merely on the activity of the mind (Prop. XVIII, Scholium). The extent to which the mind's ideas are ordered in this fashion determines the extent of its adequate knowledge.

The basis of this conception of sense perception and, indeed, of Spinoza's whole analysis of knowledge, is the principle that "*the idea of every mode, in which the human body is affected by external bodies, must involve the nature of the human body, and also the nature of the external body*" (Prop. XVI). This follows from the status of the body as a finite mode which, as such, is determined by its network of relations with external bodies, and from the conception of the mind as the idea of the body, which reflects in the realm of thought everything that occurs in the world of extension. The key implication of this principle is that the human body provides the focal point from and through which alone the human mind can perceive its world.

This has two further consequences, one positive and the other negative, which Spinoza presents in the form of corollaries. The first, and positive, corollary, is that "the human mind perceives the nature of a variety of bodies, together with the nature of its own." From this we can conclude that sense perception *does* provide us with an awareness of external bodies. The fact that the mind is defined as the idea of the body does not therefore imply that the only object which a given mind can represent is its own body, but only that it has these other ideas in virtue of the idea of its own body.[15] The second, and negative, corollary, is that "the ideas, which we have of external bodies, indicate rather the constitution of our own body than the nature of external bodies." This is precisely the principle which underlies the above-cited analysis of error. Since the perceptual awareness of external bodies is a function of the state of one's own body or, more precisely, of one's sensory apparatus, this awareness only provides information concerning how a body appears, and this, strictly speaking, is as much a fact about the constitution of one's own body as about the nature of the external body.

This obviously provides the basis for the analysis of the inadequacy of our knowledge insofar as it is based on sense experience, but before developing this theme in a systematic form, Spinoza presents some of the important implications of this principle for the science of psychology. Since the ideas in the mind involve the nature both of one's own body and of external bodies, and since the order and connection of ideas is identical with the order and connection of things, it follows that the laws determining the relations of ideas in the mind must reflect the laws concerning the relations between bodies in the realm of extension. A foundation is therefore laid for a mechanistic psychology which formulates universal laws concerning the relations of ideas, and Spinoza proceeds to treat both imagination and memory in these terms.

Spinoza often uses the term "imagination" in a very broad sense to characterize all thought, including sense perception, wherein the order of ideas in the mind reflects the order of affections in the body (caused by external objects). Ultimately, this covers all thought which is according to the "common order of nature." These bodily affections are called "the images of things" and their corresponding ideas the "imaginations of the mind" (*mentis imaginationes*) (Prop. XVII, Scholium), so that the whole process of thought based on these ideas can be entitled "imagination."[16] In the present context, however, Spinoza's concern is mainly with imagination in the more limited and usual sense of the mind's propensity to form ideas of absent objects. Depending on the circumstances in which it occurs, and the conclusions which are drawn from it concerning the idea of the absent object, this propensity can be viewed either as a power or defect of the mind. In either case it is perfectly natural and is explicable in terms of a general principle which constitutes a kind of psychological version of the law of inertia: "*If the human body is affected in a manner which involves the nature of any external body, the human mind will regard the said external body as actually existing, or as present to itself, until the human body be affected in such a way, as to exclude the existence or the presence of the said external body*" (Prop. XVII).

The same line of thought is applied to memory, understood as the mind's ability to recall the idea of a past object on the basis of a present image or impression. Its principle, which is a consequence of the law governing the operation of the imagination, is that "*if the human body has once been affected by two or more bodies at the same time, when the mind afterwards imagines any of them, it will straightway remember the others also*" (Prop. XVIII). As noted in the scholium, memory in this sense is really a process of association, and the law which Spinoza here presents concerning the operation of memory is precisely the same as that which subsequent philosophers and psychologists have termed the law of the association of ideas. Furthermore, for Spinoza, as for these later thinkers, the importance of this principle lies in the fact that it provides an explanation as to how the mind moves from the thought of one thing to the thought of another thing that stands in no logical connection with the first. This basis is simply habit, which is itself the product of past associations in experience.[17] To cite one of Spinoza's own examples, a soldier, upon seeing the tracks of a horse, will tend to think of a horseman, and then of war, while a farmer, seeing the same tracks, will naturally proceed to the thought of a plough and a field. In neither case is the transition logical, and it thus does not lead to genuine knowledge. Nevertheless, in both cases it is natural and predictable; for, as Spinoza concludes, "every man will follow this or that train of thought, according as he has been in the habit of conjoining and associating the mental images of things in this or that manner" (Prop. XVIII, Scholium).

Having articulated the basic principle underlying sense perception and described two of the fundamental operations of the mind with regard to its sensible ideas, Spinoza is ready to proceed to his treatment of perceptual knowledge *per se*. First of all, he points out, on the basis of the preceding analysis, that the mind's knowledge of the body depends on the body's having been affected by external bodies (Prop. XIX). Put in more modern terms, this means simply that a person's awareness of his own body depends on external stimuli. But since the mind is the idea or mental correlate of the body, what holds of one applies likewise to the other (they are both "in God" in the same manner) (Prop. XX). Now Spinoza proceeds to argue, albeit somewhat incongruously in light of his theory of attributes: *"The idea of the mind is united to the mind in the same way as the mind is united to the body"* (Prop. XXI). This idea of the mind, or "idea of the idea," is nothing but the mind's awareness of itself, that is, self-consciousness. Thus, just as the mind is aware of its body, so also it is aware of itself. The human mind, in other words, is self-conscious (Prop. XXII). In this brief series of succinct propositions Spinoza therefore provides a basis for understanding how the human mind, as the idea of the body, can become conscious both of its body and of itself.

Furthermore, since it has already been established that the mind is only aware of the body insofar as it has been affected or modified by external bodies, it likewise follows, on the basis of the above principles, that the mind does not know itself, or is not self-conscious, except insofar as it is aware of these modifications (Prop. XXIII). External stimuli are therefore required for the awareness of the mind as well as of the body. Apart from external stimuli of some sort, self-awareness is simply impossible. Nevertheless, the ideas correlated with such stimuli do not provide the mind with adequate knowledge of the parts of its own body (Prop. XXIV). This is merely Spinoza's way of making the obvious point that a person's perception, sensation or immediate feeling (all three being used here synonymously) of the state of his own organism does not provide him with any scientific knowledge thereof.

It is further obvious, by precisely the same line of reasoning, that the ideas correlated with these stimuli do not provide us with any adequate (scientific) knowledge of the external objects which interact with and stimulate our organism (Prop. XXV). This much was clear from the analysis of imagination, which showed that such ideas, those termed "imaginations" or "mental images," only represent the object as it *appears*, not as it *really is* in itself. The same analysis also showed, however, that it is only through the medium of these ideas that the human mind can form the idea of the actual existence of an external object (Prop. XXVI). Such knowledge, in other words, requires perceptual evidence or experience.

On the basis of these considerations, Spinoza is able to arrive at some interesting and paradoxical conclusions. Since the idea of one's own body depends on the idea of external bodies, and since it has been established that ideas of the latter class are inadequate, it follows that the same holds for the idea of one's own body (Prop. XXVII), and hence that the knowledge of one's own body possessed in this manner is similarly confused (Prop. XXVIII). But the difficulty does not stop here; for since what holds for the ideas of the body applies equally to the idea of the idea, which has already been shown to be equivalent to the mind's idea of itself, it can also be concluded that such ideas do not provide adequate knowledge of the human mind (Prop. XXIX). The initial outcome of Spinoza's analysis of knowledge thus seems to be a radical and hopeless skepticism, which is further extended to include knowledge of the duration of one's own or external bodies (Props. XXX-XXXI). The human mind, as a finite mode, seems only able to apprehend the world and itself through the distorting perspective of its own body, and to be totally unable to perceive things in the manner of an infinite intellect.

Yet no sooner does Spinoza arrive at this seemingly skeptical conclusion than he begins to qualify it. This result, he notes, follows only insofar as the mind "perceives things after the common order of nature" and is "determined from without . . . by the fortuitous play of circumstances." It does not follow "at such times as it is determined from within, that is, by the fact of regarding several things at once, to understand their points of agreement, difference, and contrast. Whenever it is determined in anywise from within, it regards things clearly and distinctly, as I will show below" (Prop. XXIX, Scholium).

The idea of being "determined from within," or self-determined, is precisely how Spinoza conceives freedom. We can thus see immediately that the epistemological problem of the possession of adequate knowledge is intimately connected with, if not identical to, the moral problem of the attainment of freedom. Nevertheless, it would seem that it is precisely this possibility, whether expressed in its epistemological or moral form, that is precluded by Spinoza's conception of the mind as a finite mode. Spinoza's present concern is therefore to demonstrate that, despite appearances, this is not the case, at least not completely, and on this basis he will proceed in the remainder of the *Ethics* to develop his moral theory.

In reference to thinking, being determined from within can only mean that the mind is guided by its own thoughts, which are ordered according to their logical relations ("the order of the intellect"), and not according to the order in which they are in the mind as the result of the body's being affected by external bodies ("the common order of nature"). The immediate problem, therefore, is to explain how the mind, as the idea of the body, whose every modification must correspond to a modification of this body, can ever be in a position to do this. The basis of Spinoza's answer lies in the claim that there are certain ideas which the human mind does possess completely and hence can conceive adequately because, unlike the ideas derived from ordinary sense experience, they do not "involve" or logically depend on ideas of particular modifications of the body. These ideas fall into two classes, corresponding to two levels of generality, and Spinoza calls them respectively *"common notions"* (Prop. XXXVIII) and adequate ideas of the *"common properties of things"* (Prop. XXXIX).

These correspond more or less roughly to the innate ideas advocated by other philosophers, which were, in fact, sometimes called "common notions."[18] Both Descartes and Leibniz appealed to this ancient theory of innate ideas in one form or another in order to explain the foundations of our rational knowledge. Their basic claim was that our knowledge of necessary and universal truths, adequate knowledge in Spinoza's sense, cannot be derived from experience. On the contrary, it was thought that the sources of such knowledge must lie in the mind and reflect its very structure, and that only this can account for its necessity and universality. This theory, however, was not construed in a naïve psychological sense. It was not maintained, as some of the critics of the theory seemed to believe, that either the infant or the untutored savage, who was a favorite of the philosophical literature of the time, was actually conscious of the "true concept of God" or the basic principles of mathematics.[19] Rather, innate ideas were viewed as dispositions which pertain universally to the human mind, but of which any given individual is not necessarily conscious. As Descartes expressed the matter in response to a critic:

For I never wrote or concluded that the mind required innate ideas which were in some sort different from its faculty of thinking; but when I observed the existence in me of certain thoughts which proceeded, not from extraneous objects nor from the determination of my will, but solely from the faculty of thinking which is within me, then, that I might distinguish the ideas or notions (which are the forms of these thoughts) from other thoughts *adventitious* or *factitious*, I termed the former *"innate."* In the same sense we say that in some families generosity is innate, in others certain diseases like gout or gravel, not that on this account the babes of these families suffer from these diseases in their mother's womb, but because they are born with a certain disposition or propensity for contracting them.[20]

Spinoza's conception of the mind as the idea of the body does not allow him to distinguish, in the manner of Descartes, between innate and adventitious ideas, between those which come from the mind and those which come from experience. From his point of view all ideas are equally innate, as they are all modifications of the attribute of thought and none is "caused" by anything in the realm of extension; and by the same token, all are equally adventitious, as each must have its physical correlate. Nevertheless, this very conception of mind does allow Spinoza to make an analogous distinction, which leads to much the same result. This is the distinction between ideas which are correlated with specific features of particular bodies, and those whose correlates are common to all bodies, or of a large class thereof. Things which are common to all bodies, and which are *"equally in a part and in the whole,"* Spinoza notes, do not *"constitute the essence of any particular thing"* (Prop. XXXVII). It follows from this that the common notions, the ideas which correspond to these things, do not arise in the mind in connection with the experience of any particular object. Hence, they do not involve or depend on the idea of any particular object, and, on the basis of his preceding analysis, Spinoza can therefore contend that the mind possesses them in their totality and understands them adequately (Prop. XXXVIII). Moreover, since these ideas correspond to what is common to *all* bodies, they, like the innate ideas of Descartes and Leibniz, are common to *all* minds. (Prop. XXXVIII, Corollary).

We have already seen that all bodies are particular modifications of the attribute of extension and are constituted by a certain proportion of motion and rest. These features, therefore, are certainly common to all bodies and are present "equally in a part and in the whole." Thus, the ideas corresponding thereto, which would seem to include the axioms of geometry and the first principles of physics, must certainly be included among the common notions. Futhermore, if we extend this line of reasoning to the attribute of thought and point to thoughts which are present equally in "a part and in the whole," that is, in all thoughts, we arrive at the laws of logic, the first principles of thought, which must likewise be regarded as common notions.[21] This brings us to the second category of adequate ideas, those of the common properties of things. These have a lesser degree of generality than the common notions and refer to properties shared only by certain bodies. Specifically, Spinoza here refers to properties that are common to the human body *"and such other bodies as are wont to affect the human body, and which is present equally in each part of either, or in the whole"* (Prop. XXXIX). The argument for the adequacy of our ideas of these common properties is basically the same as for the common notions. Their commonality enables the mind to grasp them completely, in the manner of an infinite intellect, and thus adequately. It is uncertain just what Spinoza has in mind here, but a reasonable interpretation, thoroughly in accord with the spirit of his enterprise, is that he is referring to the first principles of physiology, while the knowledge of the corresponding ideas of these common properties would yield the basic laws of psychology.[22] Although the details of this analysis are highly obscure, and Spinoza never completed the further elaboration which he promised, the basic point emerges with sufficient clarity. It is simply that insofar as the mind possesses such ideas, and deduces its other ideas from them (Prop. XL), it will know its objects truly or in an adequate manner.

One detail, however, could not be left to the projected future work. In order to avoid complete misunderstanding, Spinoza felt it necessary to distinguish between his common notions and adequate ideas of the common properties of things, the very foundations of scientific reasoning, and the universals or general terms of the scholastics. These latter are of two kinds. The first are the so-called "Transcendentals" such as "Being, Thing, Something." These are the most general concepts of all, applicable to all genera. The second are the various genera and species themselves into which all substances in nature fall. As already noted, Aristotelian science proceeded largely by classifying substances in terms of such universals, and Spinoza's basic contention is that not only do such concepts not yield adequate knowledge of the nature of things, but they reflect the limits of the imagination rather than the power of the intellect. The mind, Spinoza points out, is only capable of distinctly imagining a limited number of things simultaneously, specifically, only as many as its body can form images of simultaneously. When these images become confused, the mind tends to form general ideas answering to these confused images. The "Transcendentals," therefore, are the most confused ideas of all, as they reflect the intellect's total inability to make distinctions. What, after all, is emptier than the concept of a mere "something"? Compare this with the notion of motion and rest, which serves as a precise quantitative principle in terms of which objects can be distinguished and explained. When we come to class concepts such as "man," "horse," "dog," the situation is similar. These merely reflect the inability of the imagination to capture the small differences between individuals, and can hardly serve as vehicles for adequate, i.e., scientific, knowledge. In short, these general ideas do not, as the Aristotelians claim, answer to the essence of things, but merely reflect what a particular individual happens to regard as important, which in turn is a function of the condition of his body. To cite Spinoza's own example:

> For instance, those who have most often regarded with admiration the stature of man, will by the name of man understand an animal of erect stature; those who have been accustomed to regard some other attribute, will form a different general image of man, for instance, that man is a laughing animal, a two-footed animal without feathers, a rational animal, and thus, in other cases, everyone will form general images of things according to the habit of his body. (Prop. XL, Scholium I)

There are thus two distinct ways in which the mind can form its general notions, and Spinoza uses this insight as a basis for distinguishing between two kinds of knowledge. These notions can, in the manner of the Aristotelians, be derived from "particular things represented to our intellect fragmentarily, confusedly, and without order through our senses." Spinoza calls such perceptions "knowledge from the mere suggestions of experience" *(cognitionem ab experientia vaga)*. Equivalently, they can be derived from signs, by which is meant hearsay or memory images, such as those derived from having read or recollected something. Both of these ways, which reflect the "common order of nature," are grouped together and termed *"knowledge of the first kind, opinion, or imagination."* This is contrasted with *"knowledge of the second kind,"* which Spinoza terms *"reason" (ratio)*, and which is, of course, based on the common notions and adequate ideas of the properties of things (Prop. XL, Scholium II).

At this point Spinoza abruptly introduces at least the possibility of a third kind of knowledge, termed intuition. Although he adds that the actual existence of this kind of knowledge will only be established later, he does note that "this kind of knowledge proceeds from an adequate idea of the absolute essence of certain attributes of God to the adequate knowledge of the essence of things." Moreover, he proceeds to illustrate all three kinds of knowledge by means of a single example:

Three numbers are given for finding a fourth, which shall be to the third as the second is to the first. Tradesmen without hesitation multiply the second by the third, and divide the product by the first; either because they have not forgotten the rule which they received from a master without any proof, or because they have often made trial of it with simple numbers, or by virtue of the proof of the nineteenth proposition of the seventh book of Euclid, namely, in virtue of the general property of proportionals.

But with very simple numbers there is no need of this. For instance, one, two, three, being given, everyone can see that the fourth proportional is six; and this is much clearer, because we infer the fourth number from an intuitive grasping of the ratio, which the first bears to the second. (Prop. XL, Scholium II)

As this example suggests, the basic difference between the second and third kinds of knowledge is that the former (reason) makes use of general principles from which it deduces its conclusions, whereas the latter (intuition) apprehends the truth in an immediate manner, without making use of any such general principles.[23] In contradistinction to the first kind of knowledge, Spinoza believes that both reason and intuition are sources of adequate ideas and necessary truths. Nevertheless, he does recognize two respects in which intuition is superior. First of all, as the description, although not the example, of intuition suggests, it, unlike reason, is able to arrive at knowledge of individual essences. Whereas the province of reason is general truths, e.g., axioms, which hold universally and do not pertain to any particular individuals, intuition proceeds from an adequate idea of the absolute essence of certain attributes of God *to the adequate knowledge of the essence of things* (italics mine). It is therefore concrete while reason is abstract. Although this is not of any immediate significance to his argument, it does become crucial in Part V of the *Ethics*, when Spinoza exhibits the preeminent role of intuition in the attainment of human blessedness. Secondly, from a purely epistemological standpoint, we can also see that knowledge from general principles alone is, in a manner of speaking, left hanging. These principles themselves require some kind of ultimate justification, and, in accordance with the principles of Spinoza's own method, this can only mean that they must be shown to be grounded in the essence of God. This is the task of the third kind of knowledge, which therefore seems to be a necessary complement to reason.

However, before descending by intuition from the eternal and infinite essence of God, it is first necessary to show how reason can ascend to a knowledge of this essence. Spinoza must therefore show that the human mind does in fact possess an adequate idea of this essence. His argument follows the already discussed refutation of skepticism and the development of the conception of a true idea as its own standard. He begins by pointing out that *"it is not in the nature of reason to regard things as contingent, but as necessary"* (Prop. XLIV). Things, after all, *are* necessary, and hence any adequate knowledge of them must reflect this fact. The imagination is therefore the source of our misguided belief in the contingency of things (Prop. XLIV, Corollary I). Moreover, to regard things as necessary is to regard them without any relation to time, and this, in turn, is to regard them as eternal. Hence, Spinoza concludes: "It is in the nature of reason to perceive things under a certain form of eternity *(sub quâdam aeternitatis specie)"* (Prop. XLIV, Corollary II).

But to conceive things in this way is to conceive them in relation to God, and Spinoza affirms that *"every idea of every body, or of every particular thing actually existing, necessarily involves the eternal and infinite essence of God"* (Prop. XLV). Given Spinoza's metaphysical principles, this conclusion is really obvious; for since all things depend on God, both for their essence and the very fact of their existence, or "the force with which they persist in existence," which Spinoza distinguishes from their duration, the idea of each actually existing thing must necessarily involve the idea of God. Furthermore, since the idea of God is, like the common notions, involved in the idea of every thing and can be apprehended either in the whole or in the part, Spinoza can conclude by precisely the same line of reasoning as used in connection with the common notions that *"the knowledge of the eternal and infinite essence of God which every idea involves is adequate and perfect"* (Prop. XLVI). Every finite thing is, after all, part of that infinite system which is called equivalently God or nature. The adequate idea of anything thus, in the last analysis, involves the idea of the whole or of God; so that we once again return to the central Spinozistic contention that the knowledge of anything in nature ultimately depends on the knowledge of God. Therefore, since it has already been established that the mind does know some things or possesses adequate ideas, Spinoza can conclude that *"the human mind has an adequate knowledge of the eternal and infinite essence of God"* (Prop. XLVII).

Although this conclusion is the logical consequence of Spinoza's argument, it is highly paradoxical from the standpoint both of traditional theology and of common sense. The key is obviously Spinoza's peculiar conception of God as the very principle of lawfulness and intelligibility. Knowledge of God is therefore really equivalent to knowledge of the lawfulness and intelligibility of nature. Why, then, do most people fail to realize this? Spinoza's answer is that this is largely because they do not correctly apply names to things (Prop. XLVII, Scholium). Specifically, they erroneously apply the name "God" to that anthropomorphic being who is really the product of their own imagination. Such a being is certainly not knowable, but it is also the case that such a being is not really God. The important thing is always to be sure that one has a proper understanding of the meaning of one's terms, and in the present instance this can be accomplished by attending carefully to the argument of the first part of the *Ethics*.

III *The Will*

In the last two propositions and concluding scholium of Part II of the *Ethics,* Spinoza turns from the intellect to the will. This short but important section not only completes the analysis of the human mind, but also provides a bridge between the metaphysical and epistemological doctrines of the earlier parts of the work and the psychological and ethical concerns of its later portions. We here find an application to the human mind of many of the same conclusions which have already been established in regard to the divine mind. Just as we have previously seen that God does not act from freedom of the will, that his actions are coextensive with his power, and that his intellect is identical with his will, so we now come to see that precisely the same things can be affirmed about the human mind.

The development of this line of thought involves a concise yet thoroughgoing critique of the traditional scholastic view of the mind, which was shared to a considerable extent by Descartes.

Central to this view is the belief that the mind contains a number of powers or faculties, which are not only distinguishable from one another, at least in function, but which also exist as capacities above and beyond their particular manifestations. Thus, the mind's volitions are explained in terms of its faculty of volition, or will, its understanding in terms of its intellectual faculty, or intellect, etc. The will is further said to be free in the sense that it possesses an absolute power of choice; and it is by virtue of this freedom of choice that man is held to be morally responsible for his actions.

Although freedom is one of the most fundamental values of Spinoza's philosophy, he certainly had no use for this traditional conception of a free will. He therefore declares categorically that *"in the mind there is no absolute or free will; but the mind is determined to wish this or that by a cause, which has also been determined by another cause, and this last by another cause, and so on to infinity"* (Prop. XLVIII). The demonstration makes clear that this result follows from the very status of the human mind as a finite mode. As such, each of its particular volitions must be determined by a particular cause; and given the cause, the effect, in this case the volition, necessarily follows. Man, in other words, may be said to choose or will something, but this choice must itself have a cause which determines it, and it is therefore not "free." But, if this is the case, then we find not only that we cannot talk about "freedom of the will" in the traditional sense, but also that there is no longer any meaning to be attached to the very notion of the will itself, as a faculty of volition, which exercises its choice, and which "might have chosen otherwise." Moreover, as Spinoza proceeds to add in the scholium, precisely the same line of reasoning suffices to demonstrate that there is no "absolute faculty" of understanding, desiring, loving or anything else. In each instance we have merely particular acts of understanding, desire or love, etc., and there is no mysterious faculty which performs these activities and exists apart from them. Quite simply put, man, like God, is what he does. His power is coextensive with his activity; and there is no room in the Spinozistic universe for any unexercised power, any "potentiality." Men, of course, believe in such things, and this is one of the basic factors underlying the prevalent belief in a free will. Here as elsewhere, however, men are the victims of their imagination. On the basis of their experience of particular volitions, they come to form the abstract idea of a volition in general, and they then proceed to mistakenly reify this abstraction, thereby giving birth to the fiction of a distinct faculty.

If there is no faculty of will, what then is volition? Can we in fact, as the first stage of the argument seems to assume, talk about distinct acts of volition? As one might expect, Spinoza's answer is an unequivocal no: *"There is in the mind no volition or affirmation and negation, save that which an idea, inasmuch, as it is an idea, involves"* (Prop. XLIX). The equation of volition with affirmation or negation shows that by volition Spinoza means, as did Descartes, the affirmation or negation of the content of a given idea. This can also be expressed by saying that an idea, as Spinoza conceives it, is really a judgment. The argument itself is based on his conception of an idea. As we have already seen, he construes ideas as acts rather than objects of thought. He can therefore claim that every idea contains an act of affirmation or negation within it. Let us consider Spinoza's own example, the idea of a triangle. His point is that we do not first entertain this idea, examine it, and then, by a distinct act of will, affirm that the sum of its three interior angles is equal to two right angles. Rather, this assertion is part of the very content of the idea of a triangle, so that in conceiving of a triangle one is already affirming this and denying its contradictory. Moreover, what is here said of this volition, i.e., the act of affirmation, can be said equally of all, "namely, that it is nothing but an idea." But since a volition is nothing apart from an idea, and since, as we have just seen, the will is nothing apart from its volitions and the understanding from its ideas, Spinoza can conclude that in man, as in God, "will and understanding are one and the same" (Prop. XLIX, Corollary).

Although he proceeds to discuss a number of possible objections to this doctrine, which are shown to rest mainly on a failure to distinguish between ideas and images on the one hand and abstractions (faculties) and realities (particular ideas) on the other, and even adds a catalogue of the advantages to morality of his doctrine, this really completes Spinoza's analysis of the human mind. The total result of this doctrine is quite revolutionary. The human mind is removed from its special place, which served only to make its activities incomprehensible, and is fully integrated into nature. As the "idea of the human body," it is not a separate substance, nor does it possess distinct and mysterious powers above and beyond its activities. Nevertheless, this does not render it totally powerless. The true power of the mind consists in its ability to understand, and this is coextensive with its possession of adequate ideas. Spinoza has here shown not only that the human mind does, in fact, possess such power, and how it does, but also that this is nothing more than its own, limited portion of the infinite power of nature. This account is obscure at many points, at least in regard to details, and Spinoza himself, as we have seen, does not pretend to have provided an exhaustive treatment of the topic. He does, however, claim that this account is complete and clear enough for his purpose, which, as he tells us at the very end of this section, was to "have laid a foundation, whereon may be raised many excellent conclusions of the highest utility and most necessary to be known" (Prop. XLIX, Corollary, Scholium). It is to these conclusions that we now turn.

CHAPTER 5

Bondage, Virtue and Freedom

THE last three parts of the *Ethics* really form a unity, and together they contain what, broadly speaking, can be characterized as Spinoza's moral philosophy. This encompasses an analysis of the human emotions and how men are subject to them (Part III); an account of the nature of human virtue, or ethics in the narrow sense of the term, which includes both the presentation of rational rules for living and an analysis of the "good life" (Part IV); and a theory of human blessedness, which provides a philosophical alternative to the traditional religious doctrine of salvation (Part V). These are the conclusions which Spinoza erects on the foundations laid in the first two parts, and they form the subject matter of the present chapter.

I *The Human Emotions*

Despite its agreement on many points of detail with previous treatments of the subject, most notably that of Descartes, Spinoza's analysis of the human emotions is one of the more interesting and original aspects of his philosophy. This originality consists largely in the thoroughgoing naturalism of his approach. We have already seen Spinoza's naturalism at work in connection with his analysis of the cognitive capacity of the mind and his mechanistic account of imagination and association. His present concern is to treat the human emotions in precisely the same way, that is, as natural phenomena. This thought underlies Spinoza's famous declaration in the preface to Part III of the *Ethics* that he will "consider human actions and desires in exactly the same manner, as though I were concerned with lines, planes, and solids." Such an approach makes possible the realization of the Cartesian ideal of a universal method, and even the modern ideal of the unity of science; for it implies that mental and physical phenomena are subject to the same set of universal laws and can be dealt with in terms of the same model of scientific explanation.[1] Spinoza himself acknowledges as much in the preface, affirming that "there should be one and the same method of understanding the nature of all things whatsoever, namely, through nature's universal laws and rules." Nevertheless, here as elsewhere, Spinoza was not guided solely, or even primarily, by theoretical considerations. Rather, his point is that only such an understanding of the emotions will enable man to avoid falling victim to them, and therewith enable him to achieve that degree of freedom of which he, as a finite mode, is capable. But before he can provide the remedy, Spinoza must first diagnose the disease, which means that he must provide an account of the basic mechanisms of the human emotions. This account brings Spinoza into direct conflict with Descartes, and it will therefore prove helpful to preface our analysis of the opening propositions of this part of the *Ethics* with a brief consideration of Descartes's doctrine as developed in *The Passions of the Soul.*

Descartes begins his account by distinguishing between actions and passions. Following the traditional view, which goes back to Aristotle, he argues that these are not two distinct things or occurrences, but merely two names for the same thing. These names are determined by the point of view from which the occurrence is considered. One and the same occurrence could be viewed as an action in relation to the agent (cause) and as a passion in relation to the patient (effect). Now the body, for Descartes, acts directly and immediately on the soul, so that what in the body is an action is in the soul a passion; and from this it follows that in order to determine the passions of the soul, it is first necessary to distinguish its functions from those of the body.

These functions are determined by means of the general Cartesian method of appealing to clear and distinct ideas. Whatever we experience as being in us, but which we also conceive may exist in wholly inanimate bodies, is attributed to the body alone, while those things which we cannot possibly conceive as pertaining to body or corporeal nature are attributed to the soul. On the basis of this principle, all physiological functions are attributed to the body, which Descartes regards as a machine, and the only function granted to the soul is thought. Thoughts, however, are of two sorts, the one being termed actions, the other passions. The former includes all of our volitions or desires, which experience teaches us proceed directly from the soul and depend on it alone. The latter encompasses "all those kinds of perceptions or forms of knowledge which are found in us, because it is often not our soul which makes them what they are, and because it always receives them from the things which are represented by them."[2]

The passions or perceptions are themselves divided into two classes. The first contains those which have the soul itself as a cause. Those include the perceptions of our desires and imaginings and of other thoughts which depend on them, in short, the mind's awareness of its inner states. The second class contains those passions which have the body as a cause, and these are in turn divided into three subgroups: (1) those which relate to external objects, e.g., sense perceptions; (2) those which relate to our own body and its parts, e.g., the sensations of hunger, thirst, pleasure and pain; and (3) those which are referred to the soul itself. The last group includes the feelings of joy and sadness, love and anger—in other words, the emotions—and constitutes the passions in the restricted sense that Descartes wished to explain under the name of the passions of the soul.[3]

This explanation is developed in terms of the interaction between soul and body. As noted earlier, Descartes held that this interaction or mutual influence occurs through the actions of the pineal gland. By means of the "animal spirits," or small particles of matter, which it both sends through the nerves to the other parts of the body and receives back again, this gland functions as a kind of messenger service between the mind and the body. When the body is affected by external stimuli, it sends its messages through the "animal spirits" to this gland, whence they are relayed to the mind and produce perceptions therein. By reversing the process and sending messages through the gland to the rest of the body, the mind is able to influence the body, and this is the basis of the Cartesian account of voluntary action. This account enables Descartes on the one hand to provide a physiological analysis of how the various passions are produced in the mind as a result of changes in the body and on the other hand to show "that there is no soul so feeble that it cannot, if well directed, acquire an absolute power over its passions."[4] This doctrine, which he shared with the Stoics, is the fundamental tenet of Descartes's moral philosophy. He attempts to justify it on the rather questionable grounds that the connection between our thoughts and motions of the "animal spirits" is due to custom, not nature. Thus, although a given emotion, e.g., fear, is generally produced in the mind as a result of particular messages sent from the body to the pineal gland, the mind, according to Descartes, has the power to break this customary connection, and to establish instead a connection between these motions and different ideas. For example, the same physiological condition which normally gives rise to fear could, by proper training, be connected with the idea of courage. There is, then, ultimately nothing to prevent the mind from attaining absolute control over its passions.

Spinoza attacks this view head-on in the preface, definitions and initial propositions of Part III of the *Ethics*. The first step in this attack is a redefinition of the notions of action and passion. Whereas for Descartes they referred to two ways of looking at one and the same occurrence, for Spinoza they characterize two distinct states of affairs. We act, he affirms, "when anything takes place, either within us or externally to us, whereof we are the adequate cause. . . . On the other hand, I say that we are passive as regards something when that something takes place within us, or follows from our nature externally, we being only the partial cause" (Def. II). As the juxtaposition of adequate and partial cause clearly suggests, this doctrine is based on the distinction between adequate and inadequate ideas. An adequate cause, we are told, is one "through which its effect can be clearly and distinctly perceived," while an inadequate or partial cause is one "through which, by itself, its effect cannot be understood" (Def. I). This distinction leads in turn to a definition of the emotions or affections (*affectiones*). As used by Spinoza, this term has reference to *both* the mind and the body. In regard to the latter, it refers to "the modifications of the body, whereby the active power of the said body is increased or diminished, aided or constrained." In regard to the former, it refers to the ideas of these modifications (Def. III). Emotions in the mental sense, which will largely concern us here, are ideas in the mind which correspond to events in the body, wherein the power of that body is affected either affirmatively or negatively. Finally, as he adds by way of explanation, if we can be the adequate cause of any of these modifications, the corresponding emotion is to be called an activity or action, otherwise it is a passion. At the very beginning of his account Spinoza therefore introduces the notion of an active emotion, and this notion will prove central to his entire ethical theory.

The immediate problem is to explain how the mind can be an adequate cause, and hence active. Given his analysis of mind, and the repudiation of the freedom of the will which this analysis entails, it is not surprising to find Spinoza affirming that *"our mind is in certain cases active, and in certain cases passive. In so far as it has adequate ideas it is necessarily active, and in so far as it has inadequate ideas, it is necessarily passive"* (Prop. I). When the mind conceives something adequately, it possesses its ideas completely and independently of any external causes. This, as we have seen, is the reason why Spinoza held that when the mind has adequate ideas, it is "determined from within" and follows its own laws (the laws of logic rather than the associations of things dictated by the "common order of nature"). From this it can be inferred that to the extent to which the mind possesses adequate ideas, it is the adequate cause of its states (emotions) and does not merely passively reflect external events. Contrary to Descartes's assumption, however, this activity of the mind does not entail any power to directly determine the body, nor passivity any power of the body to determine the mind. Both are precluded by the doctrine of attributes, from which we can conclude that *"body cannot determine mind to think, neither can mind determine body to motion or rest or any state different from these, if such there be"* (Prop. II).

As Spinoza proceeds to note, in the long and significant scholium to this proposition, the problem with Descartes, and with all of those who believe that the mind can influence the body through some mysterious act of will, is simply that they have not adequately understood the nature of body. "No one," he writes, "has hitherto laid down the limits to the power of the body, that is, no one has as yet been taught by experience what the body can accomplish solely by the laws of nature, in so far as she is regarded as extension." In view of Descartes's prodigious efforts to provide a purely mechanistic account of human physiology, and his consequent conception of the body as a machine, it might seem doubtful that Spinoza is here referring to Descartes. Nevertheless, this is precisely the case. What Spinoza seems to have specifically in mind is Descartes's claim that we can determine the functions of the mind or soul by attributing to it everything which we cannot clearly and distinctly conceive as pertaining to the body, i.e., everything which we cannot explain in mechanistic terms. From Spinoza's standpoint, this whole approach is far too facile, as it neglects a great truth which has

already been established, namely, "that from nature, under whatever attribute she be considered, infinite results follow" (Prop. II,
Scholium).

But what about our ordinary experience? Does this not provide
ample evidence of the mind's ability to exercise control over the
body? Again Spinoza's answer is a categorical no. "Experience," he
points out sarcastically, "abundantly shows that men can govern
anything more easily than their tongues, and restrain anything more
easily than their appetites." Moreover, people only tend to believe
that they are free in regard to their moderate appetites and desires
which they are able to control, but not with regard to their stronger
desires and more violent appetites, which often prove irresistible.
Yet this distinction is illusory, and it stems from an ignorance of true
causes. The truth of the matter, according to Spinoza, is that there
simply is no such thing as a volition or mental decision distinct from
a bodily appetite, through which an individual either resists or
yields to that appetite. On the contrary, he asserts:

A mental decision and a bodily appetite, or determined state, are simultaneous, or rather are one and the same thing, which we call decision, when
it is regarded under and explained through the attribute of thought, and a
conditioned state, when it is regarded under the attribute of extension, and
deduced from the laws of motion and rest. (Prop. II, Scholium)

In order to fully understand this doctrine, we must see it in connection with the analysis of volition in the sense of the affirmation or
negation of the content of a given idea. The point there was that this
was not to be considered something extrinsic to the thought itself,
which the mind could or could not do, but rather as part of the
content of the thought. We now find that precisely the same thing is
affirmed in regard to desires. As a finite modification of thought, any
desire is determined by a cause, specifically by an idea. The "mental
decision" to engage in or forego any course of action is therefore not
a mysterious act of will, but simply another name for a specific
desire. As such, it is as determined as the bodily appetite which it
reflects in the attribute of thought.

The problem of understanding human action is therefore radically
shifted from the form in which it arose in Descartes. The question is
no longer whether or how consciousness can effect changes in the
bodily mechanism. This very possibility has been ruled out on

metaphysical grounds (the doctrine of attributes). Instead, the central issue is whether the mind can ever be the sufficient or adequate cause of its desires. Moreover, once the question is posed in this manner, it admits of an affirmative answer. This occurs whenever these desires follow from, or are caused by, adequate ideas. We can express the same point in non-Spinozistic terms by saying that the mind acts, as opposed to merely being the passive victim of circumstances, whenever its desires, and hence its decisions, are grounded in rational considerations, e.g., when it desires a particular food because of the knowledge (adequate idea) that it is nutritious. In Spinoza's own terms, *"The activities of the mind arise solely from adequate ideas; the passive states of the mind depend solely on inadequate ideas"* (Prop. III).

We have seen enough to realize that in the first three propositions of this section, and the last two of the preceding, Spinoza has developed what amounts to the outlines of a psychology wherein human thought and activity is to be understood without any reference to the notion of a will. It should also be obvious, however, that if such a radical program is to succeed, Spinoza must introduce an alternative principle that can adequately account for the dynamics of human behavior. This function is fulfilled by his conception of *conatus*. The *conatus* of a thing is simply its effort to persist in its own being. This effort pertains to the nature of every finite mode, and in man, who is conscious of such an effort, it becomes the desire for self-preservation. Spinoza therefore comes down on the side of Hobbes, and many others, who view the desire for self-preservation as the basic motivating force in human behavior. In characteristic fashion, however, Spinoza does not affirm this on the basis of an empirical knowledge of human nature, but rather deduces it from the very status of man as finite mode. Such an approach enables Spinoza to affirm not merely that this desire happens, as a matter of fact, to be basic to man, but that it constitutes his very essence.

Spinoza establishes this fundamental tenet of his anthropology in an indirect manner. First, arguing in universal terms, he notes that it is a self-evident truth that *"nothing can be destroyed, except by a cause external to itself"* (Prop. IV); from which it also follows that things which are naturally contrary, and capable of destroying one another, cannot exist in the same object (Prop. V). This is an application of the principle of inertia, and it can be illustrated by a physical object, or finite mode of extension, which is constituted by a particular proportion of motion and rest. Any change in this proportion would result in the destruction of the thing, but since the thing simply is this proportion, and endures as long as the proportion lasts, this change cannot come from the thing itself. It must therefore be due to an external cause. The theory of *conatus* emerges from the reformulation of this line of thought in positive terms, whereby mere inertial force or resistance is conceived as an actual endeavor.[5] Since nothing internal or intrinsic to a thing can destroy it, and since it is naturally opposed to anything capable of taking away its existence, it can perfectly well be said that *"everything, in so far as it is in itself, endeavours to persist in its own being"* (Prop. VI). Now, by the essence of anything, Spinoza means "that, which being given, the thing is necessarily given also, and, which being removed, the thing is necessarily removed also; in other words, that without which the thing, and which itself without the thing, can neither be nor be conceived" (*Ethics* II, Def. II). This description of essence fits perfectly a thing's *conatus*, and thus Spinoza can conclude: *"The endeavour, wherewith everything endeavours to persist in its own being, is nothing else but the actual essence of the thing in question"* (Prop. VII). Moreover, precisely because it constitutes the essence of the thing, this endeavor does not last for a determinate period of time, but continues for as long as the thing endures (Prop. VIII).

It only remains to apply this principle to the human mind. Such a mind, we have learned, is composed of both adequate (clear and distinct) and inadequate (confused) ideas. Since the mind's *conatus* constitutes its very essence, it must be reflected in all of its ideas; and since the human mind is self-conscious (contains the "ideas of the idea"), it must be aware of this endeavor. Thus Spinoza affirms: *"The mind, both in so far as it has clear and distinct ideas, and also in so far as it has confused ideas, endeavours to persist in its being for an indefinite period, and of this endeavour it is conscious"* (Prop. IX). This result is of great importance, for it establishes the universality of the *conatus* principle for the explanation of human behavior. All such behavior, whether it be an "act of the mind," that is, a rational decision, based on adequate ideas of the end to be achieved and the means to be employed, or a passive response to external stimuli, based on blind impulse and imagination (merely inadequate ideas), is an expression of the effort of the individual in question to preserve his own being.

From this we can readily see the absolute impossibility, for Spinoza, of what other philosophers have described as "disinterested" action. Man can no more help striving to preserve his being than a stone can help falling when it is dropped. This simply is his nature, and nothing, including man, can violate the laws of his own being. When viewed from a psychological standpoint this endeavor can be called will (*Voluntas*), so that one can, in a manner of speaking, say that man "wills" to preserve his being. There is nothing undetermined or free about this will, however, and, as in the previous analysis, this "act of will" is nothing more than the mental decision accompanying the bodily appetite. The notion of appetite (*Appetitus*) is therefore basic in the characterization of an individual's *conatus*. This refers to the endeavor for self-preservation viewed in relation to *both* the mind and the body. Construing it in this broad sense, Spinoza claims that appetite is "nothing else but man's essence, from the nature of which necessarily follow all those results which tend to its preservation; and which man has thus been determined to perform" (Prop. IX, Scholium). Appetite in this sense can also be called desire (*Cupiditas*). The only difference is that desire implies consciousness, so that desire can itself be defined as "appetite with consciousness thereof." One can therefore equally well say, as Spinoza does in fact say at the end of his analysis, that "*desire* is the actual essence of man."[6] Spinoza's concern is not with the precise terms, as *conatus,* appetite, desire and even will are treated as roughly equivalent, but with making it clear that all of man's behavior is grounded in the endeavor to preserve his being.

At first glance this conception of *conatus* as the endeavor on the part of a thing to preserve its being may seem to conflict with the frequent description of the same *conatus* as the thing's effort to *increase* its power or force for existence. Moreover, this latter conception was already implicit in the "official" definition of the emotions wherein, as we have seen, Spinoza referred specifically to the increase or diminution in the organism's active power or power of acting (*agendi potentia*). This power is the force through which the body maintains its existence (its particular proportion of motion and rest) throughout its interaction with other bodies in its environment. Spinoza also equates this force with a thing's "perfection," but with regard to living organisms, with which we are at present concerned, it can perhaps be more easily understood as the organism's level of vitality. This force or vitality can be viewed as the very principle of organic unity. When it sinks below a certain level, the organism is overcome by its environment; its particular proportion of motion and rest is destroyed; and it can be said to die.[7] The endeavor of an organism to preserve its existence is therefore identical with the effort to increase its perfection, power of acting, force for existence or level of vitality. The only difference is that the initial formula refers to the organism in isolation, while the latter, which is much more relevant to the emotional life of man, considers it as involved in a constant struggle for existence with other beings in its environment.[8] From this point of view, anything that lessens an organism's power lessens its ability to preserve its being, and anything that increases this power enhances its ability.[9]

Spinoza's basic concern is with the emotions, and especially the passions, insofar as they are ideas in the mind which correspond to the changes in the level of vitality of the body. Essential to this analysis is the familiar conception of the mind as the idea of the body. From this we can now see that its fundamental endeavor or basic desire must be to affirm the existence of the body. Just as the body, in its endeavor to persist in its being, tends to reject any change or effect contrary to its nature, so the mind tends to reject the *idea* of anything contrary to the existence or well-being of the body (Prop. X). The mind, in other words, cannot spontaneously entertain the thought of anything destructive of the body and, consequently, of itself. Spinoza thus rules out in advance, as a psychological impossibility, anything like a Freudian death wish. Furthermore, since the power of thought in the mind is a function of its ability to affirm the existence of the body, it also follows that *"whatsoever increases or diminishes, helps or hinders the power of activity in our body, the idea thereof increases or diminishes, helps or hinders the power of thought in our mind"* (Prop. XI). The human mind is therefore determined by its very nature to attempt, as far as possible, to conceive things which are beneficial to the body (Prop. XII).

These general principles or universal laws of the mind's *conatus* provide the basis for the explication of the primary emotions: pleasure, pain and desire. All are closely associated with the transition from one state of perfection or level of vitality to another. Pleasure or joy (*Laetitia*) is the *"passive state wherein the mind passes to a greater perfection,"* and pain or sorrow (*Tristitia*) is the *"passive state wherein the mind passes to a lesser perfection"* (Prop. XI,

Scholium). One's pleasures and pains therefore reflect the changes brought about in one's organism through its interaction with the environment, and as Spinoza notes in his subsequent analysis, the source of pleasure and pain lies in the transition itself, not in the state at which one arrives.[10]

The status of desire is considerably more complicated. Although Spinoza affirms that desire, pleasure and pain constitute the three primary emotions, instead of describing what he now means by desire, he simply refers to the previous description of it as "appetite with consciousness thereof." The problem is that desire in this broad sense in which it is equivalent to *conatus* is not so much itself an emotion as the very basis of the emotions, including pleasure and pain. Man, however, not only has desire in this broad sense, in which it is really more appropriate to say that man *is* desire, but he also has particular desires, e.g., wealth, power, health, knowledge, etc. These particular desires, which are specific determinations of the fundamental desire or *conatus*, are obviously directed toward whatever the mind feels is beneficial to the body and to itself, that is, toward whatever it regards either as a source of pleasure or as a means for avoiding pain. But desire in this sense seems clearly to be dependent on the emotions of pleasure and pain and not to be fundamental. For as Spinoza himself later admits, there are as many kinds of desire as there are kinds of pleasure and pain, and there are as many kinds of these as there are objects by which we are affected (Prop. LVI). Nevertheless, although it does seem clear that Spinoza uses the notion of desire in two distinct senses, and that his discussion is rather confusing, it is still possible to see why desire, in the sense of the desire for a particular object, is regarded as a distinct and primary emotion.[11] The point here is simply that while a particular desire depends on what the mind deems to be either pleasurable or at least a means for avoiding pain, the desire itself is not a pleasure or a pain. We cannot therefore account for the emotive life of a man simply in terms of pleasures and pains but must also include desires, which function as the basic motivating forces in human behavior.

The claim that pleasure, pain and desire are primary emotions implies that all of the other emotions, the so-called "derivative emotions," can be explained in terms of them. The actual systematic working-out of this thesis with regard to a whole catalogue of emotions, taken mostly from Descartes, occupies the great bulk of this part of the *Ethics*. We obviously cannot here follow the details of this analysis and see how it applies to very many specific emotions, but we can at least delineate the basic principles on which this discussion is based. A crucial point to keep in mind is that pleasure, pain and desire, as just described, relate directly to present objects, which cause the modifications in the body to which the respective passions in the mind correspond. The derivative emotions all turn out to be species or combinations of pleasure, pain and desire, which are directed in various ways either to objects which are not at present existing and affecting the body, or to objects which are not themselves directly the cause of its modifications.[12]

This can be illustrated by the two most basic derivative emotions, love and hate. We have already seen that the mind attempts, as far as it is able, to conceive of those things which increase or help the power of activity of the body. From this, and from his whole analysis of imagination and memory, Spinoza is able to infer that *"when the mind conceives things which diminish or hinder the body's power of activity, it endeavours, as far as possible, to remember things which exclude the existence of the first-named things"* (Prop. XIII). The very *idea* of an object can thus itself be a source of pleasure or pain, even if the object is not actually present, and this provides the basis for Spinoza's analysis of love and hate. The former, he argues, "is nothing else but *pleasure accompanied by the idea of an external cause,"* and the latter "is nothing else but *pain accompanied by the idea of an external cause."* Moreover, like any other species of pleasure and pain, these passions are inseparable from the effort to possess and keep present to oneself the object of love, and to remove and destroy the object of hatred (Prop. XIII, Scholium).

Given this conception, Spinoza can hold that the human mind is capable of feeling love or hatred toward any number of things, and much the same can be said in regard to two other key derivative emotions, hope and fear, which are defined respectively as an inconstant pleasure or pain *"arising from the image of something future or past, whereof we do not yet know the issue."* These passions, like everything else in nature, do not arise capriciously, but in accordance with universal and necessary laws. Within the context of his analysis, Spinoza presents two such laws, both of which are based on the previous analysis of the imagination. The first of these has been called the "law of the association of emotions."[13] According to this law, an object which has never been itself the cause of pleasure, pain or desire may become such by being associated with one that has. This association could be based on similarity, contrast or contiguity. For instance, the mind necessarily tends to love objects which resemble those that it already loves, hate those that contrast sharply with them, and love and hate in turn those things which it commonly finds together with the objects which it loves and hates. The second basic law can be called the "law of the imitation of the emotions."[14] This law serves to explain how an object which is neither an essential or accidental (through association) cause of pleasure, pain or desire, may become such if it happens to cause them in other human beings whose emotions we naturally tend to imitate. Here Spinoza deals for the first time with the social nature of man, and explains emotions such as sympathy, pity and joy in the well-being of others.

These laws, however, deal only with the mind insofar as it is passive, that is, only insofar as it is the inadequate or partial cause of its affections. To this extent it is primarily subject to external causes, as a result of which "like waves of the sea driven by contrary winds we toss to and fro unwitting of the issue and of our fate" (Prop. LIX, Scholium). Nevertheless, although Spinoza repudiates the Cartesian conception of the power of the mind in terms of a free will, he no more believes that the above account tells the whole story of the emotive life of the mind, than that the analysis of sense perception and imagination told the whole story of its cognitive life.

Accordingly, at the end of his long analysis of the passions, Spinoza briefly introduces and describes the active emotions. *"Besides pleasure and desire, which are passivities or passions,"* he notes, *"there are other emotions derived from pleasure and desire, which are attributable to us in so far as we are active"* (Prop. LVIII). These emotions are grounded in the mind's adequate ideas. When the mind conceives anything adequately, it is necessarily also aware of itself. It is therefore aware of its power or activity, and this gives rise to an active emotion of pleasure. This emotion is basically the same as that which other philosophers have regarded as "intellectual pleasure," although Spinoza is careful to point out that the source of the pleasure is the mind's sense of its own activity, not the nature of the object. Similarly, desire as an active emotion is simply rational desire or the endeavor to preserve one's being insofar as the endeavor is guided by adequate ideas (scientific knowledge). There is, however, no active analogy to pain, the third primary emotion.

This emotion reflects a diminution in the mind's power or activity, and, as we have seen, this can never be the result of the mind's activity or adequate ideas, but merely of its being determined by external forces and possessing inadequate understanding (Prop. LIX).

The account closes with the suggestion that all of a person's actions which stem from active emotions can be ascribed to "*strength of character (fortitudo).*" This, in turn, is divided into "*courage (animositas)*" and "*highmindedness (generositas).*" Courage is defined as "*the desire whereby every man strives to preserve his own being in accordance solely with the dictates of reason.*" As we shall soon see, courage, construed in this broad sense, is equivalent to virtue as a whole; although here it is referred solely to those actions which are concerned with the good of the agent. As such, it is contrasted with highmindedness, which is defined as "*the desire whereby every man endeavours, solely under the dictates of reason, to aid other men and to unite them to himself in friendship*" (Prop. LIX, Scholium). This governs our actions when we are concerned with the well-being of others, and it provides the basis of the social virtues. Within the confines of the third part of the *Ethics*, however, Spinoza does little more than describe and affirm the possibility of these active emotions, through which the mind can escape being a slave to its passions. The actual demonstration of this claim and the development of its implications for the understanding of the moral life are the aims of Part IV of the *Ethics*, which deals with the nature of virtue.

II *Human Virtue*

The full and revolutionary implications of Spinoza's naturalism emerge with his analysis of virtue. Most moral philosophers, as well as the "man in the street," have operated with a presupposed conception of moral perfection and goodness. These are viewed as absolute values which man "ought to," and therefore can, realize. Within the Judeo-Christian tradition, this view has often but not always been linked to the conception of man as created with a free will by a transcendent Deity in order to fulfill certain divine commandments. The eternal destiny of the individual is then linked to his success or failure in fulfilling these commandments. This religious ethic has competed in the West, for at least the last three hundred years, with a secular theory wherein the theological trimmings are removed but wherein it is still affirmed that man has a free will; that there are absolute moral values; and consequently, that there are certain duties which man is obligated to perform. The conscientious performance of these duties is called virtue and is deemed worthy of praise, while the failure to perform them is considered morally blameworthy.

We have seen enough of Spinoza's philosophy to realize that it contains a thoroughgoing critique not only of the doctrine of the freedom of the will, but of this whole moral outlook, in both its secular and religious forms. This outlook, and the conception of man which it implies, is a product of the imagination. It therefore rests on inadequate ideas, and more specifically on a failure to recognize that man, as a finite mode, is a part of nature and that all of his desires, values and actions are necessary consequences of his endeavor to preserve his being. From this standpoint it is pure nonsense to talk about any absolute standard of goodness or perfection to which man "ought" to conform. The analysis of the emotions has already made it quite clear that "goodness" is a function of desire; so that "in no case do we strive for, wish for, long for, or desire anything, because we deem it to be good, but on the other hand we deem a thing to be good, because we strive for it, wish for it, long for it, or desire it" (*Ethics* III, Prop. IX, Scholium). In the preface to Part IV of the *Ethics,* we are told that perfection and imperfection are likewise relative concepts ("merely modes of thinking"). They therefore have no reference to the actual nature of things, but merely to the things as considered in connection with certain human purposes or desires.

It might appear from this that Spinoza is undermining the very possibility of a morality, and such, indeed, was the way in which his views were generally regarded by his contemporaries. Spinoza, however, did not view the situation in this light. Rather than undermining morality, Spinoza offered what he took to be a new and more adequate way to understand it, one based on the true nature of man. Thus, although he repudiated traditional notions of perfection, goodness and virtue, regarded as absolute values totally independent of human desires, he certainly deemed it both possible and important to provide alternative versions of these conceptions.

The key to Spinoza's reformulation of the basic moral concepts is the undeniable fact that while all men are determined by nature to seek their own preservation and happiness, not all men are equally adept at attaining these goals. In fact, most men for Spinoza, as for Thoreau, "lead lives of quiet desperation." This is simply because they are slaves of their passions, and hence not in control of their lives (not free). We can therefore set before ourselves an ideal of life or standard of human perfection, and this will be that type of character and mode of living through which man is most in control of his life and best able to preserve his being. Such a life will be that of the "free man." Now by the *good* in this context can only be meant "that which we certainly know to be useful to us" (Def. I), and by *evil* "that which we certainly know to be a hindrance to us in the attainment of any good" (Def. II). Both good and evil are therefore viewed exclusively in terms of the human *conatus.* Similarly, virtue, from this perspective, is no longer viewed in the traditional manner primarily as disinterested or altruistic behavior, but in Spinoza's own words: "By *virtue* (*virtus*) and *power* I mean the same thing; that is (III, vii), virtue, in so far as it is referred to man, is a man's nature or essence, in so far as it has the power of effecting what can only be understood by the laws of that nature" (Def. VIII).

The equation of virtue with power reflects the original Latin meaning of the term, rather than the traditional ethical meaning which we have come to associate with it. On this analysis, virtue is essentially nothing more than the ability to act according to one's nature, to be self-determined, to be oneself the source of one's states. This, in turn, is equivalent to the ability to act in the sense of being an adequate cause. The virtuous man for Spinoza is thus the man who has power over his own emotions, who is not merely a slave to his passions. Moreover, since virtuous behavior, so construed, involves, by definition, an increase in one's power of acting, such behavior is inherently and necessarily pleasurable. Virtue is therefore identical with happiness, and this enables Spinoza to affirm, in opposition to many religious ethics, that virtue is its own reward.

The essential feature of Spinoza's theory of virtue, however, is its connection with knowledge. This connection is based on the analysis of what it is to be an adequate cause. As we have already seen, man can only be an adequate cause, and hence act in the full sense of the term, insofar as he has adequate ideas. The logic of Spinoza's position thus leads directly to the identification of virtue and knowledge. Only if he lives "under the dictates of reason," to use Spinoza's frequent expression, can man control his passions, realize his true being, and achieve human perfection. The real power in human existence is therefore the power of reason, not will. Reason, to be sure, can never, for Spinoza, replace desire as the motivating force in human behavior. Man is essentially desire, and hence cannot cease desiring. He can, however, through the possession of adequate ideas, i.e., the exercise of reason, come to understand his desires and their causes, discern what is truly useful for his self-preservation, and live accordingly. He can, in short, desire rationally. The possession of adequate ideas is therefore at one and the same time *both* the ultimate goal of all human endeavor, in the sense of being that state in which man most fully realizes his essence or acts, *and* the *means* through which he can alone arrive at this goal.

Nevertheless, Spinoza was under no illusions as to the extent of this power. Human perfection is a relative notion, and its achievement a rare and difficult feat. Thus, the first eighteen propositions of this part of the *Ethics*, which is significantly entitled "Of Human Bondage," deals in a thoroughly realistic fashion with the limits of the power of reason in its conflict with the passions. The entire discussion is prefaced by an axiom which sets the tone for what follows: "There is no individual thing in nature, than which there is not another more powerful and strong. Whatsoever thing be given, there is something stronger whereby it can be destroyed."

Man is just such an individual thing in nature, and as such he cannot be conceived without other things, and is to that extent always passive (Prop. II). Furthermore, it follows from this, together with the above axiom, that *"the force whereby a man persists in existing is limited, and is infinitely surpassed by the power of external causes"* (Prop. III). Man, therefore, cannot be the adequate cause of all of his modifications, that is, he cannot cease being a part of nature (Prop. IV), and from this Spinoza is able to conclude that "man is necessarily always a prey to his passions, that he follows and obeys the general order of nature, and that he accommodates himself thereto, as much as the nature of things demands" (Prop. IV, Corollary). It thus becomes very difficult to see just what room there is in the Spinozistic universe for the power of reason, and this difficulty is compounded by the claim, at the very beginning of the analysis, that *"no positive quality possessed by a false idea is removed by the presence of what is true, in virtue of its being true"* (Prop. I). Truth is therefore not in its own right a weapon against false or inadequate ideas, from which it seems to follow that it cannot serve as a weapon against the passions. Spinoza is led to this conclusion by his conception of falsity as a mere privation of knowledge. We have already seen that insofar as false ideas are referred to God, or seen in their total context, they become true. If, therefore, this alleged positive quality of a false idea were to be removed by what is true, it would be removed by itself, which is obviously absurd. This can be further understood in light of the previous analysis of the relation between reason and imagination. There we saw that the possession of the adequate scientific idea of the sun does not remove but merely enables us to understand the imaginative idea which we have of it as a disk in the sky about two hundred yards away. Generalizing from this example, Spinoza concludes that "imaginations do not vanish at the presence of the truth, in virtue of its being true, but because other imaginations, stronger than the first, supervene and exclude the present existence of that which we imagined" (Prop. I, Scholium).

The difficulty increases when we realize that this conclusion holds not only for imaginative ideas but for emotions as well. As an idea wherein the mind affirms of the body either a greater or lesser force of existence than before, an emotion can only arise in the mind when the body is affected in such a way that its force is increased or diminished. In non-Spinozistic terms, every emotion is correlated with a physiological change in the organism's level of vitality. Such a change can only occur when the body is affected by an external force, and once occurring, this new state tends to preserve itself (according to the principle of *conatus* or inertia), until the body is affected in a contrary manner by another external force. For example, a state of pleasure will tend to persist until it is replaced by another feeling through a subsequent physiological change. But, since it is the corresponding modification in the attribute of thought, precisely the same can be said of the emotion, and Spinoza can therefore assert that "*an emotion can only be controlled or destroyed by another emotion contrary thereto, and with more power for controlling emotion*" (Prop. VII).

Finally, by combining both of these propositions, Spinoza is led inescapably to the conclusion that "*a true knowledge of good and evil cannot check any emotion by virtue of being true, but only in so far as it is considered as an emotion*" (Prop. XIV). Once again Spinoza appears to have arrived at an impasse. Just as in his analysis of knowledge, it would seem to be impossible to explain how the human mind, as the idea of the body, could ever exert any power over the passions.

We find, however, that this very proposition, which expresses the essence of the difficulty, also suggests the means to overcome it. The key to the solution lies in the distinction between "a true knowledge of good and evil" considered merely insofar as it is true, and this same item of knowledge, considered insofar as it is an emotion. But how can knowledge possess an emotive force such that it can function as an actual determinant of human behavior? Spinoza's answer to this crucial question is to be found in the claim that *"the knowledge of good and evil is nothing else but the emotions of pleasure or pain, in so far as we are conscious thereof"* (Prop. VIII). The proof of this proposition turns on the notion of an idea of an idea. First of all, he notes, we call a thing good or evil insofar as it is either an aid or a hindrance to the preservation of our being. The signs whereby we recognize this are the emotions of pleasure and pain, and the knowledge of good and evil is nothing but the mind's awareness of these ideas (pleasure or pain). This knowledge is therefore an idea of an idea. As such, Spinoza argues, it is not actually distinct from the original idea, but is merely the same idea *qua* consciously apprehended. From this Spinoza concludes that such knowledge possesses the entire force of the pleasure or pain which it apprehends, and this force is ultimately what enables knowledge to function in the requisite manner. This emotive force, which pertains to knowledge by its very nature, is the basis for understanding the power of reason.

Yet reason remains at best a fragile power, and Spinoza proceeds to underscore this fact by providing a brief analysis of the power of the emotions. We see first that the relative strength of an emotion is a function of the modality and temporal location of its object. For example, an emotion toward an object viewed as present and necessary is stronger than one toward an object viewed as future and possible or contingent (Props. IX-XII). These general principles are then applied to the "emotion arising from the knowledge of good and evil" (rational desire). This application shows in general that such desire can be checked by many other emotions by which we are often assailed (Prop. XV). More specifically, it shows that rational desire for a future object can be more easily overcome than a similar desire for a present object (Prop. XVI); that rational desire directed towards a contingent object is weaker still (Prop. XVII); and finally, that, all things being equal, a desire arising from pleasure is stronger than one arising from pain (Prop. XVIII). By means of this analysis, which is based on his theory of the emotions, Spinoza attempts to explain in his own terms, without recourse to the notion of will or the Christian conception of a sinful nature, a fundamental fact of moral experience, viz., the great difference between knowing what is good, right or useful and being able to do it.

After establishing that reason has some, albeit a very limited, power to control the passions, Spinoza turns abruptly to the question of "what course is marked out for us by reason, which of the emotions are in harmony with the rules of human reason, and which of them are contrary thereto" (Prop. XVIII, Scholium). In answering these questions, Spinoza provides a general account of the nature of human virtue and of the proper goal of the rational life, together with an analysis of some specific virtues, both real and purported. These answers constitute Spinoza's moral philosophy in the narrow and usual sense of the term.

The account is, of course, based on the conception of man as essentially *conatus* or desire for self-preservation. Hence, it begins with the assertion that *"every man, by the laws of his nature, necessarily desires or shrinks from that which he deems to be good or bad"* (Prop. XIX). Now, virtue has been seen to be the power to act according to the laws of one's nature, from which it follows that the more an individual is able to seek and obtain what is useful to him, i.e., preserve his own being, the more virtue he possesses, while the more he neglects his own true interests, the more he is subject to external forces rather than to the laws of his own nature (Prop. XX). Thus, unless overwhelmed and deranged by external forces, every individual desires to live (Prop. XXI), and no desire can be viewed as more basic (Prop. XXII), nor any good as "higher" than the preservation of one's being (Prop. XXV). Spinoza, however, is far from equating mere survival with virtue; as if a person could be called virtuous who through fortuitous circumstances, and without really knowing what he was doing, managed to pursue the prudent course. The important point is that this result must follow from the individual's own *activity*. He must be the adequate cause, which means that his behavior must be grounded in adequate ideas (Prop. XXIII). A person who behaves in this manner is said by Spinoza to "act in accordance with the dictates of reason," from which it follows that "*to act absolutely in obedience to virtue is in us the same thing as to act, to live, or to preserve one's being (these three terms are identical in meaning) in accordance with the dictates of reason on the basis of seeking what is useful to one's self*" (Prop. XXIV).

But what is truly useful to man? What goal does the man motivated by rational self-interest seek to obtain? The answer immediately suggested by the preceding analysis would seem to be simply life, or perhaps life accompanied by good health and the maximal possible amount of pleasure. Spinoza's moral philosophy would then turn out to be a rational egoism or hedonism of a particularly crude sort. This, however, is far from the case. Spinoza's actual contention is that we desire under the dictates of reason not merely to live but to *understand,* and that the only things which are deemed useful from this point of view are those that are conducive to our understanding (Prop. XXVI). This is, indeed, a paradoxical result, and even more paradoxically, Spinoza proceeds to establish it on the basis of the very principle of self-preservation with which it seems to conflict. According to this principle, Spinoza argues, the mind, like everything else in nature, endeavors to persist in its being and to perform those activities which follow from the law of its being. This implies that insofar as a given mind is governed by reason, or acts according to the dictates of reason, it will endeavor to remain in that state and to perform those activities which follow from it. But the essence of reason in regard to our mind is clear and distinct conception (understanding). Thus, the fundamental endeavor of a mind which is governed by reason will be to understand, and it necessarily only regards those things as useful which are conducive to its understanding. Spinoza here accomplishes the complete intellectualization of virtue. The end of human life is the exercise of the intellect and nothing more. From this it follows that "*we know nothing to be certainly good or evil, save such things as really conduce to understanding, or such as are able to hinder us from understanding*" (Prop. XXVII). Moreover, since the highest object of knowledge is God, the very source of intelligibility, Spinoza also concludes that "*the mind's highest good is the knowledge of God, and the mind's highest virtue is to know God*" (Prop. XXVIII).

This uncompromising intellectualism implies that the ordinary moral and social virtues such as benevolence have no absolute worth and are only valuable to the extent to which they contribute to the power of the mind. Spinoza, however, believes that they do contribute significantly to this power, and he therefore gives at least some of them great importance. "To man," he writes, "there is nothing more useful than man—nothing" (Prop. XVIII, Scholium). The point is that man needs the help of other men if he is to realize his full intellectual potential. On the basis of this principle, Spinoza's moral theory is transformed from an intellectualistic egoism into a philosophy which emphasizes the social nature of man, and which argues, on the basis of the principle of self-preservation, for the necessity of a genuine concern for the well-being of others.

As usual, Spinoza casts his argument in a metaphysical form, deducing men's need for one another from general principles concerning the relations between all finite modes. The starting point of his analysis is the assertion that no individual thing which is entirely different from our own nature can either help or hinder us in any way (Prop. XXIX). This follows from the even more general principle that things which have nothing in common (expressions of different attributes) cannot enter into causal relation. Since they cannot affect one another at all, it is obvious that they cannot affect one another either advantageously or adversely. Things which do share something in common with us can either help or hinder us, that is, can augment or check our power of activity. Something can be harmful if it disagrees with, or is contrary to, our nature (Prop. XXX). This would apply to things whose efforts to preserve their own being conflict with our efforts to preserve our being. On the biological level one could here probably think of things such as poisonous foods or predatory animals. If, however, a thing is in harmony with our nature, by which is meant that its effort to preserve its being coincides with our effort to preserve our own being, then it is always useful to us (Prop. XXXI). Remaining on the biological level, one might here think of nutritious foods and friendly or useful animals.

In applying these principles to man's social relationships, Spinoza's major concern is to demonstrate that insofar as men live in harmony with reason, they live in harmony with one another, and are therefore beneficial to one another. First, however, he argues that insofar as men are subject to the passions, they differ from, and are not in harmony with, one another. This is because men are then determined by external things and their passions differ according to the nature of the determining objects. They are therefore at least potentially in conflict (Props. XXXII-XXXIV). Now, against this view, one might object that two people can often love and desire the same object, and thus share something in common, while at the same time obviously being in a state of conflict. Spinoza counters this by pointing out that although both may love or desire the same object, they really do not share the same emotion. The one person has the idea of the loved object as present or in his possession, and the other has the idea of the same object as absent. Hence, the one will feel pleasure and the other pain, and *this* difference is the basis of their conflict (Prop. XXXIV, Scholium). Under the guidance of reason, however, the situation is far different. In such circumstances men's actions follow from the laws of human nature alone, not those of external objects. They thus are not in conflict with one another. Moreover, since what reason tells us is good or bad, necessarily is such, it follows, according to Spinoza, that "men, in so far as they live in obedience to reason, necessarily do only such things as are necessarily good for human nature, and consequently for each individual man" (Prop. XXXV).

The outcome of this analysis is the claim that when men, under the dictates of reason, pursue their own self-interest, the result is mutually beneficial. This view has obvious affinities to the famous doctrine of Adam Smith, offered a century later in defense of a capitalistic, free enterprise system. According to Smith, the pursuit by each individual of his own economic self-interest (profit) in a free market, and in competition with others, leads ineluctably, albeit somewhat mysteriously, to the common good. Unlike the vision of man and society offered by capitalism, however, the Spinozistic conception is decidedly noncompetitive, and even anticompetitive.[15] Although each pursues his own self-interest, men living under the guidance of reason cannot come into competition with one another. Ultimately this is because the highest good towards which they all strive is, unlike wealth, common to all. This good, as we have already seen, is understanding, and Spinoza feels that an individual's increase of understanding does not come at the expense of others, but can only be to their benefit. There can thus be no jealousy, envy or competition among genuine seekers after truth; quite the contrary: "*The good which every man, who follows after virtue, desires for himself he will also desire for other men, and so much the more, in proportion as he has a greater knowledge of God*" (Prop. XXXVII).

Spinoza offers two arguments in defense of this thesis, the one strictly utilitarian, the other psychological and based on his theory of the emotions. The utilitarian argument, which is implied rather than stated, holds that whoever lives under the guidance of reason, and thus pursues understanding as the highest good, necessarily desires that others do so likewise for basically two reasons. One is that similarly motivated individuals would not molest him out of envy, jealousy and fear, the emotions with which philosophers have traditionally been greeted; and the other, that like-minded individuals would be of positive assistance in one's pursuit of wisdom. The psychological argument seems rather like an appeal to what is now called "positive reinforcement" and is based on the analysis of love provided in the previous section. This analysis showed that a good which an individual loves or desires for himself will be loved more constantly and with a stronger emotion if he sees that others love it also. It is for this reason that men necessarily desire that others love what they themselves love. In the case of those who are driven by their passions this often leads to conflict, for the "good" in question cannot, by its very nature, be possessed by all. This does not occur, however, with regard to a good desired by those living under the guidance of reason. Here the good can be shared by all, so that mutual desire serves to unify rather than to alienate men.

Insofar as he is rational, man is therefore necessarily a social animal. While seeking his own true good, he also seeks the good for others, and desires the society of those who share his concern. Yet, as Spinoza was fully aware, "it rarely happens that men live in obedience to reason, for things are so ordered among them, that they are generally envious and troublesome one to another." Nevertheless, Spinoza continues, thereby articulating the basic principle of his political philosophy, even in regard to the common run of men, who live according to their passions rather than reason, society is not only beneficial but actually necessary. Man is by nature a social animal, and in light of this basic contention Spinoza concludes with uncharacteristic emotion:

Let satirists then laugh their fill at human affairs, let theologians rail, and let misanthropes praise to their utmost the life of untutored rusticity, let them heap contempt on men and praises on beasts; when all is said, they will find that men can provide for their wants much more easily by mutual help, and that only by uniting their forces can they escape from the dangers that on every side beset them: not to say how much more excellent and worthy of our knowledge it is, to study the actions of men than the actions of beasts. (Prop. XXXV, Corollary, Scholium)

The demonstration of the superiority of the life of reason and of the social nature of man leads to a discussion of specific virtues. Spinoza's account is once again an application of his basic conception of man as a part of nature, whose very essence is the desire for self-preservation. The virtues discussed are themselves emotions or states of mind, and their value is determined by ascertaining their relation to this desire. Since pleasure is, as we have seen, an emotion which reflects, in the attribute of thought, an increase in the body's power of activity, while pain is an emotion which reflects precisely the opposite condition, it follows that pleasure in itself is always good and pain is always bad (Prop. XLI). Every organism necessarily desires pleasure and man is no exception. It is crucial, however, to distinguish between pleasure which reflects the well-being of the organism as a whole and mere stimulation (*Titillatio*) or localized pleasure. The latter may, for obvious reasons, be bad, and its opposite, grief (*Dolor*), may be beneficial, if it serves to restrict stimulation, thereby preventing it from becoming excessive and hindering one's ability to function (Prop. XLII).

This attitude toward pleasure determines the hedonistic, anti-ascetic tone of much of Spinoza's moral philosophy. Rejecting the Calvinistic austerity of many of his countrymen, Spinoza found nothing wrong with the simple enjoyment of life. "Assuredly," he writes, in obvious reference to the Calvinists, "nothing forbids man to enjoy himself, save grim and gloomy superstition."[16] Pleasure, after all, reflects perfection (power), and hence "to make use of what comes in our way, and to enjoy it as much as possible . . . is the part of a wise man." Nevertheless, these pleasures must be enjoyed in moderation and with regard to the well being of the organism as a whole. This entire attitude towards pleasure is aptly expressed in Spinoza's concluding reflections:

I say it is the part of a wise man to refresh and recreate himself with moderate and pleasant food and drink, and also with perfumes, with the soft beauty of growing plants, with dress, with music, with many sports, with theatres, and the like, such as every man may make use of without injury to his neighbour. For the human body is composed of very numerous parts, of diverse nature, which continually stand in need of fresh and varied nourishment, so that the whole body may be equally capable of performing all the actions, which follow from the necessity of its own nature; and, consequently, so that the mind may also be equally capable of understanding many things simultaneously. (Prop. XLV, Corollary II, Scholium)

We can see from this that all of the emotions can be divided into three classes. There are some which are intrinsically good and can never become excessive; some which are intrinsically bad; and finally, a large group of emotions which are good if experienced in moderation, and bad if enjoyed excessively. Among the emotions which are always good and can never become excessive, Spinoza includes not only pleasure *per se*, which we have already discussed, but also mirth, which is the opposite of melancholy (Prop. XLII), and self-approval, insofar as it is grounded in reason. Spinoza's account of the latter is highly interesting and clearly reveals the anti-Christian orientation of his moral philosophy. Pride or self-approval without any rational basis is, of course, harmful and is to be avoided at all costs. But insofar as this self-approval arises from an adequate idea of one's power, it is the "highest object for which we can hope," for it is simply the conscious awareness of one's virtue (Prop. LII).

Under the category of the intrinsically bad emotions, Spinoza gives first place to pain, and its frequent concomitant, hate. Closely associated with these, and rejected in equally unqualified terms, are emotions such as envy, derision, contempt, anger and revenge. All of these are bad because they are inimical to the power of the organism and result in actions which alienate man from his fellowmen. More interesting is the fact that Spinoza here locates many of the traditional religious "virtues," e.g., hope, fear, humility, repentance and pity. All of these emotions reflect ignorance and a lack of power in the self. None of them, therefore, can be regarded as really good, and none has any place in the life of reason. Nevertheless, in a concession to human frailty Spinoza does note significantly: "As men seldom live under the guidance of reason, these two emotions, namely, Humility and Repentance, as also Hope and Fear, bring more good than harm; hence, as we must sin, we had better sin in that direction" (Prop. LIV, Scholium).

Paramount among the emotions which can be either good or bad, depending on whether or not they are experienced in moderation, are stimulation, which has already been discussed, desire and love. The difficulty with the latter two emotions lies in their connection with stimulation. Love or desire, if directed toward an object which stimulates or gratifies a part of the organism or one of its appetites at the expense of the well-being of the whole, can be excessive and hence harmful. This includes pathological states such as avarice, ambition and gluttony. Spinoza himself, however, seems to have given first place in this category to lust or erotic love. Contrary to his generally anti-ascetic attitude, Spinoza tended to view sexual desire as an unmitigated evil, indeed, as a form of madness! (Prop. XLIV, Scholium)

Part IV of the *Ethics* culminates in what amounts to an encomium of the life of reason, which now becomes equated with freedom. It begins with the assertion, which is already implicit in what has preceded, that none of the passions which have been accorded a kind of provisional value for those who do not live according to the dictates of reason, e.g., hope, fear, shame, compassion, humility and repentance, would have any use, "if men could easily be induced to live by the guidance of reason only" (Prop. LVIII, Scholium). This follows from the already established connection between acting rationally and "acting" in the full sense of the term. Although a passion may more or less accidentally (Spinoza's term is "blindly") aid in the preservation of our being, it is always possible for the same goal to be more efficiently accomplished by reason without the aid of the passions (Prop. LIX).

In developing this theme, Spinoza initially views reason in a purely utilitarian fashion, as a force through which human well-being can be achieved. Here we see first of all that a rational desire cannot be excessive. Such a desire is the very essence of man insofar as he acts; so that if such a desire were excessive, it would mean that human nature had exceeded itself, which is absurd (Prop. LXI). Equally important, however, is the ability of reason to view things from the standpoint of eternity, and hence to ignore temporal considerations. Thus, ideally at least, a thoroughly rational man would be totally free of any conflict between immediate and long-range goals. He could clearly and distinctly conceive the effects of all of his actions, and he would thus never succumb to our usual inclination for the present good, but would automatically choose the greater good or the lesser evil, whether this was to be found in the immediate present or in the distant future (Prop. LXII).

The utilitarian, hedonistic dimension of Spinoza's position is, however, soon eclipsed by the more concrete depiction of the life of the free man. The basic feature of such a person, as Spinoza describes him, is his affirmative attitude toward life. This attitude is seen to follow directly from the nature of rational desire. Since such desire is grounded in a knowledge of what is truly beneficial, and hence pleasurable to man, it naturally leads one to seek good directly, and only indirectly to shun evil insofar as it stands in the way of the realization of some good (Prop. LXIII, Corollary). Moreover, since by evil is meant the knowledge of pain, and since pain is always a passive state based on inadequate ideas, the knowledge of evil is always inadequate (Prop. XXIV). Thus, if the human mind possessed only inadequate ideas, it would form no conception of evil (Prop. XLIV, Corollary). This, of course, cannot be the case, and so the free man can be said to pursue the greater good and avoid the lesser evil (Prop. LXV), but it does help us to understand why emotions such as hate and fear have no place in the life of the free man. This whole line of thought, which is quite literally a philosophical defense of the "power of positive thinking," culminates in the famous reflection that *"a free man thinks of death least of all things; and his wisdom is a meditation not of death but of life"* (Prop. LXVII).

Finally, Spinoza comes to the description of the free man in action, that is, in his concrete relations with other men. Here, more than anywhere else in the *Ethics*, his analysis reflects his own experiences and practices, as much as his metaphysical principles. The first point to be made is that while living among the ignorant, as, indeed, he must, the free man will endeavor as far as possible to avoid receiving favors from them (Prop. LXX). This is necessary if he is to maintain his blessed freedom and avoid becoming dependent on the passions of others. Yet Spinoza also recognizes that there are distinct limits to the feasibility of such a procedure. (The fate of the De Witts may very well have been a factor here.) "For though men be ignorant," he notes, "yet they are men." Spinoza's reasoning here is still basically pragmatic and utilitarian. The point is that we might very well find ourselves in a situation where we need the help of others. Thus, while we should strive to retain our independence, we should also make sure that we do nothing to antagonize anyone, as a haughty refusal to have any dealings at all would most assuredly do. Courtesy to others, including the ignorant, is therefore an essential ingredient in the free man's behavior, as, indeed, it was in Spinoza's.

Once again, however, Spinoza goes considerably beyond the utilitarian, pragmatic level. There is such a thing as genuine gratitude and respect, but this is a feeling which only one free man can feel for another (Prop. LXXI). This is both because only the free man is thoroughly useful, and only the free man has the intellectual capacity to recognize this usefulness. Between free men a level of friendship and gratitude is therefore possible, based on a pure goodwill, which differs radically from the fickle sense of gratitude of those who are led by their passions. Moreover, because the free man possesses such a pure goodwill, Spinoza also claims that he never acts fraudulently, but always in good faith (Prop. LXXII). As he goes on to affirm in the demonstration of this proposition, this holds without exception; so that even if the preservation of his very life depended on being deceitful, the truly free man would refrain from doing so.

We have here another of the great paradoxes of Spinoza's thought. An account of the moral life which begins by anchoring virtue completely in self-preservation and equating it with power, ends by proclaiming a sublime ideal of self-sacrifice! Spinoza's reasoning here would seem to be based on his rather broad interpretation of the notion of self-preservation and on his emphasis on the necessity of the social dimension of human existence. When viewed from the standpoint of reason—which is the standpoint of eternity—self-preservation, like everything else, has no reference to temporal duration. Thus, the free man, who by definition lives according to the dictates of reason, does not simply do whatever he can in order to live as long as possible. That would be the attitude of one who is the slave of his passions and fears death. The free man does, to be sure, strive to preserve himself, but he is concerned with what is essential to his being, viz., his rationality and autonomy. He could therefore be perfectly willing to risk his life in order to preserve that aspect of his being. But, as we have already seen, reason teaches men to seek the society of others, such society being necessary for the development of reason itself. From this Spinoza is able to conclude that reason could never teach us to act fraudulently, for if it could teach us, it could similarly teach all men to do likewise, "in which case," Spinoza notes, "reason would persuade men not to agree in good faith to unite their forces, or to have laws in common, that is, not to have any general laws, which is absurd" (Prop. LXXII). More succinctly put, Spinoza's point is that since reason teaches us the necessity of society for the development and preservation of reason itself, reason could never advocate a state of affairs (anarchy) which would be destructive of its own nature.

Given the above result, the final proposition of this section is obvious: *"The man, who is guided by reason, is more free in a State, where he lives under a general system of law, than in solitude, where he is independent"* (Prop. LXXIII). The free man for Spinoza, as for Rousseau after him, is not the isolated hermit, but the citizen. As such, he not only chooses to live according to the laws of his country, which are therefore not viewed as impediments to freedom, but he also takes an active role in its political life, something which, as we have seen, Spinoza himself endeavored to do.

III *Human Blessedness*

The difference between the life of the slave and that of the free man has been described in vivid terms. The latter is guided by reason, and the former is driven by his appetites, which are themselves determined by inadequate, imaginative ideas of external objects. In common with many moralists, Spinoza thus maintains that the virtuous, good, happy or free life (these terms being used more or less interchangeably) is the life of reason. In opposition to most traditional moralists, however, Spinoza also claims that the possibility of reason governing the passions is not to be explained in terms of some mysterious power of the will or in the inexplicable ability of the mind to act upon the body (in the manner of Descartes). We learned instead that only a stronger and contrary emotion can destroy or control a given emotion, and hence, that the possibility of reason controlling the passions depends on reason itself, or adequate ideas, possessing an emotive force. This general possibility was itself justified through the analysis of the emotions, but nothing specific was said about how this was to take place, nor has anything yet been said concerning the victory of the power of reason. These are the tasks of the last part of the *Ethics*, which therefore falls into two rather distinct portions. The first twenty propositions present some specific guidelines, practical precepts, or (to use Spinoza's own term) "remedies," through which the understanding can, to some extent at least, gain control of the emotions and bring human behavior under the dictates of reason. The last twenty-two propositions show how human blessedness culminates in the "intellectual love of God" (*amor intellectualis Dei*) and explains in what sense the mind can be said to be eternal. While the former are among the most straightforward and practical, the latter are undoubtedly the most mystical-sounding and diversely interpreted series of propositions in the entire work.

Spinoza begins by laying down the basic principle in terms of which the entire discussion is to proceed: "*Even as thoughts and the ideas of things are arranged and associated in the mind, so are the modifications of body or the images of things precisely in the same way arranged and associated in the body*" (Prop. I). This follows immediately from the identity of the order and connection of ideas with the order and connection of things, and it has been aptly called the "metaphysics of the remedy"; for it allows Spinoza to claim that the mind can have control over the modifications of the body, even though they do not interact.[17] As the proposition makes clear, the modifications or affections in question are the images of the external things which affect the body and which determine its appetites. According to the above principle, it follows that insofar as the ideas in the mind are ordered in the manner of the "order of the intellect," the images and appetites, which are their physical correlates, will be similarly ordered. Rational thought will thus necessarily correspond to moderate and not excessive appetites.

The practical problem is how to produce the desired condition, and its resolution really requires nothing more than the explicit focusing on a number of points which have already been established. In his general approach Spinoza follows Descartes in affirming that the key lies in the mind's ability to break established patterns of association and to replace them with new ones. Unlike Descartes, however, he views these associations as holding between ideas and not between ideas and corporeal states, e.g., Descartes's "animal spirits." His analysis of the remedies for excessive love or hate is a case in point. These emotions, it will be recalled, were defined respectively as pleasure and pain accompanied by the idea of an external cause. The imagined external cause of one's pleasure or pain is the object of the emotion, and the way to overcome any such emotion is to sever it from this *idea* of the external cause (Prop. II). This can be accomplished by uniting it to the thought of another cause. For example, hate towards a particular individual who has done some harm can be overcome, or at least considerably diminished, by thinking of the harmful action as at most a contributing factor in one's pain, and as itself conditioned by a prior cause, and this in turn by a prior cause, etc. In short, rather than focusing one's attention on the unique object of hate, one comes to see it merely as a determined part of a causal chain. To do this is to form a clear and distinct idea of the emotion, and thus Spinoza can claim that *"an emotion, which is a passion, ceases to be a passion, as soon as we form a clear and distinct idea thereof"* (Prop. III).

Furthermore, since *"there is no modification of the body, whereof we cannot form some clear and distinct conception"* (Prop. IV), that is, no modification which we cannot, to some extent at least, understand in terms of general laws or "common notions," and since an emotion is an idea of a modification of the body, it follows that there is no emotion of which we cannot form some clear and distinct idea (Prop. IV, Corollary). This is Spinoza's rather oblique way of stating that every emotion is capable of being understood scientifically, and he is in effect recommending that we endeavor to cultivate a detached, scientific attitude towards our own emotional life. There are, of course, severe limits to our ability to do this, but to the extent to which we are capable of achieving it, we can assume control not only of our loves and hates, but also of our desires and appetites.

This ability is enhanced by certain features of our emotional makeup which give some advantage to the rationally grounded, i.e., active, emotions in their struggle with the passions. First of all, we note that, all other things being equal, our strongest emotions are toward things which we regard as free (Prop. V). For example, we love or hate an individual with greater intensity if we believe that he is solely responsible for our condition and acted out of free choice. The knowledge of the necessity of a state of affairs, which is chiefly what we derive from a "clear and distinct conception," inevitably serves to weaken the force of an emotion. Our tendency to respond passionately to things is based largely on a sense that they might have been otherwise. We feel saddened by the loss of a good that we feel we might have possessed, but this feeling is mitigated, if not completely overcome, by the recognition that this loss was inevitable. Furthermore, since rationally grounded emotions are, by their very nature, directed toward the common properties of things, it follows that if we take time into consideration, these emotions will be stronger than passions which are directed toward an absent object (Prop. VII). The object of the former kind of emotion (nature and its universal laws) is always present, and the emotion can therefore remain constant. While obviously less intense at a given moment than the hope, fear, disappointment or regret generated by the thought of an absent object, its constancy enables it, in the long run, to overcome the latter. In other words, the greater endurance of a rationally grounded emotion more than compensates for its lack of intensity.

Finally, while it is obviously true that *"an emotion is stronger in proportion to the number of simultaneous concurrent causes whereby it is aroused"* (Prop. VIII), such an emotion turns out to be less harmful than an equally powerful emotion which is attributed to fewer causes or to a single cause (Prop. IX). Once again Spinoza seems to primarily have sexual love in mind. His point is that emotions of this nature lead to an obsessive concern with a few objects or one particular object and therefore hinder the mind from engaging in its characteristic activity, thought. Fortunately, however, an emotion fostered by a large number of different causes is stronger, and since this is precisely the kind of emotion associated with the scientific attitude (which is concerned with that which is common to *all things*), the healthy emotion has the power to overcome the obsessive concern with particular objects. On this basis, Spinoza is able to conclude confidently that *"so long as we are not assailed by emotions contrary to our nature, we have the power of arranging and associating the modifications of our body according to the intellectual order"* (Prop. X).

The problem is that we cannot always remain in that idyllic condition of detached observation. We are still parts of nature, and as such cannot totally avoid being assailed by dangerous emotions. Nevertheless, we can minimize this danger if, while in a detached state of mind, we can prepare for it by framing "a system of right conduct, or fixed practical precepts" which we can commit to memory and later apply in the manner of a rule of thumb as the situation demands. Spinoza believes that by so doing we can train our imagination to more or less react in appropriate ways, and, on the basis of this assumption, he proceeds to lay down just such a set of rules for the development and maintenance of a healthy character (Prop. X, Scholium).

These rules turn out to be basically conventional bits of popular wisdom, although Spinoza does succeed in giving them his own characteristic twist. For example, we have already learned that hatred should be overcome by love, and in order that "this precept of reason may always be ready to our hand in time of need," Spinoza suggests that we reflect often on human wrongs and how they may best be prevented by highmindedness. In so doing, we shall come to associate the idea of wrongness with that of love or highmindedness, so that when a wrong is close to us, we will tend to respond with the proper emotion. Similarly, if we constantly reflect on the necessity of things, we shall be better able to control the anger or hate in our reactions to personal injury; and if we reflect on courage as a means of overcoming fear, we shall be better prepared to meet the ordinary dangers of life. Most important of all, we must train ourselves that "we may always be determined to action by an emotion of pleasure." This is the ultimate expression of the power of positive thinking. Spinoza's point is that the proper way to free ourselves from an obsessive attachment to an unobtainable goal, be it a sexual partner, wealth, power, etc., is *not* to constantly harp over the harmful features of such a goal. The negative approach succeeds only in breeding an attitude of envy or resentment, and, as Spinoza acutely notes, all of the faults which we have convinced ourselves are to be found in the lover who has jilted us miraculously disappear as soon as we find ourselves back in his or her good favor. Hence, the only way to actually overcome, as opposed to temporarily repress, these emotions is to think positively about things, to concentrate on men's virtues rather than their faults.

The ultimate positive thought, and therefore the ultimate remedy against the passions, is the love of God. Through this love, and this love alone, the mind is able to assume control of its emotive life and organize its bodily appetites. The special power of this emotion is based on its connection with the third kind of knowledge (intuitive knowledge), and on the fact that it can be suggested by and conjoined with all of our physical states. Basic to the latter point is Spinoza's contention that the more things a given emotion can be associated with, the more frequently it can be evoked, and the more constantly it can occupy the mind (Props. XI-XIII). Since there is no modification of the body or physical state of which the mind cannot form some clear and distinct idea, and since to conceive something clearly and distinctly is to conceive it in relation to God, it follows that the mind is able to refer all of its bodily modifications to the idea of God (Prop. XIV). This idea can therefore be associated with all of these modifications.

The real key to the argument, however, is the contention that this third kind of knowledge is more potent than the second kind (Prop. XXXVI, Scholium). Although Spinoza does not explain himself any further, one can assume that its greater power over the emotions is a function of its greater explanatory power. First of all, by comprehending particular things (individual essences), including the inquiring self, it goes beyond abstract generalities and shows how general principles relate concretely to particular instances. Secondly, by comprehending these particular things in relation to God, it grasps them in terms of the very source of their intelligibility. It is, therefore, the highest conceivable level of understanding, and, as such, must be the expression of the highest or most perfect activity of the mind, and the source of the greatest intellectual satisfaction. From this we can readily conclude that this activity will be accompanied by the greatest possible joy, and since this joy is conjoined with the idea of God as its cause, Spinoza can call this activity the "love of God" and claim that *he who clearly and distinctly understands himself and his emotions loves God, and so much the more in proportion as he more understands himself and his emotions*" (Prop. XV). Finally, since this love is fostered by, and associated with, all of the states of the body, Spinoza is likewise able to conclude that it must necessarily hold the chief place in the mind (Prop. XVI).

The love of God, so construed, is "the highest good which we can seek for under the guidance of reason" (Prop. XX). In order to fully understand this, it is necessary to consider this love in a little more detail, and especially to distinguish it from the kind of love recommended by the religious tradition. Such consideration shows that the decisive characteristic of Spinozistic love is its unrequited character. Since God is without passions, He cannot feel pleasure or pain. Consequently, He cannot be said either to love or to hate (Prop. XVII). Thus, the person who loves God in the manner recommended by Spinoza cannot, like the religious man, expect to be loved in return (Prop. XIX). For the same reason this love cannot be turned into hate (Prop. XVIII), nor can it *be stained by the emotion of envy or jealousy*" (Prop. XX). Such unhealthy, negative emotions are always the result of unfulfilled expectations, and in relation to the God of Spinoza this can never occur.

Against this it might very well be objected that this God, who is the cause of all things, must also be the cause of pain and thus could very well become an object of hate. Spinoza, however, anticipates and dismisses such an objection. His argument is that "in so far as we understand the causes of pain, it to that extent (V. iii.) ceases to be a passion, that is, ceases to be pain (III. lix.); therefore, in so far as we understand God to be the cause of pain, we to that extent feel pleasure" (Prop. XVIII, Scholium). Spinoza is not here making the absurd claim that one can get rid of pain simply by acquiring a knowledge of its cause. Nor is he *merely* claiming with the Stoics that, through the knowledge of the necessity of a pain, we are better able to bear it. This certainly is part of Spinoza's view, but he also wishes to suggest in a positive vein that the adequate knowledge of a pain is not itself a pain, but like any adequate knowledge, it is an expression of the mind's activity, and hence a genuine source of satisfaction.

Now, with the delineation of the chief good for man, one might reasonably expect the *Ethics* to end. However, after a brief summary of the remedies for the passions, including the knowledge and the love of God, which is now explicitly related to the third kind of knowledge, Spinoza suddenly proclaims: "And now I have finished with all that concerns this present life. . . . It is now, therefore, time to pass on to those matters, which appertain to the duration of the mind, without relation to the body" (Prop. XX, Scholium). Moreover, as he goes on to assert: *"The human mind cannot be absolutely destroyed with the body, but there remains of it something which is eternal"* (Prop. XXIII). The *Ethica Ordine Geometrico Demonstrata* thus ends with the proclamation of the eternality of the human mind. Although apart from one passage wherein they are equated, Spinoza consistently uses the term "eternal" instead of the traditional religious expression "immortal," this doctrine seems to stand in obvious contradiction to the central teachings of the *Ethics*. [18] Have we not seen that the human mind is merely the idea of the body and that the order and connection of ideas is the same as the order and connection of things; and does not this clearly imply that the human mind cannot exist apart from the body?[19]

In order to understand the meaning and function of this doctrine of the eternality of the mind, as well as the sense of some of the language which Spinoza uses in the above passage, we must first realize that, despite appearances, he has not yet accomplished all that he set out to do. He has, to be sure, provided us with an elaborate analysis of the nature and causes of the human predicament, viz., man's bondage to the passions, as well as with some remedies against this predicament. These remedies all involve knowledge, of both the second and third kinds, with the third kind being more "potent." Accordingly, knowledge, even the knowledge of God, has so far functioned as a force for controlling the bodily appetites, and thus escaping bondage to the passions. But the avoidance of bondage is not identical with the attainment of freedom. The negative must be complemented by the positive, remedies against the passions by a doctrine of salvation or blessedness. This blessedness will, of course, turn out to consist entirely of intellectual activity, especially the activity connected with the third kind of knowledge. In establishing this, however, Spinoza must move from a consideration of reason (construed in a broad sense to include both the second and third kinds of knowledge) as a force for dealing with the passions, that is, reason as a means, to the life of reason as an *end in itself* and as constituting human blessedness. This account of the life of reason will be based on the already established ability of the human mind to transcend, by means of its adequate ideas, its status as part of the "common order of nature," and to conceive things "according to the order of the intellect," wherein it is said to participate in the "infinite intellect of God."

Spinoza here uses traditional religious and theological expressions, namely, the "present life" and the "duration of the mind, without relation to the body" in order to indicate this basic shift in concern. The "present life" in this context is merely the life of conflict with the emotions.[20] Since this conflict is between the adequate ideas in the mind and the bodily appetites, it can certainly be said to concern the mind as it is in relation to the body. Thus, in moving from a consideration of the efficacy of reason as a means, to an analysis of rational activity as the source of intrinsic and ultimate satisfaction (blessedness), Spinoza is, indeed, in a certain sense turning from "all that concerns this present life," and to a consideration of the "mind, without relation to the body." As suggested above, this will lead to a further consideration of the implications of the power of the mind to transcend, through its adequate ideas, its status as a part of nature, and to view things "under the form of eternity," but it will not involve any claim concerning an afterlife wherein the mind can somehow exist in a disembodied state.

The real problem is caused by the reference to duration.[21] Spinoza does not merely say that he will consider the mind apart from the body, but that he will consider its duration in this context. This strongly suggests at least the possibility of some kind of survival and "eternal life" in a disembodied state. Yet no sooner does

Spinoza introduce this possibility than he teaches us how it is to be understood. Thus, in the very next proposition, he affirms that "*the mind can only imagine anything, or remember what is past, while the body endures*" (Prop. XXI). This result obviously follows from the previously established connection between both memory and imagination and bodily functions. Apart from the correlation between the ideas in the mind and these functions, there can be neither memory nor imagination. But without memory we can have no notion of personality or of personal identity. This is a difficulty which also arises with regard to theories of reincarnation. What sense, after all, does it make to say that one is the same person as an individual who lived any number of years ago, if there is no possible recollection of that individual's experiences? Memory, if not actually constitutive of personal identity, is at least an important component thereof.[22] Thus, if the duration of the mind apart from the body is without memory, it can hardly be viewed as a survival of the personality.[23] Certainly, the popular notion of personal immortality and of an "afterlife" wherein one is rewarded or punished for one's behavior in this "present life" would seem to presuppose that we can remember our past deeds. Otherwise there would not seem to be much justice in the rewards and punishments. We can therefore conclude that by explicitly excluding memory from the mind as conceived in this state, Spinoza is giving to the reader a clear signal that he is not presenting anything like the traditional notion of personal immortality.

Moreover, as if this were not enough, Spinoza proceeds to point out that the eternality of the mind is not to be confused with its duration, and that the latter can only be said to continue as long as the mind is united with the body (Prop. XXIII, Scholium). Indeed, this is precisely what one would expect him to say, as he repeatedly distinguishes between eternity and duration. The former is defined in the very beginning of the *Ethics* as "existence itself, in so far as it is conceived necessarily to follow solely from the definition of that which is eternal" (*Ethics* I, Def. VIII), and in the explanation attached to this definition, he points out that existence of this kind (by which he means eternal existence), is an eternal truth, and is not to be confused with, or explained in terms of duration, even though this duration be conceived as endless.[24] In short, eternity, for Spinoza, is equivalent to timeless, necessary being, and has nothing at all to do with "lasting through an infinitely long time."[25]

Given this conception of eternity, it follows that if Spinoza is to establish his thesis, he must show that there is a sense in which the human mind expresses or involves timeless, necessary being, and this is precisely what he sets about to do. The starting point of this argument is the claim that despite the lack of memory and imagination, "*nevertheless in God there is necessarily an idea, which expresses the essence of this or that human body under the form of eternity*" (Prop. XXII). This argument turns on the distinction between essence and existence, which Spinoza developed in the first part of the *Ethics*, wherein he argued that God is the cause of both the essence and existence of things (*Ethics* I, Prop. XXV). The essence of a thing, as we have already seen, is equivalent to the thing itself (*Ethics* II, Def. II). Here, however, it is equated with the thing insofar as it is deduced or follows from the relevant attributes and infinite modes. It is, in other words, the basic nature of the thing, as seen in light of these general principles. For example, the essence of a body would be that particular proportion of motion and rest which constitutes its being. The actual existence of a thing is defined in terms of its duration, and this is determined not by the attributes and infinite modes, but by external factors, i.e., other finite modes. Since the essence of a thing (here the human body) follows from, or is conceived in terms of, an attribute of God, Spinoza contends, in virtue of his doctrine of attributes, that there must likewise be an idea in God corresponding to this essence, and that this idea expresses an eternal truth.

So far there is nothing particularly strange or unexpected. In the very next proposition, however, Spinoza proceeds, allegedly on the basis of his conception of the human mind as the idea of the body, to claim that this concept, idea, or eternal truth "which expresses the essence of the human body," also appertains to the essence of the human mind. Thus, although we cannot in fact assign duration to the mind except while the body endures, "yet, as there is something, notwithstanding, which is conceived by a certain eternal necessity through the very essence of God (last Prop.); this something, which appertains to the essence of the mind, will necessarily be eternal" (Prop. XXIII).

The problem with this argument is not with the contention that the idea in God, which corresponds to the essence of the body, is eternal. This eternality, as well as the very existence of such an idea, follows from the doctrine of attributes. Rather, the problem concerns just how this idea in God can belong to the essence of the human mind, which would seem to be necessary if Spinoza is to prove his claim. Spinoza attempts to establish this on the basis of the status of the mind as the idea of the body. There is, however, nothing eternal in *this* idea, which consists merely in the affirmation of the actual existence of the body, and hence, as Spinoza admits, only endures as long as the body endures. It would seem that the only way in which the idea in God can belong to the actual nature of the human mind is through the mind's ability to conceive it, i.e., to have an adequate idea of the essence of its body. Now, as we have seen, and as Spinoza will further emphasize, to have an adequate idea of something is to conceive "under the form of eternity," and when one does this, one can be said to be part of the infinite intellect of God. But the eternality of the human mind then turns out to be equivalent to its ability to conceive of itself and its body as eternally necessitated, that is, to understand itself by the third kind of knowledge. It is obvious, however, that this ability is not itself "eternal," i.e., does not last forever, so that what is strictly speaking eternal is only the content or object of such thought.[26]

Having established his claim about the eternality of the mind, Spinoza proceeds to make explicit the connection between this eternality and the third kind of knowledge. Such knowledge is claimed to be *"the highest endeavour of the mind, and the highest virtue"* (Prop. XXV), as well as the source of the highest possible mental satisfaction (*Mentis acquiescentia*) (Prop. XXVII). The attainment of this kind of knowledge is thus equated with the attainment of human perfection. But since this, like the second kind of knowledge from which it arises (Prop. XXVIII), involves understanding things "under the form of eternity," Spinoza contends that it cannot occur *"by virtue of conceiving the present actual existence of the body, but by virtue of conceiving the essence of the body under the form of eternity"* (Prop. XXIX). The ability to understand things by the third kind of knowledge is thus connected with precisely that feature of the mind through which it was previously held to be eternal. This connection is made even more explicit with the claim that *"the third kind of knowledge depends on the mind, as its formal cause, in so far as the mind itself is eternal"* (Prop. XXXI). Finally, in the scholium to this proposition, we learn not merely that the mind's ability to know things by the third kind of knowledge depends on the eternality of the mind, but that the mind *is* eternal, precisely to the extent to which it conceives things in this manner. We thus see once again that by the eternality of the human mind, Spinoza means nothing more than the mind's ability to transcend the inadequate, imaginative knowledge to which it is subjected in virtue of its relationship to the actual existence of its body, and to conceive things, and especially its own body, "under the form of eternity."

Moreover, Spinoza not only equates the mind's ability to conceive things by the third kind of knowledge with its eternality, but also with its blessedness. This equation, which is the true culmination of Spinoza's philosophy, is accomplished by showing how this kind of knowledge gives rise to the "intellectual love of God" (amor intellectualis Dei). We have already seen the love of God at work in the first part of this section, wherein it served as the supreme remedy against the passions. That love was, to be sure, intellectual, although Spinoza did not then characterize it as such. But as a force for controlling the bodily appetites, as a weapon in the moral struggle, its function was "this-worldly" in the religious sense. Indeed, it can be construed as the Spinozistic analogue to the Christian conception of divine grace as an aid in the struggle with sin. Now, having finished his analysis of that struggle, i.e., "with all that concerns this present life," Spinoza turns again to the love of God, and shows that it in itself constitutes human blessedness. Viewed in this context, it provides the Spinozistic alternative to the Beatific Vision.

The connection between the third kind of knowledge, the intellectual love of God and human blessedness, is made very directly. The point, once again, is simply that the understanding of anything in this manner is a positive source of joy, and that since this knowledge involves understanding the thing in question in relation to God, the joy is accompanied by the idea of God as its cause (Prop. XXXII). As before, the equation of this situation with the love of God depends on Spinoza's rather peculiar conception of love as pleasure accompanied by the idea of an external cause. Love in this sense can be directed not only toward persons or animals, but also toward inanimate objects or works of art. Anything at all which can serve as a cause of pleasure can, for that very reason, be an object of love. The pleasure—or, better, mental satisfaction—associated with the third kind of knowledge is the pure joy of knowing. God is the cause of this joy in the sense that He is the ultimate object of knowledge and source of the very intelligibility of things. In the last analysis, then, the intellectual love of God, which is equivalent to human blessedness, turns out to be essentially nothing more than the delight in the intelligible as the intelligible, which accompanies the mind's satisfaction with its own power of cognition.[27]

Given this conception of love, we can understand Spinoza's mystical-sounding and paradoxical claims that *"God loves himself with an infinite intellectual love"* (Prop. XXXV) and that *"the intellectual love of the mind towards God is that very love of God whereby God loves himself, not in so far as he is infinite, but in so far as he can be explained through the essence of the human mind regarded under the form of eternity; in other words, the intellectual love of the mind towards God is part of the infinite love wherewith God loves himself"* (Prop. XXXVI). Having just been told that God does not love, and hence, that man's love of God is unrequited, one is certainly taken aback by these assertions. There is, however, no real contradiction, but only another example of Spinoza's tendency to express his rationalistic thought in religious terms. Since the human mind has been shown to be a modification of the attribute of thought and, in regard to its adequate ideas, part of the infinite intellect of God, the mind's love of God is equivalent to God's love of himself, so modified. This claim, in other words, reduces to an elaborately expressed tautology, and there is no reason to believe that Spinoza wished it to be construed in any other way.[28] By expressing himself in this convoluted and paradoxical manner, Spinoza is, in effect, saying to the theologians that this is the only way that one can understand their central contention that God loves man.

When we look beneath the theological cloak in which Spinoza presents his moral philosophy, we see that what it basically points to is the equation of both virtue and blessedness with knowledge. Virtue is power, and man's power for Spinoza, as it was in a very different sense for Bacon, is a function of his knowledge. Moreover, the very exercise of this power, i.e., rational thought, is the ultimate source of satisfaction, as it is that activity through which man realizes his true being or "acts" in the special Spinozistic sense of the word. This is, however, a rather aristocratic or "elitist" doctrine, as it would seem to restrict virtue and blessedness to a select few, viz., the philosophers, while condemning the great mass of mankind to a life of misery and bondage.

Now, Spinoza was obviously bothered by this problem; for as we shall see in our study of his political philosophy, he was constantly torn between his democratic sentiments and his scorn of the superstition and ignorance of the multitude (the typical intellectual's plight!). The same tension and an ultimate decision in favor of the "wise," is reflected in the metaphysical solution to the problem of blessedness which he provides in the *Ethics.* The key to this solution is the notion of degrees of eternality. "We feel and know that we are eternal," he writes (Prop. XXIII, Scholium), apparently with reference to all men and not merely the philosophers. Just as we earlier saw that the human mind (meaning thereby every human mind) *"has an adequate knowledge of the eternal and infinite essence of God,"* so we now see that, in consequence of this very knowledge, every mind has at least a vague insight into the true order of things, and some vestiges of "intellectual love" (the feeling which accompanies this insight). But as was the case with the knowledge of God, most men confuse this genuine insight with their imaginative ideas. In this instance, "they confuse eternity with duration, and ascribe it to the imagination or the memory which they believe to remain after death" (Prop. XXXIV, Corollary, Scholium).

Thus, while all minds have an eternal part or aspect, not all minds are eternal to the same extent.[29] The difference between minds and the degree of freedom and blessedness that they possess is a function of the extent of their adequate knowledge. The greater the extent of one's adequate knowledge, the less one will be subjected to the imagination and the ensuing passions, especially the fear of death (Prop. XXXVIII). This fear and the associated emotions, which would seem to be connected with the imaginative view of immortality, can, to be sure, never be completely overcome. But for the mind which has attained to the third kind of knowledge, "the part thereof which we have shown to perish with the body (V, xxi), should be of little importance when compared with the part which endures" (Prop. XXXVIII, Scholium). What perishes, of course, are the imagination and associated emotions, while what "endures," i.e., constitutes the true actuality of such a mind, is rational thought.

Spinoza's whole philosophy is epitomized in the last proposition of the *Ethics. "Blessedness is not the reward of virtue, but virtue itself; neither do we rejoice therein, because we control our lusts, but, contrariwise, because we rejoice therein, we are able to control our lusts"* (Prop. XLII). In order to understand this assertion, which contains an explicit attack on the religious conception of salvation as "reward," we need only to keep in mind the connection between blessedness and knowledge on the one hand, and knowledge and power on the other. Spinoza's point is simply that we do not acquire this knowledge by first controlling our lusts or passions, but that we only have the power to control these to the extent to which we already possess adequate knowledge. Thus, whereas the ignorant man is perpetually tormented by his passion and never achieves genuine peace of mind or freedom, "the wise man, insofar as he is regarded as such, is scarcely at all disturbed in spirit, but, being conscious of himself, and of God, and of things, by a certain eternal necessity, never ceases to be, but always expresses true acquiescence of his spirit." Such then is the good, the particular form of human existence, to which the *Ethics* points the way. It is certainly hard to achieve, but as Spinoza reflects in his famous closing words:

Needs must it be hard, since it is so seldom found. How would it be possible, if salvation were ready to our hand, and could without great labour be found, that it should be by almost all men neglected? But all things excellent are as difficult as they are rare. (Prop. XLII, Scholium)

CHAPTER 6

Man and The State

WE have learned from the *Ethics* that, despite his *conatus*, or fundamental drive for self-preservation, man is essentially a social animal. This conclusion was based on the realization that "to man there is nothing more useful than man—nothing." From this we were led to see that man can achieve freedom or blessedness only in association with other men. The difficulty, however, is that men are at best imperfectly rational, and the great bulk of men hardly rational at all. They are therefore guided by what their imaginations tell them is the good, rather than by what actually is such. Accordingly, they cannot live in society with one another unless they are subjected to a common set of laws and a sovereign power to enforce these laws. Human society, in other words, is possible only in a state. But this seems to preclude the possibility of achieving that very freedom which requires socialization in the first place. The problem of freedom is thus central to Spinoza's political thought, just as it was to his metaphysical and moral theory. While it was the task of the *Ethics* (at least one of its most important tasks) to investigate the nature and limits of human freedom, and to show how it was possible in the face of the thoroughgoing determinism of nature, the major concern of Spinoza's political philosophy is to explain how freedom can be realized in a state, which by its very nature demands absolute obedience to law.

Spinoza's basic conviction is that such freedom is both possible and desirable; indeed, that "the purpose of the state is really freedom."[1] But he also believes that liberty (freedom in the political context) can be achieved only if each individual surrenders all of his power to the state. Again, the parallel to the metaphysical doctrine of the *Ethics* is striking. There the great lesson was that one can only achieve genuine freedom (autonomy or self-governance) by realizing that he is a completely determined part of nature; that he has no free will; and that all of his actions follow universal and necessary laws. Here, freedom is achieved through complete subjection to the laws of the state. In both cases, freedom and subjection to law are intrinsically connected rather than opposed. As a consequence, Spinoza was led to affirm that the most absolute state, meaning the state with the most power over its citizens, is the best state, and, paradoxically enough, that this condition is realized in a democracy.

These thoughts are developed in the *Theological-Political Treatise* and the *Political Treatise*, which, although differing greatly in style and tone, contain, with one significant exception, much the same doctrine. The former work, which we have already discussed in connection with Spinoza's life, was a polemical piece, addressed to the events of the time. Within the context of a devastating attack on the authority of the Bible, and hence on the authority of the clergy, he there provided a classical defense of the principles of freedom of thought and speech. The latter work, which Spinoza never finished, is basically a textbook in political science. Adopting the dispassionate, analytic method of the *Ethics*, which considered human behavior as subject to a set of universal and necessary laws, the *Political Treatise* attempts to deduce from these basic laws of human nature the true causes and functions of the state. On the basis of these considerations, it then proceeds to show how any regime must be organized—whether it be a monarchy, aristocracy or democracy—if it is to endure and preserve the peace and freedom of its citizens.

As a political thinker, Spinoza was influenced by many factors, not the least of which were his study of Machiavelli and his personal observation of the political events of his time in the Netherlands. The chief influence, however, was undoubtedly provided by Thomas Hobbes. Spinoza's political philosophy can be profitably seen as a continued dialogue or debate with Hobbes. We shall therefore begin our consideration of Spinoza's political thought with an analysis of the assumptions which he shared with Hobbes concerning the nature, legitimacy and origin of political power. This will enable us to see precisely the points at which the two men diverge, and thus to better understand Spinoza's unique contribution to the history of political philosophy as well as some of the limitations of his theory. Finally, we shall consider Spinoza's own application of his principles in his discussion of the best constitution for each type of government, which occupies the bulk of the *Political Treatise*.

I *The State of Nature and Civil Society: Hobbes and Spinoza*

As thoroughly modern men, imbued with the scientific outlook, both Hobbes and Spinoza thought that political philosophy must be based on an accurate assessment of human nature. Both therefore condemn much of traditional political philosophy for erecting utopias which men are not fit to inhabit. Nevertheless, in so doing, both thinkers make extensive use of many of the basic conceptions of the very line of traditional political thought which they criticize. These include the notions of natural right, natural law, the state of nature, and the social contract. In order to understand their political thought it will therefore be necessary to consider these traditional conceptions at least briefly.

All of these conceptions have roots in Greek thought, and all have been used at various times in history in support of a wide variety of political theories. In modern times, however, their main function has been in support of political liberalism. By liberalism is here meant the view which advocates two closely related doctrines: (1) that the *sole* end of the state is to enhance the lives of its individual citizens; and (2) that all government is by consent of the governed. From these principles it is generally inferred that any governmental power which is not used for this purpose, or which is not established by consent, either explicit or tacit, is illegitimate and can be justifiably resisted.

The doctrine of natural rights is one of the chief pillars of this line of thought. The basic contention of this doctrine is that all men are born with certain rights, which therefore pertain universally to man *qua* man, and consequently, that the state neither confers these rights, nor can legitimately deny them. The Declaration of Independence captures this thought by describing such rights as "inalienable," and it cites "life, liberty, and the pursuit of happiness" as examples thereof. Since all men possess such rights, "all men are created equal"; and since any violation of these rights by a governmental power is in principle illegitimate, any such violation can be said to justify civil disobedience or even revolution.

The notion of natural law has its roots in Stoic philosophy and Roman law, and during the Middle Ages it was used in support of feudalism. Yet it has also played a central role in classical liberal thought, wherein it is closely associated with the theory of natural rights. Within this context, natural law is generally construed as a set of universally valid moral rules, which are grounded in either reason or the will of God, depending on whether the theory in question is secular or religious. These rules function as criteria or norms for judging the morality of the actions both of individuals and of states. This doctrine holds that the "positive," i.e., actual, laws of every state *ought* to conform to these rules, and that the sovereign, who is often thought to be "above the law" in the sense of the civil or positive laws, is nonetheless obliged to follow these rules, which constitute a "higher law." Together with the theory of natural rights, this doctrine obviously provides a powerful tool for judging the legitimacy of political institutions and the exercises of sovereign power.

Much the same can be said about the theory of a social contract. The roots of this theory reach back to the Sophists of ancient Greece. The Sophists appealed to an original contract as a means of justifying their conviction that all laws, and even society itself, are the products of human conventions and have no divine authority or sanction. In its subsequent history, however, the notion of the social contract has come to include two distinct doctrines, which, although closely connected, are not always held together. The first of these, which is called the "social contract proper" or "pact of association,"[2] asserts that the state originated when a group of individuals, living in a "state of nature," agreed to join together and collectively submit to a sovereign power. It is thus a theory of the origin of the state; and it is grounded in an individualistic, asocial conception of human nature. Society or political organization, in this view, is not "natural" but is the result of an express decision on man's part to leave his original asocial condition, which is termed the "state of nature."

The second form of this theory affirms the need for a contract of government or "contract of submission,"[3] wherein the people contract with the sovereign concerning the conditions of rule. On this theory, the people pledge their obedience to the sovereign in return for the promise of protection and good government. If the sovereign fails to keep his part of the bargain, his claim to allegiance is at an end and the people are no longer bound to obey. The contract in this form is thus not an agreement among the people themselves, but one between the people who are already organized into a society, and the sovereign. As such, it serves to define the conditions of sovereignty and obedience, thereby providing a basis for theories of limited sovereignty, as well as liberal principles in general.

By ingeniously reinterpreting each of these notions, Hobbes used them in support of a theory of absolute sovereignty, the most efficient form of which is held to be monarchy. Far from serving to justify the rights of the individual over and against the state, as in liberal thought, they become, in Hobbes, the very means for denying that he has any such rights. Central to his analysis is the notion of the social contract, and like other contract theorists, Hobbes begins his argument with a consideration of the state of nature. Unlike some theorists, however, he does not regard the state of nature as an actual historical situation before the advent of civil society. Rather, he uses it to refer to the condition of man as he is everywhere and at all times apart from the restraints and protection provided by a state.

Hobbes's description of man in a state of nature, which is really an analysis of human nature, is reminiscent of much that we have already seen in Spinoza. Hobbesian man is both thoroughly determined and thoroughly egotistical. His fundamental drive is for self-preservation, although Hobbes also grants a basic role to vanity in the motivation of human behavior.[4] In this state, Hobbes argues, man has a "natural right" to do whatever he deems necessary for his self-preservation. But since everyone else equally possesses such a right, which is limited only by one's power, and since everyone else is motivated by the desire to appropriate everything necessary to preserve his being and impress others, it follows that this state is one of perpetual conflict, in which no one really possesses any rights in the sense of guaranteed protection.[5] Hobbes expressed this thought by characterizing the state of nature as a state of war of "every man, against every man," and he describes the life of man in such a state as "solitary, poore, nasty, brutish, and short".[6]

The whole point, of course, is that such a state of affairs is intolerable and is to be avoided at all costs. Moreover, Hobbes believed that reason provides us with certain rules which, if followed, will enable us to avoid it. With typical audacity, he equated these rules for survival with natural law, or the "laws of nature," and even with the "divine law." There are some fifteen such rules, but we need only consider here the first two, which form the basis of his theory of the social contract and consequently of his doctrines of sovereignty and political obligation. The first and most fundamental of these laws of nature is the maxim that "peace is to be sought after, where it may be found; and where not, there to provide ourselves for helps of war."[7] The basic question is thus how peace is to be achieved, which is equivalent to the question of how man is to escape from the state of nature. The answer is provided by the social contract. The necessity for such a contract emerges when one realizes that the basic source of conflict in the state of nature is the unlimited right therein of all men to all things which they deem necessary for their self-preservation. Reason therefore dictates that peace can only be achieved if everyone voluntarily relinquishes or transfers some of his rights. Such a mutual transference of rights is a contract, and when it includes a promise of future performance, it is called a covenant.[8] The formation of such contracts or covenants thus seems to provide the path through which men can escape from the state of nature.

Hobbes thought that covenants create obligations where none existed before, but he also realized that in a state of nature one has no assurance that others will respect the agreement. In order for a covenant to be valid, it is therefore necessary that a sovereign power be recognized, capable of enforcing such agreements. But this can only be achieved if the multitude covenant among themselves to surrender all of their rights to such a sovereign power. By such an act, which is what Hobbes means by the social contract, the multitude of wills becomes one will, and the multitude itself a commonwealth. This contract, therefore, is not between the people and the sovereign (the pact of subjection of traditional liberal theory) but among the people themselves. Moreover, the result is not a limited, but an absolute sovereign whose very will is law. The absolute nature of the sovereign power follows from the absolute nature of the surrender of rights on the part of the people. In contracting among themselves, the people voluntarily give all of their own right or power to the sovereign, and thereby create for themselves an obligation of total obedience. Behind this severe theory, which seems to justify the most unyielding depotism, lies the conviction that sovereignty must be either absolute or nonexistent, and that if nonexistent, chaos and civil war necessarily prevail. Having experienced civil war in England, Hobbes evidently felt that it is the greatest conceivable social evil, and hence, that any form of government, no matter how oppressive, is preferable to it.

At first glance, Spinoza's political philosophy seems to be an only slightly modified version of Hobbes's. As in the *Ethics*, man is viewed as part of nature, completely subject to its laws, and, like everything else in nature, his basic endeavor is to preserve his own being. Moreover, since he does this according to the laws of his nature, not out of free will, and since the laws of his nature are, as the *Ethics* has shown, the laws of God, man does this by "sovereign natural right." Thus Spinoza, like Hobbes, reinterprets the notion of natural right, and broadens its meaning to encompass whatever an individual does in accordance with the laws of his nature. But since everything that an individual does is a necessary consequence of the laws of his nature, it follows that everything that he does is right! Whether the individual in question acts according to the dictates of reason or is driven by his passions, whether he is motivated by sympathy for his fellow man or sheer malice, are all beside the point. Either way he is acting according to the laws of his nature, and he has no power to do otherwise. Moreover, given this deterministic, amoral starting point, Spinoza does not hesitate to conclude

that the right and laws of nature, under which all men are born and for the most part live, forbids nothing but what nobody desires and nobody can do: it forbids neither strife, nor hatred, nor anger, nor deceit; in short, it is opposed to nothing that appetite can suggest.[9]

This interpretation of "natural right" is even more radical than Hobbes's, who limited the right of an individual to do whatever he deems necessary for his self-preservation. This would seem to rule out at least some kinds of actions, such as those which are grounded in mere vanity and which the individual knows will not enhance his self-preservation. One can therefore contend that despite his naturalism, there yet remains a trace of the old, moral meaning of natural right in Hobbes.[10] Spinoza is thus the more consistent naturalist, and this will prove to be crucial for his whole critique of Hobbes and for the development of his positive alternative to the Hobbesian Leviathan state. For him, an individual's natural right is limited only by his power and, indeed, is identical with this power. It is thus Spinoza, not Hobbes, who affirms unequivocally that "might makes right."

Spinoza's conception of the state of nature follows logically from this basic premise concerning natural right. Men in this condition strive, as they do everywhere, to preserve their own being. Here, however, there is no authority except that which is grounded in fear, and no basis for mutual trust. Men are therefore naturally enemies, and in such a situation literally "anything goes." Spinoza expresses this latter point by contending, against Hobbes, that men have a natural right to break promises. Since there is no external authority or power to enforce obedience, it is both natural and rational for an individual to honor an agreement only insofar as it is profitable for him to do so. But since he is the only judge of its profitableness, Spinoza reasons:

So if he judges that his pledge is causing him more loss than gain—and it makes no difference whether he judges truly or falsely, for to err is human—then, since it is the verdict of his own judgment that he should break it, he will break it by the right of nature.[11]

Spinoza does not go quite so far as Hobbes and equate the state of nature with a state of war, but he does affirm that in this situation man is always subject to the threat of war and thus has no security. Ultimately, this is due to the fact, already noted by Hobbes, that the isolated individual is really powerless; that he is unable to preserve his being, either in the sense of fully protecting himself from attack by others, or adequately fulfilling his needs. Moreover, since right is equivalent to power, Spinoza can also say with Hobbes that, despite his unlimited natural right, the individual in this situation really has no rights at all. The hopelessness of this situation renders necessary the transition to civil society, which is regarded by both Hobbes and Spinoza as the condition in which alone man can effectively exercise his right or power. However, in his analysis of the benefits to be derived from membership in civil society, Spinoza goes considerably beyond Hobbes. He does this by supplementing the latter's emphasis on security and escape from a state of war, with a consideration of the positive benefits and advantages to be derived from such membership. These benefits range all the way from an increase in material comfort, gained through the division of labor, to the possibility of philosophy itself; and all of this reflects the rather un-Hobbesian notion that nothing is more useful to man than man himself. The actual mechanism of this transition from a state of nature to civil society is, however, somewhat uncertain, as Spinoza offers divergent accounts in the *Theological-Political Treatise* and the *Political Treatise*.

In the former work Spinoza sides with Hobbes in appealing to the social contract as the means whereby man moves from a state of nature to civil society. Unlike Hobbes, however, he seems to regard this as an actual historical occurrence. For example, in repudiating the notion that despite the lack of civil law, man in a state of nature still stood under obligation to God, i.e., natural law, Spinoza asserts that the state of nature is prior in both time and nature to religion.[12] Moreover, after reflecting on man's misery in this condition, wherein man must constantly be on guard against every other man, Spinoza suggests that

each must have firmly resolved and contracted to direct everything by the dictate of reason alone (which no one dares to oppose openly lest he appear to lack understanding), to bridle his appetite when it suggested anything harmful to another, to do to nobody what he would not wish done to himself, and, finally, to defend his neighbour's right as if it were his own.[13]

Above and beyond this, however, these same individuals seem to have already realized what we have just learned, viz., that men can only be expected to honor a contract as long as they deem it advantageous to do so; and therefore, that a lasting union of men cannot be built upon a foundation as fragile as good faith. Consequently, they must have further agreed that each individual should transfer all of his right to society as a whole. Since society as a whole, rather than any individual or group thereof, as in Hobbes, is given the power by this pact of submission, the resulting state is called a democracy. Nevertheless, society thus empowered will possess the natural right or sovereign power to work its will upon its individual members, "and everyone will be bound to obey it either in freedom of spirit or from fear of the supreme penalty."[14]

In the *Political Treatise*, on the other hand, not only is all reference to such a pact of submission dropped, but also it is affirmed that "since all men, savage and civilized alike, everywhere enter into social relations and form some sort of civil order, the causes and natural foundations of the state are not to be sought in the precepts of reason, but must be deduced from the common nature or constitution of men."[15] It is thus not reason, but some common passion such as hope or fear, which leads men to join together.[16] Consequently, the origin of society must be seen as the inevitable outcome of human passions, not as the product of deliberate design by rational men. Within this changed perspective, the requirement of complete submission and obedience to sovereign power is still maintained, but it is now viewed as a necessary condition for the existence of an enduring state, not as an historical event through which the state was created.

This change can be seen either as the result of a genuine development in Spinoza's thought[17] or, as is more likely, as a reflection of the exoteric polemical character of the *Theological-Political Treatise*.[18] Since this work is to a large extent historical, and since in its political portions it focuses on the Hebrew commonwealth or theocracy, which was, after all, alleged to have originated at a particular moment in time with an explicit covenant, it would be natural for Spinoza within this context to treat the origin of the state *as if* it were an historical event. The important point, however, is that the thesis that the state began with an explicit covenant between rational individuals is not only not required by, but is actually incompatible with, the basic outlines of Spinoza's philosophy. We have already seen that it is a cardinal tenet of the *Ethics* that the life of reason is only possible in a society. One could therefore hardly expect Spinoza to assume that the existence of rational, autonomous, "free" individuals was a precondition for society itself. Moreover, as Spinoza makes quite explicit, if men were in fact led by the dictates of reason, the sanctions imposed by a state would be unnecessary, and a society of rational men would never submit to them. Finally, as we have also seen, Spinoza explicitly rejects any notion of an obligation independent of utility, such as seems to be required by the historical or factual form of the contract theory.[19]

Nevertheless, apart from all questions about an historical contract, it remains the central teaching of Spinoza's political philosophy, a teaching common to both works, that the very possibility of a civil society requires the total surrender by each individual of his right, i.e., power, to society as a whole. In the resulting state, as in the state of nature, men are still governed by hope and fear and by the desire to preserve their being, but in the civil state "all fear the same things, and all have one and the same source of security, one and the same mode of life."[20] In order for this to be possible, it is absolutely crucial that the surrender include the right to decide what is just or unjust. If the multitude is to be guided "as if by one mind, and, in consequence, the will of the commonwealth be taken for the will of all, what the commonwealth decides to be just and good must be regarded as having been so decided by every citizen."[21] Only by such means can anarchy be avoided. For if individuals retain the right of private judgment, there is no common standard of justice to which one can appeal, and therefore no unifying social bond. "Thus," Spinoza concludes, "no matter how unfair a subject considers the decrees of the commonwealth to be, he is bound to carry them out."[22]

A more uncompromising argument for absolutism can hardly be imagined. An individual seems to have no rights except for those granted to him by the state. Anyone who attempts to reserve additional rights for himself, or who challenges the authority of the state, is to be regarded as an enemy of the state and treated as such. Yet, we are struck with the paradox that the same philosopher who argued in this manner, also claims that the goal of the state is liberty; champions the freedom of thought and speech; and holds, at least in one of his works, that democracy is the best form of government. The reconciliation of these claims is the basic task of any interpretation of Spinoza's political philosophy, and it is to this task that we now turn.

II   *The Limits and Uses of Political Power*

We have already suggested that Spinoza arrived at these results through an adoption of a more consistently naturalistic, "amoral" position than Hobbes himself. The best place to begin is thus with a consideration of Spinoza's own account of the relation between his thought and that of Hobbes. Fortunately, such an account is available; for in a letter to his friend Jarig Jelles, who evidently requested information on just this point, Spinoza writes:

With regard to Politics, the difference between Hobbes and me, about which you enquire, consists in this, that I ever preserve the natural right intact so that the Supreme Power in a State has no more right over a subject than is proportionate to the power by which it is superior to the subject. This is what always takes place in the State of Nature.[23]

By the claim that, unlike Hobbes, he preserves natural right intact, Spinoza apparently means that he consistently equates right with power, while Hobbes does not. This point is well taken, at least as a criticism of Hobbes, and underlines a basic inconsistency in the argument through which Hobbes establishes his absolutistic conclusions. This inconsistency concerns the weight given to contracts, which in turn reflects an inconsistency in Hobbes's conception of natural law. As we have already seen, Hobbes equates natural law with a set of precepts or practical maxims which a rational being ought to follow if he desires to escape from a state of nature. They are, therefore, essentially rules for self-preservation, maxims of prudence. This is quite different from the traditional conception of such laws as a body of "higher laws," or moral principles, above and beyond the civil laws of any state, to which both the citizens and the sovereign are morally obligated. With his conception of man in the state of nature, and his correlative notion of sovereign power as the source of all law and justice, Hobbes, like Spinoza, repudiates *this* doctrine of natural law. Nevertheless, when discussing the social contract, Hobbes contends that it creates an unconditional obligation to obey, and he justifies this in terms of the "law of nature" that covenants ought to be kept.[24] Such an obligation, it turns out, is independent not only of the wisdom and justice of the sovereign's commands, but also of his power. Thus, the very same law of nature which teaches us what to do for our self-preservation, places us under an absolute obligation to obey the sovereign power, even when doing so is obviously not in our best interests.

This partial moralization of natural law was no doubt motivated by Hobbes's deep conviction that civil war is an unmitigated evil, to be avoided at all costs. But given his conception of man as driven by a desire for self-preservation, he obviously cannot maintain this obligation to obey the sovereign in an unqualified form. Since, in his view, an individual enters into the social contract only in order to preserve his being, that individual cannot be expected to abide by it when to do so threatens his very life. Hobbes is therefore forced to admit that an individual has a "right" to resist the sovereign power when his life is in immediate danger.[25] Furthermore, he cannot stop with this single exception, but must acknowledge many other "rights" which an individual reserves for himself and which the sovereign power cannot justifiably threaten. Thus we are told that the subject reserves for himself the right to resist for "bodily protection, free enjoyment of air, water and all necessaries for life";[26] that a subject cannot be commanded to kill a parent; and that "there are many other cases in which obedience may be refused."[27] These, and other passages which add further qualifications, reflect the tension between the naturalistic and the "moral" elements in Hobbes's theories of natural right and provide vivid illustrations of the contradictions that emerge when he attempts to unite both elements in support of his theory of absolute sovereignty.[28]

Spinoza avoids these pitfalls by the simple expedient of eliminating all reference to a moral element which creates an obligation above and beyond the actual arrangement of power. The key to his position lies in the recognition that the right of the sovereign, like that of everything else in nature, is coextensive with his power, and that since this power is not infinite, neither is his right. The sovereign, in other words, does not have the right to do what he does not have the power to do. Now, sovereign power is largely exercised in the promulgation of laws and regulations, and Spinoza's point is that there are some laws which a sovereign literally does not have the power to enforce. This conclusion is derived from the realization that everyone is motivated by the desire for self-preservation and, consequently, will always choose that course of action which he believes to be most advantageous. People who live according to the dictates of reason will recognize the desirability of obeying the law, but since such individuals are few and far between, the force of the law rests largely on its sanctions, that is, fear of punishment or hope of reward. By properly applying these sanctions, a sovereign can, of course, gain considerable control over a populace. There are, however, at least according to Spinoza, certain acts which run so counter to human nature that no threat or promise of reward can lead an individual to perform them. As examples of such acts Spinoza cites forcing a man to testify against himself, torture himself, kill his parents, or to make no attempt to avoid death.[29] Laws or commands requiring these or similar deeds are therefore of no effect, and thus, "keeping natural right intact," one can claim that the sovereign has no "right" to assert them.

Spinoza, however, does not stop with such extreme cases, which by themselves do not go very far toward mitigating the evils of tyranny. He also shows a keen awareness of the inherent limitation of legislative power with regard to beliefs and private morality. Such things should not, because they cannot, be legislated. As he notes in the *Theological-Political Treatise:* "He who seeks to determine everything by law will aggravate vices rather than correct them. We must necessarily permit what we cannot prevent, even though it often leads to great harm."[30] But if this holds true for obvious evils, such as extravagance, envy, greed and drunkenness, which a government might legitimately wish to eliminate, "much more then must we allow independence of judgment; for it is certainly a virtue, and it cannot be suppressed."[31] Spinoza thus argues for freedom of thought not only on the basis of its benefit for society, a view which we shall consider shortly, but also because a government is powerless to prevent it. This belief may seem somewhat naïve in light of our current knowledge of thought control and "brainwashing," but Spinoza himself was not totally unaware of the ability of a government to influence public opinion. He nevertheless felt that there were distinct limits to this power, and that in the last analysis a man cannot be forced to believe otherwise than he believes or to judge otherwise than his reason dictates.[32] Laws governing opinion are therefore ineffectual and a violation of natural right.

Above and beyond this, Spinoza also recognized that there are some things which a government can accomplish by brute force, but that in doing them it inevitably undermines its own authority. Since a government cannot do these things with impunity, Spinoza argues that it does not, strictly speaking, have the power or right to do them.[33] Behind this claim is the contention that for a law to be effective, that is, to command obedience, it must not do too much violence to the public's sense of what is to its own advantage. Although a government can for a time, by the use of force and propaganda, institute policies which run completely counter to the prevailing public opinion, the attempt to do so will succeed only in arousing widespread opposition, which will lead in the end to the government's own downfall. Public opinion, or what the majority regards as in its own best interests, thus functions as a real check on governmental power. To function effectively, and even to stay in power, a government must consider the will of the people.

Spinoza's political philosophy, however, is not primarily devoted to telling us what a government cannot do at all, or what it cannot do with impunity, but with determining what it *ought* to do, if it is to realize the end for which it was established. In basic agreement with Hobbes, Spinoza defines this end as peace and security, and he also acknowledges that this cannot be achieved without a force strong enough to guarantee compliance with the law. Unlike Hobbes, however, he further contends that the state ought not to be construed merely as a device for preventing men from killing one another, but also as a positive instrument, having an essential role to play in the creation of the conditions necessary for a meaningful human existence. "A commonwealth," he writes, "whose subjects are restrained from revolting by fear must be said to be free from war rather than to enjoy peace"; and again: "A commonwealth whose peace depends on the apathy of its subjects, who are led like sheep so that they learn nothing but servility, may more properly be called a desert than a commonwealth."[34] The point of all this is that peace is not to be construed with Hobbes as the mere absence of war, for the sake of which almost any degree of tyranny and oppression would be tolerable, but rather as a positive condition in which man can exercise his virtue. The goal of the state is thus to create this condition, a view which Spinoza clearly affirms in his conclusion to this discussion: "Thus when I say that the best state is one in which men live in harmony, I am speaking of a truly human existence, which is characterized, not by the mere circulation of blood and other vital processes common to all animals, but primarily by reason, the true virtue and life of the mind."[35]

By identifying the "truly human existence" with the life of reason, Spinoza is underlining the basic practical conclusion of the *Ethics*. But if man is to properly exercise his reason, and thus to achieve the freedom described in the *Ethics*, it is obviously necessary for him to develop an independent judgment. A regime which proscribes opinions is therefore not one in which man can readily realize his true nature and live a fully human life. This is the point of the already cited claim in the *Theological-Political Treatise* that "the purpose of the state is really freedom." Here freedom must be understood primarily as the freedom of thought and speech, and it is argued that while governmental power can and ought to be used to limit the actions of subjects, it should not be used to limit their thoughts (which is impossible) or their freedom to express these thoughts. Moreover, not only is the suppression of these basic freedoms harmful for the individual who is attempting to live according to the dictates of reason, but it is also harmful to the state itself. In recognition of both the history of the Dutch Republic and of the Marranos in Spain and Portugal, Spinoza contends that attempts to suppress these freedoms succeed only in producing hypocrites and martyrs. The great lesson of Spinozistic political science is thus:

If honesty, then, is to be valued above servility, and sovereigns are to retain full control, without being forced to yield to agitators, it is necessary to allow freedom of judgment, and so to govern men that they can express different and conflicting opinions without ceasing to live in harmony.[36]

Finally, the emphasis on freedom of thought and expression leads Spinoza in the *Theological-Political Treatise* to his conception of democracy as "the most natural form of state," meaning thereby the form which comes "nearer to preserving the freedom which nature allows the individual."[37] The point here is that although a democracy, like any form of government, requires that every individual transfer his natural right to the sovereign and agree to obey the laws, it at the same time gives him a say in determining these laws which he is obliged to obey. Every citizen therefore has, at least in theory, an equal voice in the affairs of state, and "in this way," Spinoza claims, "all remain equal as they were before in the condition of nature."[38] Moreover, in no other form of government are the benefits of freedom more apparent. Since every citizen has a stake in the decision-making process, and since the will of the majority becomes law, a democracy must not merely tolerate, but actually require, freedom of thought and expression. A democracy, in other words, more than any other form of government, has a vested interest in the rationality of its subjects; and for that reason it would seem to be that form of government under which one could most readily lead the kind of life described in the *Ethics*.

Here, then, is the liberal element in Spinoza's political thought, that element in virtue of which he differs most profoundly from Hobbes and stands firmly in the tradition of Locke and Rousseau as one of the founders of modern liberal democratic thought. Yet, in coming to grips with Spinoza's political philosophy, one must constantly keep in mind that this liberal element is found in an uneasy juxtaposition with another strand which is much more akin to Hobbes. This other, less than liberal, strand, is reflected in the demand for total obedience and in the adoption of the Hobbesian doctrine that the state, as the source of civil law, can in the strict sense do no wrong. Spinoza, to be sure, attempts to avoid some of the more unpleasant consequences of this view with his already discussed analysis of the limits of governmental power. We saw there that in order for a law to be effective, it must not clash too violently with the majority's sense of its own best interests. A law requiring universal suicide would be universally disobeyed, and any government which tried to enforce such a law would be "rightly" overthrown. The problem with this is that the multitude seldom, if ever, operate under the guidance of reason. What the majority at any time regards as advantageous is not necessarily so, from which it follows that there can easily be valid laws, approved at least tacitly by the majority, which are nevertheless grossly unjust and yet demand obedience.[39]

Spinoza himself was very much aware of this problem, and his attempts to deal with it reveal the deepest motivations of his thought, as well as its basic conflicts. Typical is the following passage from the *Theological-Political Treatise,* where an effort is made to reconcile the right of free speech with the demand for total obedience to the law:

For example, suppose a man shows that some law is contrary to sound reason, and thus maintains that it should be repealed; if he at the same time submits his opinion to the judgment of the sovereign (which alone is competent to pass and repeal laws), and meanwhile does nothing contrary to what that law demands, then, of course, he ranks with all good citizens as a benefactor of the state. But if he breaks the law in order to accuse the magistrate of injustice and to stir up mob hatred against him, or makes a seditious attempt to repeal the law against the magistrate's will, he is simply an agitator and a rebel.[40]

This passage expresses in graphic form the limits of Spinoza's political philosophy, limits which seem to follow from his rigid separation of thought and action. It therefore makes clear that despite his great advance over Hobbes in finding room for the rights of the individual in an authoritarian state, he was not able to show how these rights could be fully reconciled with political power and the demand for total obedience to the law. When confronted by an unreasonable or "unjust" law, an individual has the "right" to reason with the authorities and try to convince them of their folly. Failing to do so, however, he must remain silent and obey. Moreover, the rational man will do so voluntarily, and the state has the right to treat as an enemy, and execute for the crime of treason, anyone who does not.

But why should Spinoza, who gave to the state the function of providing the social conditions necessary for the realization of human freedom and rationality, so narrowly limit the rights of the individual against the state? Otherwise expressed, why, according to Spinoza, should a rational man obey a law which he knows to be counter to his true self-interest? The answer lies in Spinoza's profound and unshakable sense of the irrationality of the multitude, a sense which constantly conflicts with his liberal political tendencies. We have already seen, from our discussion of the *Ethics,* that the life of reason is not attainable by the masses, and that human freedom is a fragile thing, difficult of attainment and easily destroyed by external forces. This belief was certainly confirmed for Spinoza by the fate of the De Witts. It was, however, not generated by that event; for we find it clearly expressed in the *Theological-Political Treatise*, where Spinoza writes, very much in the spirit of Hobbes: "There is no doubt that devotion to country is the highest form of piety a man can show; for once the state is destroyed nothing good can survive, but everything is put to hazard; anger and wickedness rule unchallenged and terror fills every heart."[41] Nevertheless, as one might expect, the sharpest expression of this point of view is to be found in the *Political Treatise*. Here, after reflecting on the fact that men are liable to passions, Spinoza concludes:

And so the more a man is guided by reason, the more free he is, the more steadfastly will he observe the laws of the state and carry out his sovereign's commands. Finally, the political order is naturally established to remove general fear and to dispel general suffering, and thus its chief aim is one which every rational man would try to promote in the state of nature; though his efforts in that state would be useless. Hence if the rational man has sometimes, by order of the commonwealth, to do what he knows to be opposed to reason, this inconvenience is far outweighed by the advantage which he derives from the actual existence of the political order: reason, we must remember, also bids us choose the lesser evil.[42]

This whole line of thought is epitomized by Spinoza's extremely negative views on revolution. As a political scientist, he points out that revolutions tend to occur whenever a tyrannical government foolishly seeks to extend its authority beyond its actual power. He denies, however, that they are ever effective in the sense of leading to a genuine amelioration of the human condition. All that ever happens is the replacement of one form of tyranny by another which is generally even more severe. In the *Theological-Political Treatise* Spinoza explicitly draws this moral from his analysis of the history of the Hebrew nation and presents it as a warning to his contemporaries. While the people held power, he notes, there was only one civil war, and even this was not bitterly contested, which made possible a peaceful settlement. "But after the people, though quite unused to kings, changed the state into a monarchy, there was almost no end to civil wars, and the battles they fought were of a fierceness unparalleled in history."[43] Moreover, lest one erroneously believe that the problem lay with the monarchy rather than with the change in government, he goes on to emphasize that it is equally dangerous to remove a monarch even though he is universally regarded as a tyrant. This is because once having become accustomed to royal power, the multitude will refuse to acknowlege any lesser authority. The removal of one tyrant thus leads inevitably to the installation of another, and Spinoza reflects: "This is why peoples, though often able to change their tyrants, have never been able to abolish them and replace monarchy by a different form of constitution."[44]

III *Forms of Government*

While Spinoza's view of human nature seems to have precluded the possibility of a beneficial change in the form of government of any given state, he also believed that each form of government could be constituted so as to ensure both the security of the state and the liberty of its subjects. The analysis and demonstration of the appropriate principles of organization (the constitutions) for each form of government is the main task of the *Political Treatise*. The account is based on the classical division of governments into monarchies, aristocracies and democracies, a division which Spinoza took to be exhaustive. The analyses of monarchy and aristocracy are complete, but unfortunately, the treatment of democracy remains a mere fragment. The entire discussion is based on the principle that for each form of government

it is necessary to organize the state so that all its members, rulers as well as ruled, do what the common welfare requires whether they wish to or not, that is to say, are compelled to live according to the precept of reason, if not by inclination, then by force or necessity—as happens when the administration is arranged so that nothing which concerns the common welfare is wholly entrusted to the good faith of any man.[45]

A. *Monarchy.* The successful functioning of a monarchy depends on its limited constitutional nature. Against Hobbes, and as a warning to the Orangists in his own country, Spinoza challenged the myth of the security and stability of an absolute monarchy. The inherent weakness of this form of government lies in the fact that "the power of one man is far too small to bear so great a burden."[46] The absolute monarch necessarily depends on others, "so that the state which is believed to be a pure monarchy is really an aristocracy in practice, but a concealed and not an open one, and therefore of the very worst type."[47] Moreover, not only is such a monarch often ruled by his advisers, who are in turn ruled by their desire to please him, but in his efforts to preserve his power, he will come to fear and oppress his own subjects. Oppression, however, is counter-productive and eventually leads to the monarch's demise.

The main goal of Spinoza's analysis is to describe those institutions which will effectively limit the monarch, so that he will be able to both preserve his power and serve the best interest of the people. The most important of these institutions is a large council, with its members drawn from all of the clans and classes of the realm. Each member of this council must be over fifty years of age, and is to serve a limited term. The body is to be so constituted that it reflects all shades of public opinion, and that the private affairs and interests of its members depend on the preservation of peace. Here again Spinoza makes no assumptions about human nature. All of these recommendations are designed to ensure that the members of the council serve the common good and are neither motivated by the desire for perpetual power nor corrupted by bribes. The primary function of this council is to defend the fundamental laws of the realm and to give advice about the administration of the state to the king, so that he may know what the common good requires. The king, for his part, "is not allowed to make a decision about any matter without hearing the opinion of this council."[48] Since the makeup of the council ensures that its majority opinion reflects the views of the majority of the populace, the king is always obliged to confirm that opinion, or, in case of a badly split council, to attempt to reconcile their differences.[49] The institution of the council thus limits the power of the king in such a way that there is at least a reasonable guarantee that he will act in the public interest.

A second essential institution in a stable monarchy is state-owned land. "The fields and the whole territory—and, if possible, the houses also—should be owned by the state, i.e. by the sovereign; who should let them out at an annual rent to the citizens, i.e. to the city-dwellers and farmers. These should be subject to no other form of taxation in time of peace."[50] This radical proposal, in virtue of which Spinoza has been described as a forerunner of Henry George,[51] was formulated in the interests of peace and security. Without a landed gentry, and with all subjects engaged in commerce, every-one will have a basically equal risk in war. The majority of both the council and the people will thus tend to disfavor war unless absolutely necessary. Such a commonwealth will therefore not involve itself in costly and destructive wars, which are among the chief causes of the undoings of states.

Finally, in agreement with Machiavelli, of whom he was a close student, Spinoza argues for the need for a citizens' militia and underlines the extreme danger of mercenary troops in a monarchy.[52] Spinoza here shows a keen awareness of the dangers of militarism, that is, of a strong professional army which can either lead the nation into unnecessary wars or be used by the monarch as a means for oppressing the people.[53] A people's militia is therefore the best protection of their liberty. Such a militia will fight only when necessary, and even then only in defense of liberty rather than out of desire for gain. Moreover, since no one is to be exempt from service in this militia, everyone will have not only an equal stake, but also an equal part in the preservation of the commonwealth. Given these, and other institutions which we have not been able to touch upon, Spinoza concludes that "a people can maintain a fair amount of freedom under a king as long as it ensures that the king's power is determined by its power alone, and preserved only by its support."[54]

B. *Aristocracy.* Whereas Spinoza seems almost grudgingly to admit that a properly constituted monarchy can function as a viable form of government, his attitude towards aristocracy is far more positive, and his discussion ends with the claim that if any state can last forever, it will be an aristocracy.[55] In fact, his whole treatment of the subject can be seen as a defense of this form of government, together with an analysis of why it failed in the Netherlands and how such failure can be avoided in the future.[56] This analysis consists largely of an appeal to certain features of the constitution of the Venetian Republic, modified so as to fit the situation in the Netherlands.

Aristocracy, as defined by Spinoza, is a form of government in which political power is held "not by one man, but by certain men chosen from the people, whom I shall henceforth call patricians."[57] While an aristocracy differs from a monarchy in respect to the number of those who are in power, it differs from a democracy with regard to the method of selection. The key point is that in an aristocracy the patricians are expressly elected, while in a democracy the right to vote, and thus political power, is automatically granted to every person who meets certain stipulated conditions. These conditions could be so stringent that very few could meet them, e.g., a very considerable amount of wealth, while those elected in an aristocracy might actually constitute a substantial proportion of the population. Nevertheless, the former would still be a democracy and the latter an aristocracy. Furthermore, not only is a large number of patricians a theoretical possibility, but it is a practical necessity if the aristocracy is to avoid either degenerating into a monarchy or splitting into factions.

Spinoza's task, as already noted, is to determine the best constitution for an aristocratic government, but before doing so he stops to catalogue the advantages which a properly constituted aristocracy has over a monarchy. These are four in number. (1) It has adequate numbers and hence sufficient power to govern. Unlike a king, it therefore does not stand in need of counselors. (2) Whereas kings are mortal, councils are everlasting. An aristocracy is thus not subject to periodic upheaval. (3) Because of old age, sickness, minority, or other causes, a king's power is often only on sufferance, but the power of a council always remains the same. (4) Finally, an aristocracy does not suffer from the extreme disadvantage of having its laws based on the inevitably fluctuating will of a single man. Consequently, in a monarchy, with its need for a supplemental council, although "every law . . . is the king's declared will . . . not everything the king wills should be law"; whereas in an aristocracy, with a sufficiently numerous council, "its declared will must necessarily be law in every case."[58]

Theoretically, the power of an aristocracy is thus much greater than that of a monarchy. In practice, however, aristocracies have been limited by the fact that the multitude have maintained a certain independence, and have therefore become an object of fear. Spinoza concludes from this that the greatest need for an aristocratic regime is that the multitude be deprived of all power, that it "retains no freedom save that which must necessarily be allowed it by the constitution of the state itself, and which is therefore not so much a right of the people as a right of the whole state, enforced and preserved by the patricians as their own exclusive concern."[59] As one commentator has pointed out, this amounts to the demand for a *dictatorship of the commercial aristocracy,* and all of the constitutional safeguards and conditions for stability which Spinoza includes in his discussion of aristocracy work toward this end.[60] Nevertheless, although such a government is in fact a dictatorship, Spinoza believed that it would inevitably be a benevolent one, and that the people would have nothing to fear:

> For the will of so large a council must be determined by reason rather than by caprice; since evil passions draw men in different directions, and they can be guided as if by one mind only in so far as they aim at ends which are honourable, or at any rate appear to be so.[61]

Once again the problem is how such a regime can best be constituted. The analysis of monarchy provides the point of departure, and the guiding question is what changes must be made in monarchial institutions in order to establish a successful aristocracy. In dealing with this question, Spinoza shows a keen understanding of the organic connection between institutions in various types of states. What is appropriate in a monarchy is not necessarily so in an aristocracy. Moreover, as he proceeds to point out, one of the basic reasons for the demise of the Dutch Republic was a failure to realize this. They mistakenly thought that all that was necessary was to get rid of the king; and they never thought of changing the underlying organization of the state.[62] The analysis of aristocracies is, however, complicated somewhat by the fact that there are two distinct kinds. One, like that of Venice, consists of a single city and its territories; another, like that of the United States of the Netherlands, consists of several relatively autonomous cities. Spinoza felt that the latter was superior, largely because of its greater power,[63] but he devotes much of his attention to the analysis of the former. Only after completing this analysis does he turn to the question of what modifications would be necessary in an aristocratic state composed of several cities.

It is absolutely essential to the success of an aristocracy in any form that the supreme council, which is composed of all of the patricians, be sufficiently strong. The recommended size is two percent of the population. The function of this council, which must meet regularly at a fixed location, is to pass and repeal laws, and to choose their patrician colleagues as well as the ministers of state.[64] But since in a stable government nothing must be left to chance, or to the good faith and rationality of the governors, Spinoza also felt it necessary that there be a supplemental body of patricians, subordinate to the supreme council, charged with the duty of seeing to it that the constitution is preserved and order maintained in the supreme council. These are called syndics, and they are in effect the watchdogs of the council. Spinoza goes into great detail concerning the appropriate number, age, involvement, and length of service of the syndics, all for the purpose of ensuring that their self-interest will lead them to pursue the general good.[65] Moreover, precisely the same principle is operative in determining the other institutions. Chief of these are the senate and judiciary. The senate, which is a second council subordinate to the supreme one, is assigned the task of transacting public business. The most important part of this business is the ordering of the fortifications of the cities and the conferring of military commissions. Since it is so directly involved with the military operations of the state, it is vital that it be composed of men who have more to gain from peace than from war.[66] The judiciary has the job of deciding disputes between private parties. It must therefore be constituted so as to be as impartial as possible, and not subject to bribes.[67]

A successful aristocracy, however, must differ from a monarchy in other areas besides the organization of its governing bodies. Thus, Spinoza advocates two institutions which he had deemed inappropriate for a monarchy, viz., mercenaries and private property. Since an aristocratic government possesses absolute power, the danger, inherent in a monarchy, of hiring foreign mercenaries does not exist; and since the people have no power and are more appropriately termed subjects rather than citizens, they can hardly be expected to serve in the army without pay.[68] A similar line of thought is used to justify private ownership. Since the people have no say in the governing of the state, without the possession of property they would have no interest in its survival. The existence of such property thus functions as an incentive to support the government.[69]

Most of the above-mentioned institutions are applicable to aristocracies of both types. The greatest modification required for an aristocratic republic composed of several cities must be in the supreme council. Here things have to be organized so that the authority of each city in the union is strictly proportionate to its power. Each city will have its own supreme council and a good deal of autonomy. The senate and judiciary form the main links between the cities, with the senate having charge of all intercity affairs. The state will, of course, have a supreme council, but this will not have a regular role in the ordinary affairs of state, and it will only convene at moments of national danger, when the very union itself is

threatened. Such an aristocracy is thus, like the United States of the
Netherlands, far more of a loose federation for common defense
than a genuine nation. Its obvious weakness would seem to lie in the
difficulty of joining together for concerted action, with the danger of
thus degenerating into a mere debating society. Spinoza, however,
was well aware of this difficulty and of the charge that this was the
cause of the demise of the United States of the Netherlands. He
nevertheless denied that this was the case, and argued instead that
its downfall was due to "its defective condition and the fewness of its
rulers."[70]

C. *Democracy.* As we have noted earlier, Spinoza's discussion
of democracy in the *Political Treatise* remains a fragment. Democracy is defined in a manner consistent with its previous contrast with
aristocracy, as a state in which the supreme council or ruling body is
composed of all of those who fulfill a certain stipulated condition.
This is opposed to one in which the members of the council are
elected. This suggests that democratic governments can take many
forms, but Spinoza tells us that he plans to deal only with what we
might call a broad-based democracy, that is, one in which all citizens who are independent and who live honestly have the right to
vote in the supreme council and to hold offices of state. The qualification of independence, we are told, is intended to exclude
women and servants, who are subject to their husbands and masters
respectively, as well as children and wards. The text ends with a
discussion of why women should be excluded from participation in a
democracy. It is based largely on the claim that women are naturally
inferior to men in terms of intellectual ability and physical strength,
although this is combined with the reflection that men are usually
attracted to women through lust, and thus cannot effectively govern
conjointly with them.[71]

Spinoza's attitude towards women makes an interesting contrast
with that of Hobbes, who, as we have seen, is generally much less
"liberal" in his views. The latter explicitly argues that women, in a
state of nature, have equal right with men, and that their "inequal-
ity of natural force" is not so great as to undermine their basic
equality with men. In support of this contention Hobbes points to
the Amazons, who actually waged war against men, and to the fact
that "at this day in diverse places, women are invested with the
principal authority."[72] Spinoza, on the other hand, seems to reflect
the feminist contention that men tend to regard women merely as

sex objects. Unfortunately, however, his comments about the intellectual inferiority of women lead one to believe that he might have thought this somewhat justified. In any event, these brief remarks, as well as the occasional references to women in the *Ethics,* make it quite clear that this is one issue on which Spinoza was not ahead of his time.

In addition to the general definition of a democracy, and the remarks concerning the exclusion of women, we do find the reflection that while an aristocracy is theoretically the best regime, as it involves the rule of the best for the benefit of all, in practice a democracy is just as good. This, we are told, is because the patricians do not in fact act for the common good, but are instead driven by their passions (a situation which, on Spinoza's own grounds, should be taken as a reflection of the inadequacy of the existing aristocratic institutions, not as a mark of the intrinsic weakness of this form of government). We are not, however, provided with any information concerning the specific institutions which Spinoza felt would be required by a viable democracy. This is certainly unfortunate, especially when we consider that the *Theological-Political Treatise* contended that democracy was the most natural form of government, and strongly suggested that it was the best form. Such a view contrasts sharply with the analysis of aristocracy in the *Political Treatise,* an analysis which emphasizes the importance of depriving the people of all power, and which clearly reflects Spinoza's abiding distrust of the masses. This analysis raises serious questions not only about the superiority of democracy, but also about whether a viable democratic regime is even possible. Perhaps, as one commentator has suggested, the *Political Treatise* remained unfinished not because of Spinoza's untimely death, but because he had come upon a problem which is insoluble in terms of his basic assumptions concerning man and the state.[73]

CHAPTER 7

Revelation, Scripture, Religion

WE have already considered the political setting and the specific concerns underlying the composition and publication of
the *Theological-Political Treatise*. Moreover, in the last chapter we
discussed many of its specifically political teachings. It is no doubt
true that the theological discussion and analysis of the Bible found in
this work are largely developed for the sake of the political message.
Spinoza's critique of revelation enables him to deny it any authority
over men's minds, and this allows him both to repudiate the preten-
sions of the Calvinist clergy and to advance his argument for freedom of thought and speech. Nevertheless, even when abstracted
from the political context, the actual analysis and critique of revealed religion found in the *Theological-Political Treatise* constitute
an important and highly influential part of Spinoza's philosophy, one
which certainly deserves consideration in its own right. This is
especially true of his critique of the Bible, in virtue of which Spinoza
is generally recognized as the founder of higher criticism or the
scientific, historical approach to the Bible. This critique, however,
is itself developed within the context of a systematic assault on the
claim of divine revelation, and it can best be understood within this
broader framework. Accordingly, we shall here first consider the
basic outlines and motivations of Spinoza's critique of revelation and
then, in light of this, discuss his general approach to the Bible.
Finally, in order to complete our account of Spinoza's view on religion, we shall touch briefly upon his attempt to distinguish between
religion and superstition and then consider the social function which
he attributes to the former.

I *The Critique of Revelation*

Spinoza's general attitude toward the claims of revealed religion
is already clear from our consideration of the *Ethics*. Basically, be-

lief in the teachings of the traditional religions, as generally construed, is equated with superstition. The source of this belief is
found in the imagination, and its hold on the mind of the masses is
explained in terms of its connection with the passions of hope and
fear. Hence, not only does Spinoza perceive that this belief lacks
any foundation in genuine knowledge, but he also holds that the
virtues which it inculcates, e.g., fear of God, a sense of guilt, sorrow, repentance, humility, etc., are totally at variance with the
virtues of the wise man. Such a critique, however, is external and
rests upon philosophical assumptions which the theologians will
simply deny in the name of a superior revealed truth. In order to
convince the theologians—and we should keep in mind that this was
his avowed concern—Spinoza must meet their arguments on their
own grounds.[1] This means that he must examine the central
theological claim that Holy Scripture, whether in the Jewish or
Christian version, contains the authoritative word of God, to which
reason must be subjected.

Now, there is, according to Spinoza, only one way in which the
authority of Scripture can be justified, and this is by means of an
appeal to Scripture itself. Ignoring the obviously circular nature of
any such process of reasoning, he therefore affirms as a fundamental
principle of Biblical exegesis that the sense of Scripture must be
taken from Scripture itself.[2] The crucial point, which is merely an
application to Biblical exegesis of the basic principle of Cartesian
method, is that nothing may be claimed to be in the text which is
not clearly and distinctly contained therein. In light of this governing principle, Spinoza rejects out of hand both the Calvinistic doctrine "that the light of nature has no power to interpret Scripture,
but that a supernatural faculty is required for the task,"[3] and the
basic tenet of Maimonidean rationalism that "if the literal meaning
clashes with reason, though the passage seems in itself perfectly
clear, it must be interpreted in some metaphorical sense."[4] Both of
these approaches are not only politically dangerous, because they
lead to the establishment of spiritual authorities, but they are also
useless for the determination of the actual meaning of Scripture,
and therefore for justifying its authority.[5]

Having rejected both of these approaches, Spinoza centers his
attention on the evidence which is traditionally adduced for the
divinity of Scripture. This evidence is of two sorts. First of all, there
is the authority of the prophets, whom Spinoza construes broadly to

encompass the Apostles, and even Christ, as well as the Hebrew prophets. This enables him to include both the New Testament and the Old Testament in his analysis. Secondly, there are miracles which allegedly serve as signs of divine revelation. Spinoza's critique of revelation thus contains a systematic analysis of both prophecy and miracles. With specific reference to Judaism, however, and perhaps in defense of his own break with the religion of his fathers, he also includes a critique of the Jewish conception of the Law and of the claim of the Jews to be the chosen people.

Prophecy, which is equated with revelation, is defined by Spinoza as "sure knowledge revealed by God to man."[6] Spinoza notes in passing that this definition could very well include ordinary knowledge, but that generally such knowledge is not attributed to prophecy. His concern is therefore solely with the extraordinary or superhuman knowledge which is traditionally held to be the unique result of prophetic insight. Following Maimonides, Spinoza agrees that prophetic insight is based on a superior imagination rather than on a superior intellect. But whereas Maimonides, the Aristotelian, used the superiority of imagination to justify a real superiority of insight, Spinoza, in accordance with the basic principles of his theory of knowledge, uses it to draw just the opposite conclusion. Once it is established that the authority of the prophets depends merely on their superior imaginative capacity, and not on their intellect, Spinoza can conclude that their views can be of no import in theoretical matters. The overall strategy and intent of the work, however, prevents him from merely deducing this result from his metaphysical and epistemological principles and requires instead that he derive it from a consideration of Scripture.

The first step is obviously to show that Scripture itself clearly teaches that prophetic power is a function of the imagination. In line with the traditional Jewish notion of the primacy of the Mosaic revelation, Spinoza shows, by means of a consideration of a number of Biblical texts, that only Moses was held to have heard a real voice or received a direct revelation from God. All of the other prophets encountered God through dreams and visions, that is, through the mediation of their imagination. The one exception to this is Christ, who "communed with God mind to mind,"[7] and whose knowledge of God is thus attributed to his intellect rather than to his imagination. On the basis of the analysis of the express teachings of Scripture, Spinoza is therefore able to conclude that, with the exception of Moses and Christ, it was only in virtue of their vivid imagination and upright character that the prophets were held to possess the "spirit of God," which is equivalent to being the recipients of divine revelation.[8]

The next step is to show that precisely because the prophets rely on their imagination, they cannot be taken as authorities in theoretical or speculative matters. This, of course, is a logical consequence of the analysis of imagination found in the *Ethics*, but we have already seen that Spinoza's strategy does not permit him to present it in this fashion. Here, however, he also obviously cannot show that the prophets themselves teach this conception of the imagination. Instead, what he can and does do is to demonstrate that not only the doctrines and conceptions but even the imagery and style of the various prophets differ markedly, and that these differences can be understood in terms of their dispositions, backgrounds and ways of life. For example, Spinoza points out that the rustic prophets such as Amos and Ezekiel tended to depict God with rustic images and in a crude style, while a far different kind of imagery and a much more polished style is to be found in the prophecies of the "courtly Isaiah." Spinoza further shows that this explains the specific differences in the visions of Ezekiel and Isaiah, and he presents these differences as a classical example of disagreement among the prophets. In his own cryptic language, which is intended to sum up the whole issue: "Isaiah saw seraphim with six wings, Ezekiel beasts with four wings; Isaiah saw Him in the likeness of a fire; each doubtless saw God under the form in which he usually imagined Him."[9]

Such discrepancies were, of course, a great source of embarrassment to the traditional defenders of the faith, and one standard tactic was to attempt to reconcile these differences by interpreting the passages in question in some nonliteral manner. Against this, however, Spinoza simply points out that by such means one could easily read anything into Scripture, "for every absurd and evil invention of human perversity could thus, without detriment to Scriptural authority, be defended and fostered."[10] The only reasonable conclusion is therefore to acknowledge frankly that the prophets disagree, and that their individual insights and visions merely reflect their own opinions and backgrounds and not some mysterious "higher" truth. However, while Spinoza uses their obvious dis-

agreement to undermine the authority of the prophets in speculative matters, he also points out that they all agree in teaching the
virtues of justice and charity. He thus concludes by granting to their
moral teachings an authority which he denies to their speculative
insights. This result, as we shall see, plays a central role in his
systematic attempt to separate theology from philosophy, and
genuine religion from superstition.

The appeal to miracles, and to reports thereof, constitutes the
second traditional basis for establishing the divine origin and authority of Scripture. Miracles are here construed as events which violate, or at least transcend, the laws of nature. As such, they function
as signs which authenticate the claims of a prophet (taken in the
broad sense) to be an emissary of God and the bearer of a divine
revelation. Since the prophets supported their teachings with miracles, these teachings and the Scripture in which they are contained
can be viewed as the authoritative word of God. Such a conception
obviously runs completely counter to the whole tenor of Spinoza's
metaphysics, and we have already seen that the argument of the
Ethics expressly rules out the possibility of anything which contravenes the universal laws of nature. As was the case with regard to
prophecy, however, his strategy does not allow him simply to refute
this conception by a metaphysical argument, but it requires that he
also show that this conception is not in accord with, or at least not
derivable from, an unbiased reading of Scripture. Nevertheless, as
he himself is forced to acknowledge, the question of miracles is not
quite the same as the question of prophecy. The nature of prophecy,
he notes, is a "purely theological question," by which is meant a
question as to what Scripture actually teaches, while the question of
miracles deals not only with this, but also with the matter of their
intrinsic possibility.[11]

Some metaphysical considerations are therefore necessary in
dealing with miracles, but Spinoza is careful to separate these considerations from the specifically anti-theistic tenets of the *Ethics*.
Here, as elsewhere in the work, his concern is to formulate the
argument in terms which the theologians might accept, or at least
will not reject out of hand with cries of "atheism." Nevertheless,
despite his conciliatory intent, Spinoza begins by describing the
common attitude towards miracles in contemptuous terms. Central
to this attitude is the belief that the power of God is somehow more
evident and worthy of adulation when manifested in unusual and

inexplicable events than when it is found in the ordinary course of nature. This power is therefore distinguished from the power of nature, and God is then viewed as a kind of royal potentate who orders things for the benefit of man. Spinoza sums up his whole attitude towards the subject by reflecting: "What pretension will not people in their folly advance! They have no single sound idea concerning either God or nature, they confound God's decrees with human decrees, they conceive nature as so limited that they believe man to be its chief part!"[12]

As this passage makes clear, one of the underlying causes of the common belief in miracles is the failure to grasp the infinity of nature, to understand "that the power of nature is infinite, and that her laws are broad enough to embrace everything conceived by the Divine intellect."[13] Students of the *Ethics* will, of course, realize immediately that their failure is itself the result of an illicit separation between God and nature. In our analysis of that work we saw that the infinity of nature follows logically from the very conception of God or nature as the one substance which contains within itself everything that is possible. ("*Whatsoever is, is in God, and without God nothing can be, or be conceived.*" *Ethics* I, Prop. XV) Since nature contains within itself everything that is possible, miracles, which by definition violate the laws of nature, are logically impossible. Moreover, this same conception of nature as an infinite and necessary system of laws was shown to be the true meaning of Maimonides's assertion that the intellect and will of God are identical. Here Spinoza begins with the acceptable theological formula: "It is the same thing to say that God wills a thing, as to say that He understands it."[14] From this he infers that the universal laws of nature reflect perfectly both the divine understanding and will. Once the theologian admits this, however, he must also admit that anything which contravenes the laws of nature would also contravene the will (and intellect) of God. In willing a miracle, God would therefore be acting contrary to His own nature, which is absurd. Thus, by a process of argument which is based on accepted theological principles, Spinoza proceeds to reduce the doctrine of miracles to an absurdity.

Furthermore, Spinoza continues, even if one were to acknowledge the existence of miracles, this could only serve to undermine rather than to confirm our knowledge of the existence of God. The point here is simply that an appeal to events which contravene the laws of nature casts doubt upon the very principles of our reasoning, and thus leads inevitably to a hopeless skepticism. If we cannot be certain of these laws or "primary ideas" (the "common notions" of the *Ethics*), then we cannot be certain of anything, including the existence of God. However, given these laws, that is, given the uniformity of nature, the existence of God can confidently be inferred. Thus, once again Spinoza turns the argument of the theologians against them, showing that it is the lawfulness of nature, and not the alleged exceptions to this lawfulness, which provides a basis for inferring the existence of God.

There is, however, another conception of miracles which is not subject to these objections. In this view, miracles are events which cannot be explained through natural causes because we, or whoever witnesses them, are not in possession of the requisite knowledge. They do not therefore transcend the laws of nature, but merely our knowledge of these laws. The notion of a miracle, taken in this sense, is certainly a meaningful one. In fact, Spinoza claims that this is precisely the sense of miracle found in Scripture: "that what is meant in Scripture by a miracle can only be a work of nature, which surpasses, or is believed to surpass, human comprehension."[15] The only problem with miracles understood in this sense is that they cannot fulfill the function attributed to them. How, after all, can any such event, which by definition surpasses human understanding, serve as a source of knowledge? Moreover, even assuming that some inferences could legitimately be drawn from such miracles, we could certainly not appeal to them to infer the existence of God. God, if He is anything, is an infinite being, and miracles are particular finite events. But from an event, viewed as an effect, we can never infer an infinite cause.[16]

Finally, in accordance with his general strategy, Spinoza supplements the philosophical critique with a further consideration of the actual Biblical teaching concerning miracles. As already noted, the Bible views miracles merely as events which surpass human comprehension. As Spinoza points out, however, this means that what counts as a miracle is determined by the particular level of knowledge possessed by the narrator or witness. But since the ancient Hebrews had a very limited amount of scientific knowledge, they naturally regarded as miraculous many events which, from the superior standpoint of seventeenth-century science, could easily be explained. Furthermore, the prevalence of miracles in the Bible is also to be explained in terms of the poetic manner of expression and the religious intent of the various authors. This intent often led the authors to ignore secondary causes and to refer things directly to God. As a result, many events are described in a way which suggests miraculous intervention on the part of God, when the authors themselves had no such thought in mind. The moral which Spinoza draws from this analysis is that the interpretation and evaluation of the Biblical miracle stories requires, among other things, an understanding of the level of knowledge, motivation and manner of expression of the authors. Far from serving as a basis for the authority of Scripture, or as a ground of faith, miracles are seen as a reflection of the limited understanding of Biblical man.

The analysis of prophecy and miracles constitutes the essence of Spinoza's general critique of revealed religion; but this is supplemented by a lengthy critique addressed specifically to Judaism, a critique which in all probability dates back to the days of his excommunication. This latter critique repudiates the claim of the Jews to be a chosen people, elected by God for a special destiny, possessing unique virtues, and, above all, subject to a special discipline (the Torah). Spinoza prefaces his treatment of this topic with a reflection which lies at the very heart of his moral philosophy: "Every man's true happiness and blessedness consist solely in the enjoyment of what is good, not in the pride that he alone is enjoying it, to the exclusion of others."[17] The Jewish people would, after all, be none the less blessed for the fact that God conferred His favors equally upon all men. The fact that the ancient Hebrews thought differently, that they prided themselves on being especially chosen, is merely a reflection of their childish understanding and rather crude moral standpoint. The implications for the contemporary Jew who might still feel that he is a member of the chosen people is obvious.

Nevertheless, the Bible does in fact speak of the election of the Jews, and once again Spinoza's overall strategy requires that he explain what legitimate sense this can have. As one might expect, this sense turns out to be consistent with the basic principles of his philosophy. First he deals with the general question of the nature of divine aid or grace. Since the "will of God" is perfectly manifest in (really identical with) the laws of nature, these very same laws can also be called decrees of God. It thus turns out to be strictly equivalent to say that everything happens according to the law of nature or the will of God. Hence, any and all human accomplishment, since it occurs according to the fixed laws of nature, can, if one wishes, be seen as the result of divine aid. In other words, the notion of divine aid is allowed, but only in a form in which it is merely another name for purely natural occurrences.

On the basis of this principle Spinoza is able to explain the peculiar achievement of the Hebrew people, in virtue of which they can be said to have been chosen by God. Denying that they possessed any superiority over the other nations in either knowledge or virtue, Spinoza concludes that their "election" can only refer to their peculiar social organization, which enabled them to survive in a hostile environment for such a long period of time. This, however, turns out to be far from complimentary; for the attribution of this organization to divine election is merely a reflection of the fact that it is inexplicable how such a crude and ignorant people could have arrived at it by rational planning. There is, or course, nothing really supernatural in all of this, but it is so incomprehensible, Spinoza ironically notes, that it could even be called miraculous![18]

This then is the only sense in which one can meaningfully talk about the Jews being a "chosen people." Even the gift of prophecy, which was traditionally viewed as a sure sign of Jewish uniqueness, or divine favor, is of no significance in this regard. For Scripture itself clearly teaches, explicitly with the story of Balaam and implicitly in many other places, that the ability to prophesy was commonly attributed to individuals of other nations. Spinoza, therefore, can reaffirm his contention that the election or superiority of the Jews concerns only their social order, and from this draw the inference "that the individual Jew, taken apart from his social organization and government, possessed no gift of God above other men, and that there was no difference between Jew and Gentile."[19] Finally, since this social order, that is, the Hebrew commonwealth, no longer exists, Spinoza arrives at the obvious conclusion that "at the present time, therefore, there is absolutely nothing which the Jews can arrogate to themselves beyond other people."[20]

It could be argued, however, that this result simply tends to ignore the obvious fact that, despite all their oppression and suffering, the Jews have managed to survive as a people with a sense of identity and a common hope for the future. Moreover, just as Christian apologists often cited the incredible growth of Christianity in the oppressive atmosphere of the Roman Empire as a sign of divine favor, and thus as evidence of the truth of the Christian faith, so too, Jewish thinkers tended to appeal to the very survival of Judaism as evidence of the divine election of the Hebrew people. Spinoza meets this issue head-on, and his treatment is a masterpiece of concise sociological analysis. Two factors are presented in explanation of Jewish survival: Gentile hatred and the sign of circumcision. Far from destroying them, the experience of hatred and oppression actually served to unify the Jews and keep them in their traditional faith. Spinoza illustrates this by noting the different fate of the Jews in Spain and in Portugal. In both countries the Jews were compelled either to embrace Catholicism, the state religion, or go into exile. In the former country, those who converted were made full-fledged citizens, with all of the rights and privileges thereof, with the predictable result "that they straightway became so intermingled with the Spaniards as to leave of themselves no relic or remembrance."[21] In Portugal, on the other hand, the Jews were forced to live apart and were considered unworthy of civic honors, and as a result they steadfastly maintained their traditional faith. Curiously enough, Spinoza seems to attach even greater importance to circumcision. With regard to this traditional Jewish rite he reflects:

> The sign of circumcision is, as I think, so important, that I could persuade myself that it alone would preserve the nation for ever. Nay, I would go so far as to believe that if the foundations of their religion have not emasculated their minds they may even, if occasion offers, so changeable are human affairs, raise up their empire afresh, and that God may a second time elect them.[22]

In order to complete his critique of traditional Judaism, Spinoza had to deal directly with the Mosaic law or Torah. It is, after all, largely on the basis of the fact that they are the recipients of this law, and not in virtue of any special moral or intellectual powers, that the Jews lay claim to being a chosen people with a unique historical mission. This law contains not only moral principles, but also rules of worship, social organization and diet. Indeed, it provides precepts governing almost every phase of one's daily life. During the Middle Ages, Jewish thinkers such as Maimonides attempted to explain and justify some of these rules which did not seem to serve any explicitly moral purpose, e.g., the dietary laws, by suggesting that they had a spiritual sense. The goal of these efforts was always to demonstrate that, apart from the laws concerning worship in the Temple, which obviously could not be observed after its destruction, all of these laws were obligatory for all Jews, as, indeed, they still are for Orthodox Jews.

The requirement to observe a large number of apparently arbitrary rules, concerning such morally indifferent matters as what one can or cannot eat, was obviously ridiculous to a philosopher of the rigidly rationalistic cast of mind of Spinoza, and it no doubt was largely responsible for his decision to completely abandon his ancestral faith. Nevertheless, rather than simply rejecting the entire corpus of Jewish law from an independent philosophical perspective, Spinoza attempts to analyze the actual significance of this law for the Hebrew people. Central to this analysis is the distinction between the divine and the ceremonial laws, both of which are contained in the revelation to Israel.

By the divine law Spinoza means those moral rules, dictated by reason, which describe what is necessary for the realization of human blessedness. This law is divine because blessedness, as we have seen from the *Ethics,* consists in the love of God, and because it follows from the idea of God which is within us. The chief precept is simply to love God as the highest good, and not out of fear or in expectation of some further reward.[23] Since this precept is universal or common to all men, and is, in fact, deduced from human nature, it is more properly described as an eternal truth than as a command. The Israelites, however, "did not adequately conceive God's decrees as eternal truths."[24] Possessed of their crude, anthropomorphic conception of the Deity, they viewed the divine law as the command of a sovereign. Thus, although the prophets taught the genuine divine law (love of God), they did not present it in its proper or spiritual sense. It was, Spinoza suggests, Christ who was sent to teach not only the Jews but the whole human race, who first taught the true sense of the law. Christ was able to do this because he possessed adequate ideas, or, in the carefully chosen language of the *Theological-Political Treatise,* he "perceived truly what was revealed."[25] Thus, Spinoza, the apostate Jew and the friend of many members of the Mennonite and Collegiate communities, gives to Christ a unique place in the religious history of the human race.

The situation with regard to the ceremonial law is somewhat different. Ceremonies are defined as morally indifferent actions, which are only called good or bad in virtue of their instituion, i.e.,

the fact that they were revealed by God. The ceremonial law therefore consists of the sum total of the morally indifferent precepts
which are contained in Jewish teaching. Since ceremonies are by
their very nature morally indifferent, they do not play an intrinsic or
necessary role in the achievement of human blessedness. This law
cannot, like the divine law, be viewed as an expression, however
inadequate, of eternal truths. The ceremonial law therefore cannot
have universal human validity. It did, however, have a particular
significance for the Jewish state, as the precepts contained therein
constituted the civil legislation of that state. In support of this claim,
Spinoza shows in great detail how various aspects of this legislation,
e.g., the laws concerning sacrifice and economic arrangements,
played a significant role in maintaining the stability of the state. The
obvious outcome of all of this is that since the significance of this law
is to be found in its function within the ancient Jewish state, and
since this state no longer exists, no contemporary Jew is under any
obligation to keep the law.[26]

II *The Interpretation of Scripture*

This thoroughgoing critique of revelation and of the special claims
of Judaism rests, to a considerable extent, on an appeal to what
Spinoza claims to be the express teachings of Scripture. The presentation and justification of the proper method for determining this
sense is therefore an integral part of Spinoza's project, forming the
subject matter of Chapters VII through XI of the *Theological-
Political Treatise*. Here Spinoza first (Chapter VII) explains the
basic principles of his exegetical method, and then, in the succeed-
ing chapters, applies these principles to the entire canon of the Old
Testament and to some of the Epistles in the New Testament. Once
again we cannot go into many of the details of Spinoza's analysis,
which reveals a deep knowledge of the Biblical text, particularly of
the Old Testament, but we can and must consider at least the main
outlines of Spinoza's revolutionary approach to the Bible.

The essence of Spinoza's approach is concisely expressed in the
famous formula: "The method of interpreting Scripture does not
widely differ from the method of interpreting nature—in fact, it is
almost the same."[27] This is, indeed, a revolutionary statement in
the history of Biblical interpretation. The Bible, which previously
had been viewed as the literal word of God, and hence as equally
sacred in every syllable, is now to be construed as a natural

phenomenon, the product of purely human capacities and endeavors. In other words, it is to be interpreted in precisely the same manner as one would interpret any other ancient text. Now with regard to any other text, the goal would obviously be to arrive at the clear intent of the author, and any interpretation which twists the sense of a given passage in order to make it conform to a previously accepted truth would be rejected out of hand. The Bible, according to Spinoza, is not to be viewed as an exception to this rule, regardless of the consequences of its application for traditional theological doctrines. Just as Descartes, in his *Discourse on Method,* has argued that the proper method in the sciences must begin with clear and distinct conceptions, which serve as the foundation of all truth, so here Spinoza, in what amounts to a discourse on the method for arriving at the true meaning of the Bible, points to the clear meaning of the text as the ultimate standard and source of interpretation.

Given this assumption, the first step in the development of a science of Biblical interpretation is to determine the proper method for the interpretation of nature, and this, Spinoza tells us in typically oblique fashion, "consists in the examination of the history of nature, and therefrom deducing definitions of natural phenomena on certain fixed axioms."[28] By the "history of nature" Spinoza seems to mean the sequence of actual events (in the language of the *Ethics* the series of finite modes). He therefore appears to be describing an essentially inductive procedure, wherein one moves from particular events to general laws ("certain fixed axioms") and from these back to the phenomena to be explained. With regard to the Bible, the phenomena requiring explanation are the particular passages under consideration. The goal is to determine the true intentions of the authors of these passages, and these intentions are to be derived from fundamental principles. These principles, or general exegetical rules, are themselves to be based on a consideration of the history of Scripture. "By working in this manner," Spinoza reflects, "everyone will always advance without danger of error—that is, if they admit no principles for interpreting Scripture, and discussing its contents save such as they find in Scripture itself."[29]

Under the general rubric of the "history of Scripture" Spinoza had in mind three quite specific things. The first of these is a linguistic or philological analysis. Since the interpretation of any text requires an understanding of its language, it is obviously necessary to investigate "the nature and properties of the language in which the books of the Bible were written, and in which their authors were accustomed to speak."[30] A thorough knowledge of the ancient Hebrew language is thus the first prerequisite for accurate Biblical exegesis, and it was no doubt with this in mind that Spinoza attempted to write a Hebrew grammar. Furthermore, Spinoza adds in a reflection which suggests considerable historical insight, this requirement holds not only for the Old Testament, but also for the New, as the latter document, although written in Greek, contains Hebrew modes of thought and speech.[31]

Secondly, it is necessary to analyze each book and to arrange its topics under appropriate headings. This will provide a general frame of reference for the interpretation of obscure passages. As an example of an obscure passage, and of the proper way to handle it, Spinoza cites two statements attributed to Moses: "God is a fire," and "God is jealous." Each of these is perfectly clear in and of itself, although taken literally they are both absurd. The problem is, therefore, to determine whether they are in fact to be understood in a literal fashion. This requires a comparison of these passages with the other relevant passages from Moses and a consideration of the ways in which these expressions were commonly used by Biblical authors. The important point, which Spinoza emphasizes against the defenders of the "reasonableness" of Scripture (the Maimonideans), is that if an alternative reading cannot be found by the above method, then the literal meaning must be accepted as the expression of the author's intent, no matter how absurd this may seem when seen from the standpoint of a more "rational" conception of God. Applying this principle to the above examples, we find that the notion of fire is used to describe anger and jealousy in the Old Testament (Job XXX, 12). We can thus easily reconcile the words of Moses, and conclude that by describing God as fire, Moses was merely trying to indicate, through a common metaphor, that God was jealous. With regard to jealousy itself, the situation is somewhat different. We can find no textual evidence in support of the claim that Scripture denies that God has passions. Hence, despite the completely unphilosophical nature of this doctrine, we must conclude that Moses actually taught that God was jealous, and not try to read some more acceptable sense into the passage by interpreting it metaphorically or allegorically.

Thirdly, one must consider certain topics relevant to the composition of each book. More specifically, we must have information about the life, times and situation of the author, as well as some knowledge of the purpose and occasion of the book in question. The crucial importance of this kind of information is obvious from the analysis of prophecy, wherein it was shown that the teachings of the prophets reflect their dispositions, circumstances and backgrounds. Finally, it is also necessary to inquire into the history of each book. This inquiry includes an investigation of how it was first received, how many different versions existed, and how it became part of the Canon. In short, it is essential to have an accurate historical knowledge of both the author and the text; for it is only in light of such knowledge that the true meaning of the text can be determined, and the "divinity" of Scripture established.

Unfortunately, a number of difficulties prevent the attainment of this knowledge, although Spinoza is quick to point out that they only concern the interpretation of the speculative teaching of the prophets, e.g., their conception of God, and not their moral teachings, which are clear even to the unlearned.[32] Among these difficulties are the very limited nature of our historical knowledge, and the almost total lack of knowledge of the nuances of the ancient Hebrew language. Moreover, above and beyond the difficulties which arise from the limitations of our knowledge, lies the problem that the very traditions and sources on which this knowledge is based are unsound. Spinoza is here referring to the received, orthodox views concerning the authorship of the various books of the Bible; the dates of their composition; their internal agreement; and the histories of their texts. The orthodox views on these matters, in both the Jewish and Christian traditions, was based on the assumption of the absolute infallibility of the text. Accordingly, each book in the Canon is regarded as a unitary work, written in its entirety by the designated author, and the text is held to have remained unaltered in the slightest from the time of its composition until the present. Such views, according to Spinoza, effectively reduce the Bible to nonsense. Thus, he includes within the *Theological-Political Treatise* a detailed discussion of the authorship and history of the main books of the Old Testament, and some brief considerations concerning some of the Epistles in the New Testament.

Typical of Spinoza's approach is his treatment of the Pentateuch, the first Five books of the Bible, often referred to as the "Five Books of Moses." Following the thinly veiled suggestion of the commentator Eben Ezra and the more explicit statements of radical critics such as Isaac de la Peyrère,[33] Spinoza points out a number of obvious reasons why Moses cannot possibly be regarded as the author of the entire Pentateuch. Furthermore, as an alternative explanation, he suggests that these books, as well as many others in the Canon, were compiled from a variety of sources by Ezra, the scribe who, together with Nemiah, is traditionally credited with the reconstruction of the Temple and the revival of the religious tradition after the exile. Spinoza believes that this explains the unity of theme and language which is found in the various books. But since this unity is far from complete, and the various books contain a number of alternative and incompatible narratives, Spinoza also suggests that Ezra did not put the finishing touches on these narratives, but merely collected them from a variety of sources "and sometimes simply set them down, leaving their examination and arrangement to posterity."[34]

The remaining books of the Old Testament, the Prophetic Books and the Wisdom Literature, are dealt with in a similar fashion, although in far less detail. Here Spinoza's general statement must suffice:

An examination of these [the Prophetic Books] assures me that the prophecies therein contained have been compiled from other books, and are not always set down in the exact order in which they were spoken or written by the prophets, but are only such as were collected here and there, so that they are but fragmentary.[35]

The New Testament, with which Spinoza did not have any great familiarity, is treated in an extremely sketchy fashion. The Gospels are completely ignored, and the main point emphasized is that the obvious disagreements between the Apostles must not be resolved by any appeal to a mystical exegesis, but should simply be recognized as a perfectly natural consequence of the fact that each of the Apostolic authors was a teacher as well as a prophet, and, as such, was concerned to communicate the Christian faith *as he understood it.* Thus, basic disagreements, such as that between James and Paul in the roles of faith and works in salvation, are not to be explained away, but frankly accepted as expressions of their different philosophical viewpoints.

Many of the inconsistencies in the various Biblical narratives to which Spinoza points were, of course, commonplace in the rabbinic tradition, and most of his specific interpretations and historical views have been rendered obsolete by subsequent research. This, however, does not minimize Spinoza's achievement in the field of Biblical criticism; for this achievement does not rest on his actual results or specific interpretations, but on the presentation of a method and a program for research through which a genuine, scientific knowledge of the Bible is alone possible.

III *Faith and Superstition*

Spinoza presents his elaborate critique of revelation, the Jewish claim to divine election, and the infallibility of Scripture as part of an endeavor to separate true religion from superstition and to determine the respective spheres of religion, so conceived, and philosophy. Moreover, as we have already seen, one of the reasons which led him to publish the *Theological-Political Treatise* was a desire to answer the charges of atheism which had been raised against him (an endeavor which, if seriously intended by Spinoza, must be ranked as one of the greatest failures in the history of Western thought). Indeed, Spinoza constantly affirms within the work that his arguments affect only superstition, that they do not undermine true religion or the public peace. Accordingly, if we are to complete our picture of Spinoza's views on religion, the analysis of his critique must be supplemented by some consideration of what he considers to be "true religion" and the function which he attributes to it.

Actually, Spinoza's position on this point is quite simple, and, in one respect at least, rather straightforwardly presented in the *Theological-Political Treatise*. Genuine or true religion, the religion taught by all of the prophets and the Apostles, is morality. This morality, however, is presented in a form in which the multitude can appreciate it. In effect, this means that the Bible presents moral principles by means of an appeal to the imagination rather than to the intellect, and hence as decrees of God rather than as eternal truths. Since the multitude are led by their imagination and are not really capable of reason, religion has a necessary social function. Such a view of religion was, of course, hardly original with Spinoza. It was already explicitly formulated by the Arabian philosopher ibn-Rushd, or Averroës, in the twelfth century,[36] and it found expression in many subsequent politically minded thinkers, most notably Machiavelli.[37] Nevertheless, although not original with Spinoza, it is still an integral part of his political thought, as it allows him at once to "save religion" and to guarantee the autonomy of philosophy.

As with his treatment of the other topics, Spinoza's strategy requires that he show that this conception of religion and its function is derived from, rather than imposed upon, Scripture. To this end he emphasizes the fact that, despite the vast disagreement in speculative matters, the Bible in its entirety teaches the same moral doctrine. This doctrine is the demand to love God above all things, and one's neighbor as oneself. But since, as it turns out, the love of God is only manifested in the love of one's neighbor, the moral teaching of the Bible is really reduced to the latter demand. Other moral doctrines found in Scripture, such as those contained in the Ten Commandments, are held to be derived from this principle. This love is therefore the genuine kernel of true religion which survives all historical and philosophical criticism. To the extent to which the Bible teaches this love, and to that extent alone, it can be viewed as the word of God. Moreover, since both the prophets and the Apostles addressed their message to the masses, this moral teaching is expressed in a simple form, easily comprehensible by everyone. The obvious implication from all of this is that one should not try to find in the Bible more than it contains. It does contain a sound moral teaching, expressed in a popular form, and this enables it to inculcate piety and voluntary obedience (really two expressions for the same thing). But it does not contain any speculative truths and should not be treated as an authority in such matters.

On the basis of this conception of the Bible as a textbook of public morality, the function of which is to inspire voluntary obedience, Spinoza proceeds to develop a doctrine of religious faith and even to delineate the basic articles of the "true Catholic faith." This faith, we are told "consists in a knowledge of God, without which obedience to Him would be impossible, and which the mere fact of obedience to Him implies."[38] The point is simply that a willingness to obey God, or what for Spinoza amounts to the same thing, a disposition to practice justice and charity towards one's neighbors, seems to entail certain beliefs. These beliefs, not taken in themselves as beliefs, but viewed as vehicles for fostering the appropriate disposition, are the articles of faith. Spinoza lists seven such "dogmas" which are alledgedly contained in Scripture. They are:

I.   That God or a Supreme Being exists, sovereignly just and merciful, the Exemplar of the true life; that whosoever is ignorant of or disbelieves in His existence cannot obey Him or know Him as a Judge.

II.   That He is One. Nobody will dispute that this doctrine is absolutely necessary for entire devotion, admiration, and love towards God. For devotion, admiration, and love spring from the superiority of one over all else.

III.   That He is omnipresent, or that all things are open to Him, for if anything could be supposed to be concealed from Him, or to be unnoticed by Him, we might doubt or be ignorant of the equity of His judgment as directing all things.

IV.   That He has supreme right and dominion over all things, and that He does nothing under compulsion, but by His absolute fiat and grace. All things are bound to obey Him, He is not bound to obey any.

V.   That the worship of God consists only in justice and charity, or love towards one's neighbour.

VI.   That all those, and those only, who obey God by their manner of life are saved; the rest of mankind, who live under the sway of their pleasures, are lost. If we did not believe this, there would be no reason for obeying God rather than pleasure.

VII.   Lastly, that God forgives the sins of those who repent. No one is free from sin, so that without this belief all would despair of salvation, and there would be no reason for believing in the mercy of God. He who firmly believes that God, out of the mercy and grace with which He directs all things, forgives the sins of men, and who feels his love of God kindled thereby, he, I say, does really know Christ according to the Spirit, and Christ is in him.[39]

The articles of this brief creed are very close to the list of "fundamentals" which were taught by the liberal Christians of the time, such as the Latitudinarians in England, and the Collegiants and Mennonites in Holland, with whom, as we have seen, Spinoza held a close association. These fundamentals were held by the above-mentioned groups to be the essential doctrines which are necessary for salvation. This approach resulted in a simplified, ethically oriented Christianity, with a considerable toleration of differences of opinion with regard to the nonessential or "indifferent" teachings of the various denominations. In reality, however, Spinoza's Averroistic conception of religion is far more radical than these liberal versions of Christianity. These groups desired to simplify doctrine in the interest of both a more sincere faith and a more harmonious society, but they still adhered in a straightforward way to this simplified faith. Spinoza, on the other hand, distinguishes sharply between the truth of these dogmas and their effectiveness in inculcating obedience. Moreover, his concern is solely with the latter. "Faith," he writes, "does not demand that dogmas should be true as that they should be pious—that is, such as will stir up the heart to obey."[40]

Nevertheless, we are here still far from the intellectual love of God of the *Ethics*, and it is only Spinoza's Averroism which can reconcile such a creed with the basic principles of his metaphysics. The God of religious faith, unlike the God of philosophy, is decked out in human attributes, and He functions as a lawgiver and judge. Moreover, the religious man views salvation as a reward for virtue, rather than virtue itself, and he requires a belief in the mercy and forgiveness of God, without which he would despair of this salvation. The point, however, is that such faith does not contradict, but rather operates on an entirely different level than, philosophical truth. Its articles are necessary to inculcate piety or virtue, not in the free man or philosopher, who lives according to the dictates of reason, but in the multitude, who can never rise above the first level of knowledge. Religion therefore appeals to the imagination. It presents moral rules as the commands of a personal God; reinforces these rules with signs and wonders; and connects them with the powerful passions of hope and fear, which are the chief moving forces for the great majority of men. In the end, true religion does not differ from superstition in its truth value, but rather merely in its usefulness for inculcating obedience and mutual love in the multitude. Supersition, by its very nature, is divisive; it breeds intolerance and social chaos. Genuine or ethically oriented religion, on the other hand, is not only a desirable social force, but actually a necessary ingredient in any society that is not composed entirely of philosophers.

It is only in light of this conception of religion that we can understand the role which Spinoza gives to religion in the state and the fact that he grants to the sovereign power supreme right in matters of public worship. First of all, this latter point, which seems to contract his advocacy of the freedom of thought, is a logical consequence of the social function which Spinoza attributes to religion. This function is to inspire voluntary obedience, and it is only appropriate that religion be under control of that power to whom obedience is due, viz., the sovereign. Secondly, far from violating the liberty of thought, such secular control serves to guarantee it. As the situation in the Netherlands made it perfectly clear to Spinoza, ecclesiastical control of public affairs was the great enemy of personal liberty. It was, after all, the Calvinist clergy that was intolerant and that demanded a share of sovereign power. Moreover, Spinoza felt that this demand for political power was not a peculiar aberration on the part of Calvinism, but rather a typical attitude on the part of any religious orthodoxy which holds that man can only be saved by adherence to its particular creed. Like Hobbes, Spinoza therefore saw in secular control over religion a check on ecclesiastical power and on the fanaticism which the exercise of such power inevitably incites in the masses. Finally, since sovereign power can control only actions and not thought, its control over religion is limited to observances or ceremonies. But since these are really indifferent, that is, they are not intrinsically connected with one's beliefs, the sovereign's control over such matters serves only to keep the public peace and does not interfere with anybody's freedom of thought. Thus Spinoza, the apostate Jew, living in a Christian country, advocates an official state religion as the best protection of the freedom of philosophy.

EPILOGUE

The Historical Significance of the Philosophy of Spinoza

A S one might expect of a thinker whose views are as complex and comprehensive as those of Spinoza, he has been interpreted in a variety of ways and has exerted an influence in many different intellectual circles. For example, he was almost universally branded an atheist by his contemporaries, yet a century later he was characterized as "a man drunk with God."[1] In addition, some have tended to see him as one of the founders of modern idealism, while others, specifically Russian Marxists, regard him as one of the great figures in the development of materialism.[2] Anything approaching an adequate treatment of his influence would naturally take us far beyond the limited scope of this study, but we can at least here note some of the main areas in which his influence has been felt.

The first figure of major significance to be decisively influenced by Spinoza was the great German philosopher Gottfried Wilhelm Leibniz. We have already suggested that the meeting between the young Leibniz and the dying Spinoza was one of the great intellectual events of the time. This is because, of all Spinoza's contemporaries, Leibniz alone was able to understand and make a creative use of the teachings of the *Ethics*. Like almost everyone else at the time, Leibniz condemned Spinoza's "atheistical" teachings as found in the *Theological-Political Treatise*. Moreover, on a superficial reading at least, his own pluralistic, ostensibly Christian metaphysical system, which he called the "Monadology," is far removed from Spinoza's uncompromising monism and naturalism. Nevertheless, one does not have to look very far beneath the surface to find a great affinity between the two philosophies. More specifically, Leibniz's own rationalistic method and associated conception of reality as a thoroughly determined, interconnected whole; his conception of substance, wherein each of the infinite number of individual substances shares the self-containedness of Spinoza's own unique sub-

209

stance; his resolution of the mind-body problem through a "pre-established harmony" which denies any interaction; and his emphasis on the notion of force, all strongly suggest the influence of Spinoza.[3] Furthermore, despite his frequent published attacks on Spinoza (which were no doubt at least partly motivated by prudential considerations), Leibniz, in a significant passage which was not published until long after his death, indicates that at one stage of his development he was actually a Spinozist.[4]

Much of the "official" eighteenth-century reaction or lack of reaction to Spinoza was the result of Pierre Bayle's enormously influential article, "Spinoza," which he included in his widely read *Historical and Critical Dictionary*.[5] In it Bayle, a Huguenot and skeptic who had settled in Utrecht after the expulsion of the Protestants from France, described Spinoza as an atheist, albeit one of exemplary character. Moreover, by means of an often gross misinterpretation of the text, he succeeded in depicting the argument of the *Ethics* as a tissue of contradictions and absurdities which could hardly be taken seriously by any rational thinker. Despite Bayle's article, however, or perhaps even partly because of it, Spinoza did exert a fairly considerable subterranean influence throughout the Enlightenment, especially in the more radical circles. The *Ethics*, to be sure, was ignored or at best misunderstood, but the *Theological-Political Treatise* was widely read and provided much of the ammunition for the deistic attacks on the claims of revealed religion.[6]

It was, however, only in the latter part of the eighteenth century in Germany that Spinoza really came into his own and was openly regarded as a major philosophical figure. This radical change in evaluation was inaugurated accidentally by the Romantic philosopher F. H. Jacobi, through his publication in 1785 of a conversation which he had had with Lessing in 1780, shortly before the latter's death. In this conversation, Lessing, who in the last decade of his life had been involved in many theological controversies, reportedly admitted to Jacobi that he rejected the orthodox conception of God.[7] Moreover, in response to Jacobi's accusation of Spinozism, he is said to have asserted: "If I should name myself after anyone, I know no other I should choose,"[8] and later, "There is no other philosophy than the philosophy of Spinoza."[9] Immediately after the publication of this conversation, Moses Mendelssohn, a longtime friend of Lessing, proceeded to "defend" his dead friend against this scandalous attack. Thus began the famous *"Pantheis-*

musstreit" (pantheism debate), which was really a debate over the significance of Spinoza's philosophy, and which played a large role in German intellectual life in the last decade of the century.[10]

The result of this debate was a fresh interest in Spinoza, an interest which was shared by literary figures such as Goethe, whose own concern really antedates this period, and the Romantic poet Novalis; by Romantic religious thinkers such as Herder and Schleiermacher; and finally, by the systematic idealistic philosophers Fichte, Schelling and Hegel. Each of these men found something different in Spinoza, and their appreciation, especially among the last-mentioned philosophers, was hardly uncritical. Nevertheless, they shared a respect for Spinoza's bold metaphysical vision; for his uncompromising determinism which somehow is not inconsistent with freedom; and, above all, for his conception of God. Rather than being dismissed as an atheist, he was now for the first time viewed as a thinker who had grasped the true nature of God, and who had described the relation between God and the world (the dependence of all things on God) in a much more profound and satisfactory manner than traditional theism.[11]

The period from the death of Hegel (1831) to the recent past witnessed something of a decline of the metaphysical spirit. System-building, in the grand manner of Spinoza, Leibniz or Hegel, was rejected as a futile endeavor by most of the philosophical world, with a resulting decline of interest in Spinoza. There are, however, significant exceptions to this. One of the most intriguing of these, at least in terms of interest in Spinoza, is Friedrich Nietzsche. In a note written in 1881 to his friend Franz Overbeck, the great historian of early Christianity, he proclaimed his somewhat belated discovery of Spinoza:

I am utterly amazed, utterly enchanted! I have a *precursor*, and what a precursor! I hardly knew Spinoza: that I should have turned to him just *now*, was inspired by "instinct." Not only is his over-all tendency like mine—namely to make knowledge [*Erkenntnis*] the *most powerful* affect—but in five main points of his doctrine I recognize myself; this most unusual and loneliest thinker is closest to me precisely in *these* matters: he denies the freedom of the will, teleology, the moral world-order, the un-egoistic, and evil. Even though the divergencies are admittedly tremendous, they are due more to the difference in time, culture, and science. *In summa:* my lonesomeness [*Einsamkeit*] . . . is now at least a twosomeness [*Zweisamkeit*].[12]

Another significant exception, with regard to both metaphysics in general and Spinoza's metaphysics in particular, is the idealistic, sometimes called "neo-Hegelian," movement which flourished in England during the last two decades of the nineteenth and the first two decades of the twentieth centuries. Inspired by Hegel and a wide variety of other influences, including Spinoza, these thinkers, of whom the best known are T. H. Green, F. H. Bradley, Bernard Bosanquet and John McTaggart, returned to the conception of philosophy as the attempt to render a rational account of the whole of reality. Many of the thinkers associated with this tradition quite naturally tended to view Spinoza as one of the great precursors of this attempt, and it is certainly no coincidence that scholars and philosophers associated with this group composed some of the most important studies of Spinoza's thought.[13] This conception of philosophy, and respect for Spinoza, was shared by another significant British thinker of the period, Samuel Alexander. Although himself a realist, Alexander was more profoundly influenced by Spinoza than any of the idealists. In his two major works, *Space, Time and Deity* (1920) and *Spinoza and Time* (1921), he developed a naturalistic metaphysical system which was basically modeled after Spinoza's, but which attempted to incorporate the results of the theory of evolution and relativity physics.

The past few years have seen a marked upsurge of interest in metaphysical questions among professional philosophers. This has not led to very many significant comprehensive speculative efforts to grasp the whole of reality in a system, but rather to more modest attempts to resolve certain problems which seem to go beyond the province of the various empirical sciences. The most important of these are the age-old question of the relation between the mind and the body and the equally perennial debate over the freedom of the will. In both of these areas, as well as in the more general field of the "philosophy of mind," philosophers have come to realize that Spinoza has significant contributions to make to contemporary discussions.

Yet for all his influence on subsequent metaphysics, as well as in the fields of Biblical criticism and political philosophy, which we have previously noted, Spinoza never founded anything resembling a school. Indeed, while there are important thinkers who have been called Cartesians (including Spinoza himself), Kantians or Hegelians, there is not a single thinker of any significance that can really be called a disciple of Spinoza or a "Spinozist." This latter expression, to be sure, had a wide currency in the seventeenth and eighteenth century as a term of abuse, but in such a way as to be applied to everyone who in any way criticized orthodox religious views, rather than as characterizing a single philosophical standpoint. Nevertheless, this failure to found a school or to gain disciples, which were the last things in the world that Spinoza wanted, does not diminish his accomplishment or lessen his significance. In particular, his critique of the Judeo-Christian conception of God, his analysis of the concept of substance, his solution to the mind-body problem, his treatment of the human emotions, and his attempt to explain the possibility of freedom within a completely determined universe are major contributions to philosophical thought. Above and beyond this, however, the general spirit of Spinoza's philosophy, if not the medieval terminology and geometrical form in which it is expressed, has been, and will continue to be, attractive to those thinkers who accept the universality of the scientific method, without (like the positivists) denying the possibility of talking intelligently about reality as a whole and who, dismissing the consolation of religious creeds, see in the exercise of reason the only basis for the salvation of man.

Notes and References

Chapter One

1. The following biographical sketch is based on accounts of Spinoza's life in some of the standard sources. These include the contemporary account *The Life of the Late Mr. de Spinoza*, generally attributed to J. M. Lucas, translated and edited by A. Wolf as *The Oldest Biography of Spinoza* (London, 1927; reissued Port Washington, New York, and London: Kennikat Press, 1970); John Colerus, *The Life of Benedict de Spinoza*, English translation (London, 1706), reprinted as an appendix to Sir Frederick Pollock, *Spinoza: His Life and Philosophy*, second edition (London, 1899; reissued by American Scholar Publications, 1966); Pollock's own account in the above-mentioned work; J. Freudenthal, *Spinoza Leben und Lehre*, second edition, edited by Carl Gebhardt, in *Bibliotheca Spinoza curis Societatis Spinozanae*, Vol. V (Heidelberg, 1927); A. Wolf, *The Life of Spinoza*, in the introduction to his edition and translation of *Spinoza's Short Treatise* (London, 1910; reissued New York: Russell and Russell, 1963); Lewis Samuel Feuer, *Spinoza and the Rise of Liberalism* (Boston: Beacon Press, 1958).

2. This material is based on the account in H. Graetz, *Popular History of the Jews*, translated by Rabbi A. B. Rhine, fifth edition (New York: Jordan Publishing Co., 1935), Vol. V, pp. 48–75, and Freudenthal, *Spinoza Leben und Lehre*, pp. 3–16.

3. For an interesting analysis of both the broad culture and the Jewish commitment of these men, see Richard H. Popkin, "The Historical Significance of Sephardic Judaism in 17th Century Amsterdam," *American Sephardi*, Journal of the Sephardic Studies Program of Yeshiva University, Vol. V, No. 1–2 (Autumn, 1971), pp. 18–27.

4. Feuer, *Spinoza and the Rise of Liberalism*, p. 5.

5. *Ibid.*, pp. 8–9.

6. Freudenthal, *Spinoza Leben und Lehre*, pp. 32 ff.

7. For a discussion of Van Den Ende and his relation to Spinoza see Feuer, *Spinoza and the Rise of Liberalism*, pp. 18–20.

8. *Ibid.*, pp. 4–9, 24–37.

9. Lucas, *The Oldest Biography*, p. 52.

10. Wolf, *Spinoza's Short Treatise*, pp. 149–150.

11. For a highly interesting discussion of the whole debate over method at the time, see Leroy E. Loemker, *Struggle for Synthesis and the Seventeenth Century Background of Leibniz's Synthesis of Order and Freedom* (Cambridge, Mass.; Harvard University Press, 1972), especially Chapter 7.

12. *The Chief Works of Benedict de Spinoza*, translated by R. H. M. Elwes, (New York: Dover, 1951), Vol. II, p. 6.

13. Freudenthal, *Spinoza Leben und Lehre*, pp. 112 ff.

14. *The Correspondence of Spinoza*, translated and edited by A. Wolf, (London, 1928; reprinted London: Frank Cass, 1966), Letter VIII, pp. 101–105.

15. *Ibid.*, Letters IX and X, pp. 105–109.

16. *Ibid.*, Letter XXVIII, p. 202. Spinoza here says that he will send to Bouwmeester the text up until the eightieth proposition of the third part. Since the third part in the final version does not have that many propositions, it is assumed that Spinoza originally intended the *Ethics* to be divided into three parts, and that the proposition referred to would thus fall within what eventually became the fourth part.

17. *Ibid.*, Letter XXIX, p. 204.

18. *Ibid.*, Letter XXX, p. 205.

19. Cf. Wolf, *The Life of Spinoza*, pp. lxxvii ff.

20. *Ibid.*, p. lxxxii.

21. *Ibid.*, p. lxxxvi.

22. *Ibid.*, p. lxxxvii–lxxxix.

23. Feuer, *Spinoza and the Rise of Liberalism*, pp. 146–147.

24. *The Correspondence of Spinoza*, Letter XLVII, p. 267.

Chapter Two

1. The classical study of the influences on Spinoza is Stanislaus von Dunin-Borkowski, *Der junge De Spinoza*, second edition (Münster: Aschendorffschen Verlagsbuchhandlung, 1933).

2. Two important discussions of this theme are E. A. Burtt, *The Metaphysical Foundations of Modern Science*, revised edition (New York, Doubleday-Anchor, 1954), and Alexandre Koyré, *From the Closed World to the Infinite Universe* (New York: Harper Torchbooks, 1958).

3. *Opere Complete di Galilee Galilei* (Florence, 1842), translated and cited by Burtt, *Metaphysical Foundations*, p. 75.

4. *Ibid.*, pp. 83–90.

5. René Descartes, *Principles of Philosophy*, Part I, Principle LI, *Philosophical Works of Descartes*, translated by Elizabeth S. Haldane and G. R. T. Ross, reprint (New York: Dover, 1955), Vol. I, p. 239.

6. *Philosophical Works of Descartes*, Vol. I, p. 150.

7. Letter to Princess Elizabeth, June 28, 1643, *Descartes's Philosophical Letters*, translated and edited by Anthony Kenny (Oxford: Clarendon Press, 1970), p. 142.

8. Descartes, *The Passions of the Soul*, Part I, Articles, XXXIV–XXXVIII, *Philosophical Works of Descartes*, Vol. I, pp. 345–349.

9. *The Principles of Descartes' Philosophy*, translated by Halbert Hains Britan (La Salle, 1961), p. 8

10. Cf. Martial Gueroult, *Spinoza I. Dieu* (*Ethique* I) (Paris: Aubier, 1968), pp. 11 ff.

11. See Spinoza's letter to Tschirnhaus, The Hague, Jan. 1675, in *The Correspondence of Spinoza*, p. 301. See also Letters XIX, XXI, LXXIII.

12. For an interesting comparison of Spinoza and Freud on this point, see Stuart Hampshire, *Spinoza* (London: Faber, 1956), pp. 106–109.

13. *The Chief Works of Benedict de Spinoza*, translated by R. H. M. Elwes (New York: Dover, 1951), Vol. II, p. 75.

14. *Ibid.*, p. 77.

15. *Ibid.*, p. 129.

16. Descartes, *Reply to the Second Set of Objections*, in *Philosophical Works of Descartes*, Vol. II, pp. 52–59.

17. One of the best examples of this was provided by Thomas Hobbes, who exerted a tremendous influence on Spinoza, not only in the area of political philosophy, but also in epistemology and psychology. In the Dedicatory Epistle to the Earl of Devonshire, attached to his *De Cive*, Hobbes advocates the application of the geometrical method to the understanding of human actions and moral problems. See Thomas Hobbes, *De Cive*, or *The Citizen*, edited by Sterling P. Lamprecht (New York, Appleton-Century-Crofts, 1949), pp. 3 ff.

18. In favor of the intrinsic connection we can cite as examples, without an effort to be exhaustive, J. Freudenthal, *Spinoza Leben und Lehre*, zweiter Teil, *Die Lehre Spinozas*, pp. 110–111; H. H. Joachim, *A Study of the Ethics of Spinoza*, (New York: Russell and Russell, 1964), pp. 12–13; Gueroult, *Spinoza I*, pp. 15 ff. Against such a connection we can cite Leon Roth, *Spinoza* (London, 1954), pp. 37–39; Hampshire, *Spinoza*, p. 21; and especially H. A. Wolfson, *The Philosophy of Spinoza* (Cambridge, Mass., 1934), Vol. I, pp. 32–60.

19. *The Correspondence of Spinoza*, Letter IX, p. 106.

20. This interpretation is most forcefully presented by Gueroult, *Spinoza I*, pp. 21 ff.

21. *Chief Works*, tr. Elwes, Vol. II, p. 35.

22. *Ibid.*, p. 34.

23. *Ibid.*, pp. 13–14.

24. The significance of genetic definitions for Spinoza is emphasized by Gueroult, *Spinoza I*, pp. 33 ff. and by Ernst Cassirer, *Das Erkenntnisproblem in der Philosophie und Wissenschaft der neueren Zeit* (Berlin: Bruno Cassirer, 1911), pp. 90 ff.

25. Cf. Harald Höffding, *Spinozas Ethica: Analyse und Charakteristik* (London and Heidelberg: Curis Societatis Spinozanae, 1924), p. 6.

26. *Chief Works*, tr. Elwes, Vol. II, p. 36.
27. *Ibid.*, p. 14.

Chapter Three

1. Aristotle, *Categoriae*, Chapter V, 4ª lines 10–12, in *The Works of Aristotle Translated into English*, edited by W. D. Ross, Vol. I, translated by E. M. Edghill (London: Oxford University Press, 1928).

2. *Ibid.*, especially Chapter V.

3. Descartes, *Reply to the Second Set of Objections*, in *Philosophical Works of Descartes*, Vol. II, p. 53.

4. Descartes, *Principles of Philosophy*, Part I, Principle LIII, *Philosophical Works of Descartes*, Vol. I, p. 240.

5. *Ibid.*, Principles LVI, LXI, LXIV, LXV.

6. This is quite forcefully argued by E. M. Curley, *Spinoza's Metaphysics: An Essay in Interpretation* (Cambridge, Mass: Harvard University Press, 1969), pp. 36 ff. Many of the views expressed in this chapter are based on his analysis.

7. For a general discussion of this whole controversy, see Gueroult, *Spinoza I*, pp. 428–461. Discussions on this point are also to be found in all of the English commentators to whom we have referred.

8. Cf. *The Correspondence of Spinoza*, Letter IX, p. 108, and *Short Treatise*, Part I, Chapter II, p. 25.

9. Cf. Curley, *Spinoza's Metaphysics*, pp. 18 ff.

10. This is claimed in an especially sharp manner by Cassirer, *Das Erkenntnisproblem*, Vol. II, pp. 119 ff.

11. Nicolas Malebranche, *De la Recherche de la Vérité*, Book III, Chapter X. The parallel is pointed out by Höffding, *Spinozas Ethica*, pp. 30–31.

12. *Philosophical Works of Descartes*, Vol. I, p. 181.

13. The famous formula *"Deus seu Natura"* (God or Nature), which indicates a strict equivalency, occurs in the preface to Part IV. *Chief Works*, tr. Elwes, Vol. II, p. 188.

14. The distinction between *natura naturans* and *natura naturata* also occurs in the *Short Treatise*, Part I, Chapters VIII and IX, pp. 56–58.

15. This division of the argument is suggested by Gueroult, *Spinoza I*, pp. 243–244.

16. *The Correspondence of Spinoza*, Letter LXXXII, p. 364.

17. *Ibid.*, Letter LXXXIII, p. 365.

18. Cf. G. H. R. Parkinson, *Spinoza's Theory of Knowledge* (Oxford: Clarendon Press, 1954), p. 64; Curley, *Spinoza's Metaphysics*, p. 45 ff; Hampshire, *Spinoza*, p. 103.

19. Cf. Curley, *Spinoza's Metaphysics*, p. 49.

20. Cf. Wolfson, *The Philosophy of Spinoza*, Vol. I, p. 322.

21. For an extended analysis of this definition, see Wolfson, *The Philosophy of Spinoza*, Vol. I, pp. 347–369.

22. The classical statement of this doctrine is by St. Thomas Aquinas, *Concerning Being and Essence*, translated by George G. Leckie (New York: Appleton-Century-Crofts, 1937), pp. 28–32.

23. Cf. *Theological-Political Treatise*, Chapter III, in *Chief Works*, tr. Elwes, Vol. I, p. 44.

24. Cf. Wolfson, *The Philosophy of Spinoza*, Vol. I, pp. 372–376.

25. Cf. *Ethics* I, Prop. XV, Scholium, and *The Correspondence of Spinoza*, Letter XII, pp. 115–122.

26. Cf. Pollock, *Spinoza: His Life and Philosophy*, p. 142; Höffding, *Spinozas Ethica*, p. 44; Parkinson, *Spinoza's Theory of Knowledge*, p. 79.

27. *On the Improvement of the Understanding*, in *Chief Works*, tr. Elwes, Vol. II, p. 37.

28. *Ibid.*

29. *Short Treatise*, Part I, Chapter IX, p. 57.

30. *The Correspondence of Spinoza*, Letter LXIV, p. 308.

31. Descartes, *Principles of Philosophy*, Part II, Prop. XXXVI.

32. Cf. Joachim, *A Study of the Ethics of Spinoza*, pp. 84–85; Gueroult, *Spinoza I*, p. 324.

33. Cf. Höffding, *Spinozas Ethica*, pp. 41 ff.

34. See Curley, *Spinoza's Metaphysics*, Chapter 2, for an extended and sophisticated development of this theme.

35. This is based largely on the analysis of Gueroult, *Spinoza I*, pp. 355–358.

36. This is suggested by Höffding, *Spinozas Ethica*, p. 45, who argues for the importance of this proposition in connection with Spinoza's psychology and ethical theory.

Chapter Four

1. Two interesting treatments of Spinoza's doctrine from this point of view are: Wallace T. Matson, "Spinoza's Theory of Mind," and Douglas Odegard, "The Body Identical with the Human Mind: A Problem in Spinoza's Philosophy," both of which appeared in the *Monist*, Vol. LV, No. 4 (October, 1971), an issue devoted exclusively to the philosophy of Spinoza.

2. Matson, "Spinoza's Theory of Mind," p. 571, discusses Spinoza's opposition to reductive materialism and to Hobbes's doctrine in particular.

3. The importance of Hobbes in this regard is pointed out by Cassirer, *Das Erkenntnisproblem*, Vol. II, pp. 99–102.

4. This is most clearly affirmed in *On the Improvement of the Understanding*, in *Chief Works*, tr. Elwes, Vol. II, pp. 12–13.

5. Matson, "Spinoza's Theory of Mind," p. 574.

6. For a detailed discussion of this topic see Robert McRae, "Idea as a Philosophical Term in the Seventeenth Century," *Journal of the History of Ideas*, Vol. XXVI, No. 2 (April–June 1965), pp. 175 ff.

7. *The Correspondence of Spinoza*, Letter LXVI, p. 310.

8. This topic is discussed in great detail by H. H. Joachim, *Spinoza's Tractatus de Intellectus Emendatione* (Oxford: Clarendon Press, 1940), pp. 74 ff.

9. Cf. Parkinson, *Spinoza's Theory of Knowledge*, pp. 110–111.

10. This account owes a good deal to the excellent discussion of this topic by Hans Jonas, "Spinoza and the Theory of Organism," *Journal of the History of Philosophy*, Vol. III (1965), pp. 43–58, reprinted in *Spinoza, A Collection of Critical Essays*, edited by Marjorie Grene (New York: Doubleday-Anchor, 1973), pp. 259–278.

11. *The Correspondence of Spinoza*, Letter LX, p. 300.

12. A thorough and interesting analysis of Spinoza's conception of truth and its relation to traditional theories is provided by Thomas Carson Mark, *Spinoza's Theory of Truth* (New York: Columbia University Press, 1972). On this issue, see also Parkinson, *Spinoza's Theory of Knowledge*, Chapter VI, "Truth and Falsity."

13. The often-overlooked possibility of an idea functioning as the ideatum or object of another idea is pointed out by Mark, *Spinoza's Theory of Truth*, pp. 61–64.

14. This is supplemented by an important account in *On the Improvement of the Understanding*, in *Chief Works*, tr. Elwes, Vol. II, pp. 24–28.

15. Critics of Spinoza on this point often argue that he uses "idea" in two incompatible senses; so that when he talks about the mind as the "idea of the body" he means by "idea" merely mental correlate, and when he talks about the mind's ideas of other objects he is using "idea" to refer to an act of thought or concept. The sharpest expressions of this view are by Pollock, *Spinoza: His Life and Philosophy*, pp. 124 ff., and H. Barker, "Notes on the Second Part of Spinoza's *Ethics*, II," *Mind*, Vol. XLVII (1938), reprinted in *Studies in Spinoza: Critical and Interpretive Essays*, edited by Paul S. Kashap (Berkeley: University of California Press, 1972), pp. 140 ff. In fact, however, the problem of knowledge, as Spinoza views it, is really to explain how an idea in the first sense can represent external objects, and the relation of these objects to the body plays a crucial part in his analysis. For a detailed discussion of this view, and a refutation of the charge of equivocation, see H. F. Hallett, "On a Reputed Equivoque in the Philosophy of Spinoza," *Studies in Spinoza: Critical and Interpretive Essays*, pp. 168–187.

16. For a detailed discussion of Spinoza's doctrine of imagination and the various senses in which he uses the notion, see Parkinson, *Spinoza's Theory of Knowledge*, pp. 138–162.

17. This line of thought is found in an especially clear form in David Hume, the great eighteenth-century Scottish empiricist and skeptic, who developed this view in both *A Treatise of Human Nature* (1739) and *An Enquiry Concerning Human Understanding* (1748). Whether or not Hume actually read Spinoza is uncertain, but his analysis of the role of habit in the

formation of our beliefs is in many ways similar to Spinoza's. Unlike Spinoza, however, Hume extended this analysis to almost the entire realm of thought, including much of what Spinoza terms the "order of the intellect," thereby arriving at his profoundly skeptical conclusions.

18. They were called such by Herbert of Cherbury in his influential work *De Veritate* (1624).

19. This line of criticism is specifically developed by John Locke in his *Essay Concerning Human Understanding* (1690), Book One.

20. Descartes, *Notes Against a Program,* in *Philosophical Works of Descartes*, Vol. I, p. 442.

21. Cf. Mark, *Spinoza's Theory of Truth*, p. 50.

22. This interpretation is advanced by Parkinson, *Spinoza's Theory of Knowledge*, p. 165.

23. Spinoza uses precisely the same example to make essentially the same point in both the *Short Treatise*, pp. 67–68, and *On the Improvement of the Understanding*, in *Chief Works*, tr. Elwes, Vol. II, pp. 9–10.

Chapter Five

1. Cf. Hampshire, *Spinoza*, especially pp. 59–62.

2. *Passions of the Soul*, Part I, Article XIX, *Philosophical Works of Descartes*, Vol. I, p. 340.

3. *Ibid.*, Article XXV, p. 343.

4. *Ibid.*, Article L, p. 355.

5. Cf. James Martineau, *A Study of Spinoza* (London: Macmillan, 1882), p. 150; and David Bidney, *The Psychology and Ethics of Spinoza*, second edition (New York: Russell and Russell, 1962), pp. 88–100, 398.

6. *Ethics* III, Definitions of the Emotions, Def. I, in *Chief Works*, tr. Elwes, Vol. II, p. 173.

7. Spinoza discusses this conception of death in an interesting scholium to *Ethics* IV, Prop. XXXIX, in *Chief Works*, tr. Elwes, Vol. II, p. 216.

8. Bidney, *Psychology and Ethics*, contends on the contrary that Spinoza simply adhered to two distinct and inconsistent theories; cf. pp. 98–99.

9. Spinoza's analysis stands in an interesting analogy with, and was perhaps inspired by, Hobbes's reflection that man's quest for power never ceases, "because he cannot assure the power and means to live well, which he hath present, without the acquisition of more," *Leviathan*, Part I, Chapter II (London: Oxford University Press, 1909), p. 75. The point for both is that man (and for Spinoza everything in nature) must constantly endeavor to increase his power merely in order to preserve his actual level of existence.

10. *Ethics* III, Definitions of the Emotions, Def. III, in *Chief Works*, tr. Elwes, Vol. II, p. 174.

11. Cf. Martineau, *A Study of Spinoza*, p. 260.

12. Cf. Wolfson, *The Philosophy of Spinoza*, Vol. II, p. 212.

13. *Ibid.*, p. 213.

14. *Ibid.*, p. 215.

15. Feuer, *Spinoza and the Rise of Liberalism*, emphasizes this aspect of Spinoza's thought. See especially pp. 40–52.

16. *Ibid.*, pp. 200–201.

17. Wolfson, *The Philosophy of Spinoza*, Vol. II, p. 265.

18. The expression "immortality of the soul" (*ziels onsterfelijkheid*) is used in the *Short Treatise*, Part II, Chapter XXIII, p. 136.

19. Most commentators have called attention to the obvious contradiction between these assertions and the central teachings of the *Ethics*, and they endeavor to explain these passages either in terms of carelessness on Spinoza's part or a concession to ordinary ways of speaking. For an analysis and critique of some of the literature on this point, see Errol E. Harris, "Spinoza's Theory of Human Immortality," *Monist*, Vol. LV, No. 4 (October, 1971). The interpretation which we offer here is close to the "standard interpretation," although rather than accusing Spinoza of carelessness, we attempt to interpret his use of theological language in light of his generally polemical stance toward the religious tradition.

20. H. H. Joachim here argues that "this present life" refers to "our life so far as we are imaginative" (*A Study of the Ethics of Spinoza* p. 296). The context of the phrase, however, makes it clear that Spinoza is referring not merely to the imaginative life per se, but to the life of conflict, which includes reason, intuitive knowledge and imagination.

21. Here Joachim argues both that this expression is "a momentary slip" and that Spinoza has two distinct senses of duration, one which is sharply opposed to eternity, and the other a "general term, of which eternal existence and temporal existence are forms" (*ibid.*, pp. 294–298).

22. The question of personal identity was first specifically raised by John Locke in his *Essay Concerning Human Understanding*, Book Two, Chapter XXVII. Locke identified the identity of a person with the continuity of memory. For an analysis of Locke's theory and its historical significance, see my "Locke's Theory of Personal Identity; a Re-examination," *Journal of the History of Ideas*, Vol. XXVII, No. 1 (January-March, 1966), pp. 41–58.

23. Spinoza himself admits as much in the same passage in which he discusses physical death. See note 7, above.

24. *The Correspondence of Spinoza*, Letter II, pp. 115–122.

25. Joachim, *A Study of the Ethics of Spinoza*, p. 298.

26. A similar interpretation is offered by Elmer Ellsworth Powell, *Spinoza and Religion* (Chicago: Open Court Publishing Co., 1906), pp. 268–269. Powell also points out that Spinoza here had some Neoplatonic predecessors who interpreted eternality in an analogous fashion.

27. *Ibid.*, p. 257.

28. *Ibid.*, pp. 263–265.

29. This whole point is well stated by Joachim, *A Study of the Ethics of Spinoza*, pp. 303–306.

Chapter Six

1. Benedict de Spinoza, *Theologoical-Political Treatise*, in *The Political Works*, edited and translated by A. G. Wernham (Oxford, Clarendon Press, 1958), p. 231. This edition contains the Latin text and English translation of the entire *Political Treatise* and the specifically political portions of the *Theological-Political Treatise*. All references to Spinoza's political writings in this chapter will be to this edition, hereafter referred to as "Wernham," while for the benefit of those who are using other editions, the references will also cite the title, chapter, and, with regard to the first work, the section.

2. J. W. Gough, *The Social Contract* (Oxford: Clarendon Press, 1957), second edition, p. 2.

3. *Ibid.*, p. 3.

4. Cf. Hobbes, *De Cive*, p. 24.

5. *Ibid.*, p. 28.

6. *Leviathan*, pp. 96–97.

7. Cf. Hobbes, *De Cive*, p. 32.

8. *Ibid.*, pp. 35–36.

9. *Political Treatise*, II, 8, Wernham, p. 273.

10. Cf. Wernham, pp. 14–15; Robert J. McShea, *The Political Philosophy of Spinoza* (New York: Columbia University Press, 1968), p. 138.

11. *Political Treatise*, II, 12, Wernham, p. 275.

12. *Theological-Political Treatise*, XVI, Wernham, p. 143.

13. *Ibid.*, Wernham, p. 129.

14. *Ibid.*, p. 133.

15. *Political Treatise*, I, 6, Wernham, p. 265.

16. *Ibid.*, VI, 3, Wernham, p. 315.

17. This interpretation is offered by Wernham, *The Political Writings*, p. 216, and by C. E. Vaughan, *Studies in the History of Political Philosophy Before and After Rousseau* (Manchester: University of Manchester Press, 1925; reprinted New York: Russell and Russell, 1960), Vol. I, p. 71.

18. This is implied by McShea, *The Political Philosophy of Spinoza*, pp. 85–90, and it is even more strongly suggested by Spinoza's own remarks (*Political Treatise*, II, 1, Wernham, p. 267), that he is merely explaining and giving a formal proof of views already expressed in the *Theological-Political Treatise* and the *Ethics*.

19. Cf. Wernham, p. 26.

20. *Political Treatise*, III, 2, Wernham, p. 287.

21. *Ibid.*, III, 5, Wernham, p. 287.

22. *Ibid.*

23. *The Correspondence of Spinoza*, Letter L, p. 269.

24. *De Cive*, pp. 43–44.

25. *Ibid.*, pp. 39–40.

26. *Ibid.*, p. 51.

27. *Ibid.*, p. 79.

28. For a discussion of this topic see McShea, *The Political Philosophy of Spinoza*, p. 142.

29. *Political Treatise*, III, 9, Wernham, p. 291.

30. *Theological-Political Treatise*, XX, Wernham, p. 235.

31. *Ibid.*

32. *Ibid.*, p. 227.

33. *Ibid.*

34. *Political Treatise*, VI, 4, Wernham, p. 311.

35. *Ibid.*, VI, 5, Wernham, p. 311.

36. *Theological-Political Treatise*, XX, p. 239.

37. *Ibid.*, XVI, Wernham, p. 137.

38. *Ibid.*

39. Cf. Gail Belaief, *Spinoza's Philosophy of Law* (The Hague and Paris: Mouton, 1971), especially pp. 73 ff.

40. *Theological-Political Treatise*, XX, Wernham, p. 231.

41. *Ibid.*, XIX, Wernham, p. 211.

42. *Political Treatise*, IV, 6, Wernham, p. 289.

43. *Theological-Political Treatise*, XVIII, Wernham, p. 195.

44. *Ibid.*, p. 201.

45. *Political Treatise*, VI, 6, Wernham, p. 315.

46. *Ibid.*, V, 5, Wernham, p. 317.

47. *Ibid.*

48. *Ibid.*, V, 17, Wernham, p. 323.

49. *Ibid.*, VII, 11, Wernham, pp. 343–345.

50. *Ibid.*, VI, 12, Wernham, p. 321.

51. Feuer, *Spinoza and the Rise of Liberalism*, p. 188.

52. Niccolo Machiavelli, *The Prince*, Chapters XII–XIII; *The Discourses*, Book Two, Chapter 20.

53. As Feuer points out, the use of a professional army and the hiring of mercenaries were policies of the Orangist Party (*Spinoza and the Rise of Liberalism*, p. 188).

54. *Political Treatise*, VII, 31, Wernham, p. 365.

55. *Ibid.*, X, 9, Wernham, p. 437.

56. Cf. Feuer, *Spinoza and the Rise of Liberalism*, especially pp. 182–192.

57. *Political Treatise*, VIII, 1, Wernham, p. 367.

58. *Ibid.*, VIII, 3, Wernham, p. 371.

59. *Ibid.*

60. Feuer, *Spinoza and the Rise of Liberalism*, p. 165.

61. *Political Treatise*, VIII, 7, Wernham, p. 373.

62. *Ibid.*, IX, 14, Wernham, p. 427.

63. *Ibid.*, IX, 14–15, Wernham, pp. 425–427.

64. *Ibid.*, VIII, 11–19, Wernham, pp. 377–383.
65. *Ibid.*, VIII, 20–28, Wernham, pp. 383–391.
66. *Ibid.*, VIII, 31–34, Wernham, pp. 393–401.
67. *Ibid.*, VIII, 37–41, Wernham, pp. 403–407.
68. *Ibid.*, VIII, 9, Wernham, pp. 373–377.
69. *Ibid.*, VIII, 10, Wernham, p. 377.
70. *Ibid.*, IX, 14, Wernham, p. 427.
71. *Ibid.*, XI, 4, Wernham, pp. 443–445.
72. Hobbes, *De Cive*, p. 106.
73. Feuer, *Spinoza and the Rise of Liberalism*, especially pp. 196–197.

Chapter Seven

1. Many of the remarks in this chapter concerning Spinoza's strategy in the *Theological-Political Treatise* are suggested by the discussion of Leo Strauss, *Spinoza's Critique of Religion*, translated by E. M. Sinclair (New York: Schocken Books, 1965), especially pp. 107–146.

2. *Theological-Political Treatise*, in *The Chief Works of Benedict de Spinoza*, translated by R. H. M. Elwes (New York-Dover, 1951), Vol. I, especially pp. 113–191. All references to this work in this chapter will be to the Elwes translation, which is the standard English version of the complete text. The Wernham version, which was cited in the last chapter, contains only the political portions.

3. *Ibid.*, p. 114.
4. *Ibid.*, p. 115.
5. *Ibid.*, pp. 115–118.
6. *Ibid.*, p. 13.
7. *Ibid.*, p. 19.
8. *Ibid.*, p. 24.
9. *Ibid.*, pp. 31–32.
10. *Ibid.*, p. 34.
11. *Ibid.*, pp. 95–96.
12. *Ibid.*, p. 82.
13. *Ibid.*, p. 83.
14. *Ibid.*
15. *Ibid.*, p. 87.
16. *Ibid.*, p. 86.
17. *Ibid.*, p. 43.
18. *Ibid.*, p. 46.
19. *Ibid.*, p. 49.
20. *Ibid.*, p. 55.
21. *Ibid.*, p. 56.
22. *Ibid.*
23. *Ibid.*, p. 60.
24. *Ibid.*, p. 63.

25. *Ibid.*, p. 64.

26. *Ibid.*, pp. 69–80.

27. *Ibid.*, p. 99.

28. *Ibid.*

29. *Ibid.*

30. *Ibid.*, p. 101.

31. *Ibid.*

32. *Ibid.*, pp. 112–113.

33. For a discussion of Isaac de la Peyrère and his relation to Spinoza, see Strauss, *Spinoza's Critique of Religion*, pp. 64–85.

34. *Theological-Political Treatise*, p. 133.

35. *Ibid.*, p. 147.

36. Averroës expresses this view most clearly in his classic work, *On the Harmony of Religion and Philosophy*, translated by George F. Hourani, Unesco Collection of Great Works, E. J. W. Gibb Memorial Series, New Series XXI (London: Luzac and Co., 1967). For a clear statement of the Averroistic position and its influence in the West, see Etienne Gilson, *Reason and Revelation in the Middle Ages* (New York: Scribner's, 1938), pp. 37–66.

37. For a discussion of Machiavelli's religious views in relation to those of Spinoza, see Strauss, *Spinoza's Critique of Religion* pp. 48–49.

38. *Theological-Political Treatise*, p. 184.

39. *Ibid.*, pp. 186–187.

40. *Ibid.*, p. 185.

Epilogue

1. Novalis, *Hymns to the Night and Other Selected Writings*, translated and edited by Charles E. Passage (New York: Liberal Arts Press, 1960), p. 72.

2. Cf. George Louis Kline, *Spinoza in Soviet Philosophy* (London: Routledge and Kegan Paul, 1952).

3. Cf. Roth, *Spinoza*, pp. 204–209. For a full-scale discussion of the whole question of the relation between Leibniz and Spinoza, see Ludwig Stein, *Leibniz und Spinoza* (Berlin: G. Reimer, 1890) and Georges Friedmann, *Leibniz et Spinoza*, second edition, revised (Paris: Gallimard, 1962).

4. G. W. Leibniz, *New Essays Concerning Human Understanding*, Book One, Chapter One, translated by Alfred C. Langley (La Salle, Illinois: Open Court Publishing Co., 1949), p. 69.

5. For a convenient English version, see Pierre Bayle, *Historical and Critical Dictionary*, selections edited and translated by Richard H. Popkin, with the assistance of Craig Brush (Indianapolis: Bobbs-Merrill, 1965), pp. 288–338.

6. Cf. Roth, *Spinoza*, pp. 199–202. For a detailed treatment of the influence of Spinoza on French thought in the eighteenth century, see Paul

Vernière, *Spinoza et la Pensée Français avant la Révolution*, 2 vols. (Paris: Presses Universitaires de France, 1954).

7. This was published by Jacobi in his *Über die Lehre des Spinoza in Briefen an den Herrn Moses Mendelssohn*. A convenient reprinting of the conversation is to be found in Gotthold Ephraim Lessing, *Gesammelte Werke*, edited by Paul Rilla (Berlin: Aufbau Verlag, 1956), Vol. VIII, pp. 616–634. For an analysis of this conversation and of Lessing's relation to Spinoza, see my *Lessing and the Enlightenment* (Ann Arbor: University of Michigan Press, 1966), especially pp. 67–79.

8. Lessing, *Gesammelte Werke*, Vol. VIII, p. 54.

9. *Ibid.*, p. 55.

10. The chief literature from this debate has been edited and published by Heinrich Scholz, *Die Hauptschriften zum Pantheismusstreit zwischen Jacobi und Mendelssohn* (Berlin: Kantgesellschaft, 1916).

11. For a general discussion of the religious thought of this period and the views on Spinoza, see A. C. McGiffert, "The God of Spinoza as Interpreted by Herder," *Hibbert Journal*, Vol. III (1904–1905), pp. 706 ff., and Friederick H. Burkhardt's introduction to his translation of Johann Gottfried Herder's *God: Some Conversations* (New York: Hafner, 1949).

12. Quoted by Walter Kaufman, *Nietzsche: Philosopher, Psychologist, Anti-Christ* (New York: Meridian Books, 1958), p. 111.

13. Among these works, all previously cited, are James Martineau, *A Study of Spinoza* (1882), Sir Frederick Pollock, *Spinoza: His Life and Thought* (1889), and the two commentaries by H. H. Joachim, *A Study of the Ethics of Spinoza* (1901), and *Spinoza's Tractatus de Intellectus Emendatione* (published posthumously, 1940). In this same category we should also include John Caird, *Spinoza* (Edinburgh and London: Blackwood, 1888), and the discussion of Spinoza's political philosophy in T. H. Green, *Lectures on the Principles of Political Obligation*, first delivered in 1879 (Ann Arbor: University of Michigan Press, 1967), pp. 49–58.

Selected Bibliography

PRIMARY SOURCES

A. Spinoza's Collected Works

Spinoza Opera, 4 vols. Ed. by Carl Gebhardt. Heidelberg: Carl Winter, 1925. The standard edition.

Benedicti de Spinoza Opera, 4 vols. bound as 2. 3rd ed. Ed. by J. Van Vloten and J. P. N. Land. The Hague: Martinus Nijhoff, 1914. An accessible and relatively inexpensive edition.

B. English Translations

The Chief Works of Spinoza, 2 vols. Tr. by R. H. M. Elwes. New York: Dover, 1951. The most complete and most readily available English version of Spinoza.

The Correspondence of Spinoza. Tr. by A. Wolf. London: Frank Cass and Co., 1966.

The Principles of Descartes' Philosophy. Tr. by Halbert Hains Britan. La Salle, Illinois: The Open Court Publishing Co., 1961. This includes as an appendix the *Cogitata Metaphysica*.

Benedict de Spinoza: The Political Works. Ed. and tr. by A. G. Wernham. Oxford: Clarendon Press, 1958. Contains the Latin text and the best English translation of the *Political Treatise* and the political portions of the *Theological-Political Treatise*.

Short Treatise on God, Man and His Well Being. Tr. by A. Wolf. New York: Russell and Russell, 1967. Also contains a life of Spinoza and a commentary on the text.

SECONDARY SOURCES

BAYLE, PIERRE. *Historical and Critical Dictionary*. Selections ed. and tr. by Richard H. Popkin, with the assistance of Craig Brush. Indianapolis: Bobbs-Merrill, 1965.

BELAIEF, GAIL. *Spinoza's Philosophy of Law*. The Hague: Mouton, 1971.

BIDNEY, DAVID. *The Psychology and Ethics of Spinoza*. 2nd ed. New York: Russell and Russell, 1962. Reprint of New Haven edition, 1940.

BRÉHIER, EMILE. *The History of Philosophy: The Seventeenth Century*. Tr. by Wade Bastin. Chicago: University of Chicago Press, 1966.

BRUNSCHVICG, LÉON. *Spinoza et ses Contemporains*. 3rd ed. Paris: Librairie Félix Alcon, 1923.

CAIRD, JOHN. *Spinoza*. Edinburgh and London: W. Blackwood and Sons, 1888.

CASSIRER, ERNST. *Das Erkenntnisproblem in der Philosophie und Wissenschaft der neueren Zeit*. Berlin: Bruno Cassirer, 1911.

CURLEY, E. M. *Spinoza's Metaphysics: An Essay in Interpretation*. Cambridge, Mass.: Harvard University Press, 1969.

DE DEUGD, C. D. *The Significance of Spinoza's First Kind of Knowledge*. Assen: Van Gorcum, 1966.

DELBOS, VICTOR. *Le Spinozisme*. Paris: Librairie Philosophique J. Vrin, 1968.

DUNIN, BORKOWSKI, STANISLAUS VON. *Der junge De Spinoza*. 2nd ed. Münster: Aschendorffschen Verlagsbuchhandlung, 1933.

DUNNER, JOSEPH. *Baruch Spinoza and Western Democracy*. New York: Philosophical Library, 1955.

FEUER, LEWIS SAMUEL. *Spinoza and the Rise of Liberalism*. Boston: Beacon Press, 1958.

FOUCHER DE CAREIL, COUNT A., ed. *A Refutation Recently Discovered of Spinoza by Leibniz*. Tr. by Rev. O. F. Owen. Edinburgh: Thomas Constable, 1855.

FREUDENTHAL, J. *Spinoza Leben und Lehre*. 2nd ed. by Carl Gebhardt in *Bibliotheca Spinoza curis Societatis Spinozanae*, Vol. V. Heidelberg, 1927.

FRIEDMANN, GEORGE. *Leibniz et Spinoza*. 2nd ed. Paris: Gallimard, 1962.

GOUGH, J. W. *The Social Contract*. 2nd ed. Oxford: Clarendon Press, 1957.

GREEN, T. H. *Lectures on the Principles of Political Obligation*. Ann Arbor: University of Michigan Press, 1967. First published, London, 1882.

GRENE, MARJORIE, ed. *Spinoza: A Collection of Critical Essays*. New York: Doubleday-Anchor, 1973. Contains an important collection of essays on Spinoza, a number of which have been referred to in the Notes.

GUEROULT, MARTIAL. *Etudes sur Descartes, Spinoza, Malebranche et Leibniz*. Hildesheim: Georg Olms, 1970.

———. *Spinoza I. Dieu (Ethique I)*. Paris: Aubier, 1968.

HALLETT, H. F. *Creation, Emanation, Salvation: A Spinozistic Study*. The Hague: Martinus Nijhoff, 1962.

HAMPSHIRE, STUART. *Spinoza*. London: Faber, 1956.

HERDER, JOHANN GOTTFRIED. *God: Some Conversations*. Tr. with an introduction by Frederick H. Burkhardt. New York: Hafner, 1949.

HÖFFDING, HARALD. *Spinozas Ethica: Analyse und Charakteristik*. London and Heidelberg: Curis Societatis Spinozanae, 1924.

HUBBELING, H. C. *Spinoza's Methodology*. Assen: Van Gorcum, 1964.

JACOBI, F. H. *Über die Lehre des Spinoza in Briefen an den Herrn Moses*

Mendelssohn in Gotthold Ephraim Lessing, *Gesammelte Werke*, Vol. VIII, ed. by Paul Rilla. Berlin: Aufbau Verlag, 1956.

JOACHIM, H. H. *Spinoza's Tractatus de Intellectus Emendatione*. Oxford: Clarendon Press, 1940.

———. *A Study of the Ethics of Spinoza*. New York: Russell and Russell, 1964. Reprint of London edition, 1901.

JOEL, M. *Spinozas Theologisch-Politischer Traktat*. Breslau: Schletter, 1870.

KASHAP, PAUL S., ed. *Studies in Spinoza: Critical and Interpretive Essays*. Berkeley, Los Angeles and London: University of California Press, 1972. Another important volume of essays on Spinoza, to many of which reference has been made in the Notes.

KLINE, GEORGE LOUIS, ed. and tr. *Spinoza in Soviet Philosophy*. London: Routledge and Kegan Paul, 1952.

LOEMKER, LEROY E. *Struggle for Synthesis and the Seventeenth Century Background of Leibniz's Synthesis of Order and Freedom*. Cambridge, Mass.: Harvard University Press, 1972.

LUCAS, J. M. *The Life of the Late Mr. de Spinoza*. ed. and tr. by A. Wolf, *The Oldest Biography of Spinoza*. Port Washington, New York, and London: Kennikat Press, 1970. Reprint of London edition, 1927.

MARK, THOMAS CARSON. *Spinoza's Theory of Truth*. New York: Columbia University Press, 1972.

MARTINEAU, JAMES. *A Study of Spinoza*. London: Macmillan, 1882.

McGIFFERT, A. C. "The God of Spinoza as Interpreted by Herder," *Hibbert Journal*, Vol. III (1904–1905), pp. 706 ff.

McKEON, RICHARD PETER. *The Philosophy of Spinoza*. New York: Longmans, Green, 1928.

McSHEA, ROBERT J. *The Political Philosophy of Spinoza*. New York: Columbia University Press, 1968.

Monist, Vol LV, No. 4 (October, 1971). An issue dedicated exclusively to Spinoza; contains a number of important papers which have been cited in the notes.

PARKINSON, G. H. R. *Spinoza's Theory of Knowledge*. Oxford: Clarendon Press, 1954.

POLLOCK, SIR FREDERICK. *Spinoza: His Life and Philosophy*. 2nd ed. New York: American Scholar Publications, 1966. Reprint of London edition, 1899; includes as an appendix John Colerus, *The Life of Benedict de Spinoza*.

POPKIN, RICHARD H. "The Historical Significance of Sephardic Judaism in 17th Century Amsterdam," *American Sephardi*, Vol. V, No. 1–2 (Autumn, 1971), pp. 18–27.

POWELL, ELMER ELLSWORTH. *Spinoza and Religion*. Chicago: Open Court Publishing Co., 1906.

ROTH, LEON. *Spinoza, Descartes and Maimonides*. Oxford: Clarendon Press, 1924.

————. *Spinoza*. London: Allen and Unwin, 1954.

SCHOLZ, HEINRICH, ed. *Die Hauptschriften zum Pantheismusstreit zwischen Jacobi und Mendelssohn*. Berlin: Kantgesellschaft, 1916.

STEIN, LUDWIG. *Leibniz und Spinoza*. Berlin: G. Reimer, 1890.

STRAUSS, LEO. *Spinoza's Critique of Religion*. Tr. by E. M. Sinclair. New York: Schocken Books, 1965.

————, and JOSEPH CROPSEY, eds. *History of Political Philosophy*. Chicago: Rand McNally, 1963. Includes essay on Spinoza by Stanley Rosen, pp. 413–422.

VAUGHAN, C. E. *Studies in the History of Political Philosophy Before and After Rousseau*. Vol I. Manchester: University of Manchester Press, 1925.

VERNIÈRE, PAUL. *Spinoza et la Pensée Française avant la Révolution*, 2 vols. Paris: Presses Universitaires de France, 1954.

WOLFSON, H. A. *The Philosophy of Spinoza*. New York: Meridian Books, 1958. Reprint of Cambridge, Mass., edition, 1934.

Index

(Authors's works are listed under their names)

233